Dear Helena,

It is a speeeeal
treat knowing you.

Much success in your
adventures!

Love,
Margin
7-1-95

FINDING YOUR NICHE ...MARKETING YOUR PROFESSIONAL SERVICE

Also by Bart Brodsky and Janet Geis:
The Teaching Marketplace

FINDING YOUR NICHE
...MARKETING *Your*
PROFESSIONAL SERVICE

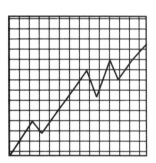

BART BRODSKY AND JANET GEIS

Community Resource Institute Press
Berkeley, California

COMMUNITY RESOURCE INSTITUTE PRESS
1442-A Walnut Street, #51
Berkeley, California 94709
(510) 525-9663

First printing: January 1992

ISBN: 0-9628464-1-4

Library of Congress Catalog Card No. 91-70347

Closing the circle: A portion of the proceeds from this book will be used to replant trees in the tropical rainforests.

Publisher's Cataloging in Publication

Brodsky, Bart, 1949-
        Finding your niche-- marketing your professional service / Bart
Brodsky and Janet Geis. --
        p.   cm.
        Includes bibliographical references and index.
        ISBN 0-9628464-1-4
        1. Professions--Marketing--Handbooks, manuals, etc. 2. Service
industries--Marketing--Handbooks, manuals, etc. I. Geis, Janet,
1950- II. Title.

HF5415.122   658.8
                                                        91-70347
                                                        MARC

*To everyone
who wants to turn an idea
into a reality.*

ABOUT THE COVER:

This photograph has gotten around. When *The San Francisco Chronicle* featured the people of Apprentice Alliance in its Sunday magazine, freelance photographer Paul Margolies retained the photographic rights. Apprentice Alliance's founder Lu Phillips wisely obtained permission from Paul to use the photograph in subsequent publicity campaigns.

Lu sent the photo to *Open Exchange,* the San Francisco Bay Area directory of services and classes which we publish. We liked the photo so much that we used it on the cover of our January 1987 edition. The public liked the photo, also; our papers moved like hotcakes out of stores and street racks. Because of this, and because of the photo's general theme, we bought the rights from Paul to use it as our book cover.

Apprentice Alliance matches experienced professionals with motivated beginners. Included are these partnerships (left to right): photographer William Porter and apprentice Angela Leaper of William Porter Architectural and Commercial Photography; apprentice Beth Nachman and caterer Patra Cianciole of Creative Catering; apprentice Michael Blumert and carpenter Don Watanabe of Watanabe and Associates.

Styling by Jan Edwards. Oh, the bird is courtesy of Terwilliger Nature Education Center.

Make your publicity photos as good as they can be. Lu has been delighted and surprised by the results of this photograph. As Lu says, "This picture lives on and on!"

ACKNOWLEDGMENTS:

Every writer needs an editor. We were fortunate enough to have had several. The following people each reviewed part or all of the early manuscript:

Richard Adelman, musician and Feldenkrais movement specialist, Oakland, CA

Tracy Dunning, corporate education consultant, Denver, CO

Douglas A. Fox, professional photographer, Evergreen, CO

Robert A. Gardner, career consultant, Oakland, CA

Jamie Jaffe, Boston Center for Adult Education, Boston, MA

Wendy Davis Larkin, marketing consultant for therapists, San Rafael, CA

Norman Prince, photographer and teacher, San Francisco, CA

Robert A. Steiner, Certified Public Accountant, El Cerrito, CA

Paul Terry, small business consultant, San Francisco, CA

Paris Williams, administrator and broadcaster, Oakland, CA

We owe these people our heartfelt thanks. Their encouragement helped us to complete this project. Their criticisms made it better. Our thanks also goes out to everybody who graciously shared their marketing stories and their photographs with us. Special thanks to Maija Vinerts for research and editorial assistance, and to Geoffrey Graham for creative design contributions. We are grateful to publishers Bernard Kamoroff and Sebastian Orfali, who helped to pave the way for others. Some of the autobiographies used herein were published originally in *Open Exchange* magazine and are reprinted by permission of the publisher. We remain exclusively responsible for any statements, errors, or omissions on these pages.

BART BRODSKY AND JANET GEIS

Contents

11.) Writing to Persuade   205

12.) Graphics With Impact   227

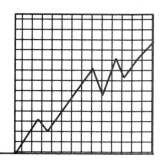

Foreword

*F*INDING YOUR NICHE...MARKETING YOUR PROFESSIONAL SERVICE is excellent! It takes you from "Exploring Career Options" through "Marketing: From Concept to Delivery," "Organizing Your Business," and more, to the details of "Sideline Teaching" and "Dealing with Commercial Printers."

Analysis and examples of nuts-and-bolts applications guide your every step, from the very first germ of your idea through the fine nuances of organization, selling, and making money on your service or class.

To present the comprehensive, practical, down-to-earth advice, the authors have pooled their decades of front line experience. The conversational tone, mixed with humor, make it both useful and a pleasure to read.

For example, "Major holiday weekends are best avoided [for your class] unless you can make a connection with the holiday theme. 'Vegetarian Singles Thanksgiving' might work. 'Christmas Eve Bookkeeping certainly would not.'"

The spirit of creativity in the book is infectious. It makes you want to run right out and set in motion those ideas that have been germinating in your fertile brain. The "how-to" information in *Finding Your Niche* is just what you need to implement your talent and ideas. It provides both inspiration and knowledge.

More than just a mechanical guidebook, *Finding Your Niche* points the way to finding joy, happiness, even love of work in your pursuit of success... the kind of love of work that the authors obviously feel about the work that they do.

You may now proceed confidently into the world to market your professional service. With *Finding Your Niche,* plus your talent, knowledge, energy, and probably far less money than you expected to have to invest to get started, you will be well on your way.

ROBERT A. STEINER, CPA

Robert A. Steiner, Certified Public Accountant, is a nationally known lecturer and author with a private practice based in El Cerrito, California.

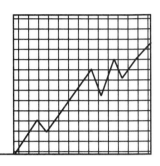

Introduction

CREATING YOUR OWN JOB on your own terms is still the American Dream. But about half of all new businesses and professional services fail within the first year. Lack of money and inexperience often get the blame. However, lots of people succeed despite starting out green and penniless. Successful people know how to dream, but they know how to plan, also. A good marketing plan can make the difference between failure and success.

Marketing is partly science and partly art. It's a skill distinct from any other expert training that you may possess. One physician said to us, "It used to be enough just to be a good doctor; now I have to be a good businessman, too!"

It's a mistake to think of marketing as an afterthought to your profession. Quite the contrary, it's the most professional thing you can do. Good marketing means that you understand the needs and wishes of your clients. If your service is highly specialized, your marketing has to be pinpoint accurate. You have to know where to find clients, what they want, what they will pay, and how to motivate them to purchase. Good marketing also can reflect your lifestyle, your social values, and even your personal commitment to clients.

This book provides you with insiders' strategies for marketing your professional service or class. It's based on the experiences of thousands of independent therapists, artists, businesspeople, specialty services, private schools, and community programs. We have over 34 years of combined experience working with such groups and individuals. Our backgrounds include publishing, school administration, advertising, and small business. Having registered over 50,000 students in a school we founded with only $5 startup capital, we are especially qualified to show you how to substitute ingenuity for money.

This book is not for Fortune 500 corporations. It's for those with inspiration and motivation, if not much cash. It's for individuals who like challenge but not unreasonable risks. It's for independent professionals and program administrators who have the freedom and the authority to test new ideas in the marketplace. If you're contemplating a new venture this book will help you get started. If your enterprise is already established this book will help you improve the "bottom line."

Here we present practical information that almost everyone can implement. Anybody can build a satisfying career doing what they love. You don't necessarily need a fat bankroll to market your own professional service. There are countless ventures that can be started for less than the cost of a night out on the town. And many of these require no special education or training other than reading, writing, and arithmetic. However, if you are fortunate enough to have special training and access to corporate resources, so much the better. This book will help you avoid common mistakes that have cost others much valuable time and money.

We'd like to hand you a sure-fire "get rich quick" scheme, but nobody honestly can guarantee success. You may have the next pet rock or the perfect aerobics workout, but you'll never know until you test your idea in the marketplace. To try takes courage. To become an acknowledged expert takes perseverance. People who sit back and wait for the world to discover them sometimes wait forever. People who are afraid to try never know failure, but they never know success either. If you are ready to try, this book will get you going. But this isn't a book about the power of "positive thinking" as such. Instead, we emphasize the positive power of information!

Here you'll find a practical guide to help you find your niche and market your professional service. Read it from cover to cover, or check it like a reference book. We detail the entire marketing process: identifying prospective clients; researching your market; getting known as an authority; conducting a promotion campaign; writing effective ad copy; producing and designing flyers, brochures, and newsletters; and how to build sideline careers writing and lecturing. We show you what's worked for others and how to apply it to your own unique circumstances. Our philosophy is that knowledge banishes fear. Accordingly, we wrote this book to empower you to succeed.

BART BRODSKY AND JANET GEIS

1

Exploring Career Options

ALL OF BUSINESS INVOLVES MARKETING. When you interview for a career position, you are selling yourself on the job market. When you ask for a raise, you are marketing your services at a higher price. If you are self-employed, your marketing decisions may be crucial to the very success of your enterprise.

All of us can benefit from a better knowledge of marketing techniques. Jobs are no longer as permanent as they used to be. Most of us will work for several employers or start several businesses during our careers. As our needs and interests change, these questions continue to surface: Big business or small? Hire out or become self-employed? Continue on the same career track or retrain in a new field? How long will the new job remain challenging and fun? As economic conditions change, how do we stay marketable?

This chapter will help you to reexamine career options from a marketing perspective. No, this is not about entering a career in marketing, but rather how marketing affects every career.

19

Self-employment or the Career Track?

The lure of a highly paid career with a major corporation typifies the American Dream. And the best companies reward innovation and creativity as never before. However, big business no longer holds the promise of lifetime security for people who choose the career track. Changing economic conditions, company restructuring, and new technologies have produced a climate of uncertainty in corporate America. Most employees will find themselves on the job market several times during their working careers, whether by choice or not.

"I didn't work for General Motors; I *was* General Motors!" Those were the words of a flabbergasted General Motors executive laid off during white-collar cutbacks in the early 1980's. It used to be that only blue-collar union jobs were vulnerable during economic downturns, but no more. The service industries—computers, banking, tenured teaching, etc.— have been hard pressed as well. The recession of 1991 saw an unprecedented increase in white collar layoffs as corporations sought to trim expenses by eliminating layers of management. Many corporations are replacing fulltime employees with independent contractors, requiring that professional and managerial people take a more market-based, entrepreneurial attitude toward their careers. For better or worse, corporate loyalty is in decline. As one laid off executive put it, "It's becoming a freelance economy." Position, status, and money are undeniable assets of big business, but job security may be a thing of the past.

> *Most employees will find themselves on the job market many times during their careers.*

The corporate career track remains a glamorous route for ambitious young professionals. However, the adventure and independence of private enterprise is attracting growing numbers of talented, highly trained individuals. For instance, after finishing his law degree, Ron had several lucrative offers to join prestigious law firms. He chose, instead, to build an independent career. That meant opening his own office, accepting the expense of rent, hiring a receptionist, and stocking his own law library. At first the receptionist took home a bigger paycheck than her employer! Clients were slow in coming, and it took a number of years to establish the practice. In Ron's case the effort was well worth the end result: success on his own terms.

The independent professional, usually working alone or with one or two others, frequently must be his own administrator, bookkeeper, receptionist, bill collector, publicist, janitor, and maybe even cook. The independent professional can take nothing in business for granted. He is responsible for budgeting, setting salaries, health care benefits, insurance, paying for vacations, setting expense accounts, and countless other little amenities and perks that many larger corporations provide routinely.

A person is lured into small business for many reasons. The corporate culture requires a certain measure of conformity; the entrepreneurial lifestyle is more freewheeling. We know many corporate refugees, people who drop out, often with great financial risk, to pursue an iconoclast dream. An accountant becomes an artist. A publicist opens a horse ranch. A scientist becomes a bodywork therapist. Corporate politics sometimes provides a nudge or a shove. Sometimes a person is derailed off his career track prematurely. Another may quit in search of work that is more personally fulfilling and fun. During child rearing, a parent may find it easier to work at home in a "cottage industry" than to continue on the career track. And sometimes what starts out as a hobby or a temporary situation can expand to become a rewarding source of income.

Consider the advantages of self-employment. The entrepreneur has personal control, autonomy, freedom to be creative, and the conviction that he is truly needed, if not indispensable, to the enterprise. An independent professional or small business owner may work longer and harder than most people in corporate jobs. However, he can schedule vacations at his own convenience, not his employer's. Perhaps he earns less money. Still, he feels that his labor is his own, and he benefits materially in direct proportion to his effort and his ingenuity. Small businesses often invite (and sometimes require!) the participation of the whole family. This is an opportunity for real community. Where your participation is vital to the enterprise, you're not likely to feel like just a cog in a big machine.

About half of all people in the U.S. work for large corporations, and the other half work in small businesses. However, most of the net gain in job formation is the result of efforts by small time entrepreneurs, not big companies. Chances are, if you are just entering (or reentering) the job market, you'll find more opportunities in small business. You'll certainly find variety. In California, for instance, 94% of businesses have fewer than fifty employees, and about two-thirds have five employees or less (California Employment Development Department 1985 survey). In these situations you'll probably be working on a daily basis with just a handful of co-workers and the boss. From here, it's not such a big step to becoming your own boss!

Self-employment requires self-discipline and motivation.

Are You An Entrepreneur?

Before you rush out and quit your present job to embark on a self-made career, ask yourself: Are you temperamentally and emotionally suited to be your own boss? It takes a good measure of self-discipline, organization, and raw motivation to work for yourself. It is not recommended for people who need an authority figure to get them moving. It requires budgeting, accounting, and an extraordinary attention to mundane details. Very few bosses can afford the luxury of hiring somebody to worry for them. And very few small businesses "run themselves." Working for yourself takes:

Courage
Marketing ability
Perseverance
Pragmatism
Self-reliance
Talent

It may take years just to define your market.

Many people love the idea of starting a new business but find out later that they don't have the temperament to withstand the pressures of running a business. Are you just flirting or are you ready to make a commitment?

In the book *Honest Business*, Michael Phillips and Salli Rasberry define "tradeskill" as the talents a person needs to succeed in small business. Tradeskill includes the ability to lessen risk, stay on course, budget time, and integrate work and play. The best way to obtain tradeskill is probably to be born into a family business. The children of white collar professionals are culturally disadvantaged compared with the children of businesspeople when it comes to tradeskill. Fortunately, tradeskill can be learned, even self-taught!

Building a business typically takes several years. It may take the first year or two just to define your market and establish your practice. One of our friends refers to this as "The Scary Beginnings." After this period, if things go well, you've established a small but solid client base and are at least breaking even. The next year or two is time to work on building your market share, expanding your business and maybe attracting more affluent clients. After a few years you get comfortable with being in business and know what clients expect of you.

By around the fifth year your business may be considered mature. You may want to keep expanding, opening branch offices or franchising. Or by now you may want to enjoy the fruits of a mature business, take more time out for yourself, delegate work to junior partners or employees. Only 10% to 20% of all businesses survive five years. Once you get this far, you're almost as likely to make it for 20 years or more.

The most successful independent professionals are also good businesspeople. If the details of business administration bore or frustrate you, probably you'd be happier working for somebody else. In this case concentrate on perfecting your skill or craft and leave the rest to entrepreneurs and marketers. But if you decide to accept the challenges and risks, then be ready to deal with these realities:

1.) Most businesses need at least a year to get going. Be prepared to support yourself with savings or by other means in the interim.

2.) New businesses, like young children, need extra attention at the beginning. Be ready to sacrifice evenings and weekends, especially around tax time.

3.) Learn new ways to budget. Income from an independent business varies with seasons, fads, and economic waves. "Make a dollar; save a dime" is good advice to see you through that inevitable lean month. Budget emergency savings just as you budget for rent and utilities.

4.) Budget time and money for promotion. Whether it's television advertising, open houses, or client calls, new businesses especially need extra promotional efforts.

5.) Expect to go through a period of testing and trial until you establish a reputation for quality and reliability. Pay your debts on time or negotiate extensions in advance. Build your reputation by being honest, fair, and consistent.

Are the risks of self-employment worth the potential rewards?

Before you invest a lot more time and money pursuing your dream, take a spoonful of caution. You know the risks: According to statistics, more businesses fail than succeed. Going on your own is hard work. Doing without a regular paycheck can be scary. If you're used to hanging out at the office cooler, you may feel isolated and alone. Are these risks worth the potential rewards?

Now don't get discouraged. We provide this reality check as a public service to counter the prevailing, overly romantic notions about small business. Our friend Robert Steiner, a self-employed CPA, wryly observes that nobody ever writes books outlining the reasons for *not* starting a small business. He's right, of course. Most of us will not pay to be deterred. Thus, most popular business books—including this one—are pep talks. The better ones encourage without fostering unrealistic expectations.

To help you decide if you are an entrepreneur, take a detailed inventory of your business skills. Updating your resume is mandatory if you are putting yourself out on the job market. You need to do almost the same thing if you plan to work for yourself. This is especially true if you intend to seek outside start-up capital. Take a personal inventory of your training and talents, likes and dislikes, strengths and weaknesses. Your list should include:

Books read
Education
Hobbies and crafts
Life experiences
People you know
Places visited
Talents
Strengths
Weaknesses

Your inventory should include social skills, such as being a good listener, having the ability to make people laugh or feel at ease, or sounding great on the telephone.

Operating a small business means wearing many different hats. You do not have to be perfect at everything. However, you do need to be aware of your limitations and weaknesses so that you can hire assistants in these areas. For example, if you hate to balance your checkbook, plan on hiring a bookkeeper as a top priority. If you shy away from confrontations, contract with a collection agency to handle overdue accounts. Concentrate your efforts where you are strong; compensate where you are weak.

You have to decide how big to grow, and how fast.

The Growing Seed or the Big Splash?

In managing a business you have to decide how big to grow, how fast, and what to risk to get there. This may depend largely on your own personality and style of doing things. It also depends upon the available human and financial resources you have.

The Growing Seed is the slow, steady approach. We also call it the grass roots, California, organic, mellow, low risk, laid back, granola and sprouts, or let-it-be approach. Minimize your initial investment. Recruit clients from your pool of friends and neighbors. Sink your roots into the community and grow with it. The Growing Seed is safe and dependable, if not always spectacular in its results.

Then there is the Big Splash. We also call it the high risk, East Coast, Big Apple, high roller, big spender, or big plunge approach. The strategy here is to spend a lot of money right up front in a gamble to capture a significant share of the market. When Gannett Publishing launched *USA Today,* they didn't expect to show a profit for at least five years. The Big Splash can work, but only if you have a big bankroll and can hold out years for return on your investment.

We usually recommend the Growing Seed approach to small businesspeople, program administrators, and independent professionals. Making a Big Splash is no good if you promptly sink to the bottom of the ocean. You're bound to make mistakes when you start out. With the Growing Seed approach your mistakes will be less expensive. So, take it slowly, at least at first, and build your confidence—and your reputation—with a track record of successes.

Service businesses are cheaper to start than manufacturing businesses. Manufacturing requires design and production facilities, warehouse storage, distribution, retailing, and inventory controls. Service businesses are labor intensive, which means that they require sweat, but not necessarily a lot of money to start. And in the service industries, individuals often can compete effectively against very large corporations.

Marketing professional services sometimes involves nothing other than the transfer of information from provider to client, usually in words and images. Here your motivation and commitment are much more important than money. Your equipment may be little more than a telephone, a pencil, and a typewriter or personal computer.

Shoestring Startups

Many services can be started as home-based sidelines: evening and weekend projects that do not require quitting your present employment. On the smallest scale, your enterprise may be little more than the outgrowth of a hobby. A coin collector, for instance, might type a newsletter on home stationery and make copies at the local copy store. It costs pennies to print and sells for dollars. It might also lead to mail-order buying and selling, sponsoring auctions and exhibitions, or historical research projects.

With or without professional degrees or extensive training, there are endless numbers of businesses that can be started on a shoestring budget of a few hundred dollars or less. There are many ways to minimize the initial risk. You can lessen expenses by working out of a spare bedroom or a corner of the living room, filing paperwork in the drawers of an unused desk, using the home phone. Hold business meetings over lunch in restaurants; the meal may be deductible and the meeting space is free.

However, there may be some limitations. City business licenses, zoning restrictions, and health department regulations all may apply to home based businesses. Many local governments are not interested in regulating the smallest scale of activities. Once your business proves viable, however, you'll want to make sure that you are in full compliance with local laws.

The number of businesses that you can start on a shoestring is almost limitless. Books such as Jay Conrad Levinson's *555 Ways To Earn Extra Money* and Entrepreneur Magazine's *184 Businesses Anyone Can Start* are loaded with suggestions. Here is our own high priority list:

Your motivation and commitment are more important than money.

Advice businesses
Business services
Craftsmaking
Direct sales
Personal and specialty services
Sideline teaching
Writing services
1001 Wild hares

The information industry requires little or no startup capital.

Advice businesses. Corporate consulting, speaking, lectures, and newsletters all comprise the advice industry. If you work now in big business, use your insider information as a springboard to going independent. Advice is an unregulated arena. No formal credentials are required as long as your advice is offered as general information, not as psychotherapy, legal, or medical diagnosis to a particular individual.

Business services. Sideline and low risk businesses include bookkeeper, graphic artist, secretary, answering service, office organizer, tax preparer, publicist, photographer, decorator, janitor. Here practical and organizational skills are valued more than credentials on paper. Other established businesspeople value competent support services. Once your business is off the ground you can sub-contract or hire employees and concentrate on administrative duties. Keep initial costs low with lease-purchase options on needed equipment. Work at home or on location at clients' businesses.

Craftsmaking. Painters and craftspeople frequently can defray the costs of their hobby with the sale of their wares. Boutiques will purchase outright or accept on consignment distinct and trendy home decorations, needlepoint, knickknacks, pottery, and the like. Minimize production costs by making display samples and a catalog brochure, and take advance orders. Also consider selling at flea markets, expos, by mail order, and ultimately to larger retail outlets.

Direct sales. Despite its lowly status, direct sales is probably the surest way to make good money with a minimal investment. It works best for motivated extroverts. Cosmetics, vitamins, exercise equipment, and scores of popular personal and professional items may be provided by distributorships. Startup kits may be inexpensive, no more than a couple hundred dollars, frequently much less. Look critically at distributorships that cost thousands of dollars; many direct sales programs require little or no capital to get started. Insist on talking with several successful distributors before investing time or money. The franchiser may or may not provide training and licenses.

Personal and specialty services. Many entrepreneurs have created successful businesses out of what other people don't like to do or don't have time to do for themselves. The list of such services is unlimited—housekeeper, caterer, floor refinisher, pet sitter, closet organizer, bill payer—you invent it! There seems to be a market for every conceivable function, from the practical to the off-beat. One clever woman started a service bringing fresh groceries to the homes of busy professionals. A communal household in one college town pays the rent by running a popular switchboard service. Western Union may be obsolete, but now we have singing "stripper-grams." Perhaps the ultimate service for the overworked yuppie is "rent a wife." Everything you need done around the house, except the sex!

Sideline teaching. Freelance and parttime teaching opportunities abound—club leader, event organizer, tutor, counselor, public speaker, high school temporary. Independent freelancers generally need no formal credentials to teach at recreation centers, churches, growth centers, and at home. Community colleges and adult schools may award temporary credentials if life and career experiences coincide with a needed subject.

Career opportunities are limited only by your imagination.

Writing services. There is a constant need for people with a command of the language, especially typists, researchers, and proofreaders. Harried university students always need term papers edited, typed, or reworked. Small press book publishers hire out for editing assignments and ghostwriting. Many typesetting shops run short staffed and will train a sincere applicant to operate computer equipment. Home-based desktop publishing services are flourishing, thanks to new, affordable computer technologies. Freelance writers can hack out a living writing for magazines and specialty publications, too.

1001 Wild hares. Try becoming a street musician, mime, or juggler. When kids lose their teeth, you can hire out as a "professional tooth fairy" and bring them quarters. If you are a good trader, check out public auctions, estate sales, and flea market vending. One Woodstock era hippie arrested too often for panhandling now makes a living selling what he finds in free boxes. At the other end of the scale, turn that vacation to Asia or South America into an import/export venture. From backyard mechanic to antique car dealer, from comic collecting to adult paper routes, the possibilities are limited only by your imagination.

We know about shoestring startups from first hand experience. We publish *Open Exchange,* a San Francisco Bay Area directory of classes and professional services. We started in 1974 with an initial investment of $4.50. That's not a typo—we spent less than $5. We advertised for teachers with handbills and in a flea market newspaper classified ad. We substituted our own labor for money. We also had the generous assistance of volunteer staff who believed in our mission. Our very first publication generated about $850 and more than broke even. By 1979 we were grossing almost a half million dollars annually. In 1980 we made a decision to reduce the size of our operation to avoid burn-out and to try other projects. Pacing ourselves turned out to be the right decision. *Open Exchange* celebrated its 17th Anniversary in Fall, 1991. With over a quarter million Bay Area readers *Open Exchange* is still growing and going strong.

"What Color is Your Package Wrapping?"

If you choose the corporate career track, Richard Bolles asks the question, *What Color is Your Parachute?* Borrowing from Bolles' book title, we'd also like to ask, "What Color is Your Package Wrapping?"

When embarking on a new career, you start by learning everything possible about your profession. You've got to know your stuff, whether it's accounting or Zen, art or medicine. If you choose to be self-employed, it's also your business to learn all about marketing.

Good marketing is a matter of style as well as substance. The benefits of your service should be perfectly clear to your prospective clients. To succeed, your business cards must be professional. Your brochures need to be crisp. Your advertising should be informative. Your presentations must be winning. How you market your service is a reflection of how you run your business. Your "package wrapping," is a reflection of its contents.

If the wrapping is wrong, the package can get lost. We've seen many excellent services fail because of poor marketing. The brochures looked amateurish, the advertising budget was wasted, or the telephone wasn't covered. All other things being equal, good marketing can make the difference between failure and success.

Good marketing is honest business.

Style, however, is no substitute for substance. Some marketers act as if promoting a service were more important than providing it. "Sell the sizzle, not the steak," they say. Don't believe it. In the long run, no amount of clever marketing can paper over the defects of a poorly run service. No amount of assurances by a particular oil company can actually clean up the Alaskan coast after a spill.

We are bothered by this apparent duality between the "dirty business" of marketing and the ethical standards of a professional. We believe that reality is more holistic. Good marketing means telling the truth. Good marketing usually is an indication of a business well run. Ideally, the wrapping is appropriate to the package.

The rest of this book is dedicated to helping you find the best wrapping for your own package, the best gift you can give to your customers.

Tudi Baskay is a member of a relatively new profession, personal organizers. Tudi calls her business Time To Organize, and she offers her services to San Francisco Bay Area residents. Here Tudi tells her story:

"Every job I've ever had has ended up the same way...you'd find me organizing the supply closet, getting the filing system in order, developing forms for easier record keeping, or arranging furniture for more efficient work-flow. Every commendation I ever got included the words 'efficient' and 'highly organized.'

"I was working in an office at a boring job. I wanted something better than that, work that would be stimulating, creative, interesting, and most of all, work that I believed in and that I could love. And I wanted to be in business for myself.

"After a lot of thought, I decided to use my organizational skills as the basis for a one woman business. Like most people, I didn't know that professional organizing existed as a career field, so I was making up a kind of work to do.

"Later, I found out that organizing is a well established career field with a professional organization, the National Association of Professional Organizers, of which I am now a member.

"I started talking about my idea to get people's reactions and input. One evening I asked my friend, Chandler, to help me develop a business and marketing plan so that I could start my business in an organized way. Chandler called me the next morning and asked me if I would sort through and organize her mother's papers. I had just accepted my first client, and Time To Organize was born. I was in business for myself, doing what I love. And I've been earning my living that way ever since.

"Here are some ideas I think are very important: That getting rid of the stress caused by disorganization is as important as the increased efficiency and productivity that organization brings; that an individual organizing plan should be developed to suit each client's personality and work habits; and that no one system is right for everyone.

"Being organized makes life easier and possessions a joy instead of a burden. I love helping people achieve those ends."

—Tudi Baskay

Stephen Altschuler is a published writer who supplements his income by offering seminars on writing and conducting walking tours throughout the San Francisco Bay Area:

"When I first saw the book, *Do What You Love, The Money Will Follow,* I felt a jolt go through me. I'd been writing and publishing feature articles since 1969, squeezing it in and around a career as a social service professional, and longing to write full time. I realized, though, when I read that title, that I hadn't focused in enough on the form of writing I really loved to do. That form is the personal experience article, which for me combines creative writing, personal growth, and making a meaningful contribution to the community. I had written and published such articles, but hadn't concentrated on them to an extent equal to my love of this form.

"It was then that I put together a proposal for a book of walks (which is the other thing I most love to do), personal reflective essays, local anecdotal history, and photography (my own and archival photos)— a book that was recently published as *Hidden Walks in the Bay Area: Pathways, Essays, and Yesterdays.*

"Feature writing was fun for a number of years, and I still do an occasional article on subjects I'm particularly interested in, but the personal essay allowed much more inner exploration, while searching for universal truths. My writing and my life became much more integral, and in the late 70's, I approached a radio station in south-western New Hampshire with a program called Backwoods Cabin, a weekly journal of a city man's (that was me) experience living in a primitive cabin in the woods, sans electricity, plumbing, phone, and the usual heating sources. They went for it and I wrote and produced that show for a year and a half, presenting short essays and original songs each week about different aspects of my inner and outer life in the woods. I knew then that this was my genre, and I continued honing this form, culminating in my current book and a sequel to the book.

"I finally felt I'd done enough of this and other writing forms to begin to teach others. My background in counseling and teaching (including a masters in counseling, credentials in psychology and education, and many years as a mental health professional) gives me a unique perspective as a writer and a teacher of this form."

—Steven Altschuler

2

Marketing: From Concept to Delivery

GENERAL ALEXANDER HAIG, ONE-TIME PRESIDENTIAL CANDIDATE and former adviser to Richard Nixon, has said, "The secret to life is marketing." The quotation is intriguing, especially considering the source. It also raises the question: What is marketing?

In common usage the words marketing, advertising, publicity, and promotion often are used interchangeably. We've heard some people say, "I don't do marketing; I just rely on word of mouth." Or, "I want to buy some publicity." In this chapter we'll explain how we define these terms. Then we'll show how you can use marketing concepts to build your business.

Marketing Defined

Marketing is the activity of bringing a product or service "on line," or available to the public, from concept to delivery. You are marketing during every phase of business: researching market needs, structuring the business, setting production methods and goals, pricing, packaging, promotion, sales, and customer service. Choosing your office location involves marketing. Picking the typeface on your business cards involves marketing. Dressing for a meeting involves marketing. Choosing the shape of the candy bar or the color of the waiting room is marketing. Marketing is conscious design. Marketing means looking at everything you do as if you were standing in your client's shoes. Our philosophy is that you should practice marketing consciously from the instant you first decide to go into business. Marketing is not just something you do as an afterthought. To paraphrase Al Haig, *the secret to business is marketing.*

Promotion Defined

Promotion is the use of mass media, direct mail, or other marketing options to reach your audience. Promotion is obvious marketing because the consumer can see and appreciate the effort and expense of a promotion campaign. Some services are more media driven than others. Some require aggressive promotion campaigns on television, radio, or in newspapers to succeed in the marketplace. Services that are new to the public often benefit from promotion that explains their use and function. Still other services seem to "sell themselves" and do not need promotion.

Generally, we define promotion to mean publicity and advertising in the mass media or direct mail. Sometimes promotion is defined in a narrower sense as a special kind of publicity and advertising. San Francisco publicist Bonnie Weiss defines promotion as "staging a special event or offering gifts or prizes to attract the public." If you go to the effort to stage a special event, you'll probably want to get as much media coverage as possible. Thus, both definitions overlap.

Publicity Defined

Publicity is free promotion that you get from the mass media—newspapers, radio, and television. You don't buy publicity and you can't control it directly. The media grants publicity because they decide that you are newsworthy, expert in your field, entertaining, or of overriding social benefit.

Publicity is public attention. Publicity can be an ego boost. Publicity may be kind or cruel. Whether you receive publicity is the decision of the media. Consider publicity to be manna from heaven, possibly a one-time shot at fame. When the spotlight shines on you, be prepared with something to say or something to sell. Enjoy publicity when you get it, but don't count on it to build your business. Even good publicity doesn't guarantee sales.

Advertising Defined

Advertising is promotion that you pay for. There are many benefits to advertising, but advertising's most important function is to boost sales. In contrast to publicity, with advertising you can carefully select your medium, target your audience, and control the content of the message. There is no one "right" form of advertising for every product or service. Some will work better for you than others. Finding out where to advertise and what to say in an ad is to some degree a matter of trial and error. At first you'll probably make many mistakes. Since advertising can be expensive, you'll want to keep your mistakes *cheap*. A good advertising campaign can be like money in the bank. However, you have to know what you're doing.

Direct Marketing Defined

Direct marketing means that you create your own "medium" and compose your own "message" to reach prospective clients. Popular direct marketing approaches include direct mail (flyers, catalogs, solicitation letters, contests, etc.); telemarketing; postering; client calls; and other direct approaches to reach prospective clients. Direct marketing is the main alternative to advertising in the major media. For many services direct marketing is the better alternative. With direct marketing you can reach a smaller, more targeted audience with a more detailed message.

Personal Marketing Defined

Personal marketing is building your business by getting known. Personal marketing emphasizes friendship and trust, being both knowledgeable and accessible. This involves circulating at parties, networking, joining clubs, and handing out business cards. Personal marketing does not necessarily mean high pressure selling, however. For professionals in business, personal marketing means being recognized as an authority. You can build an "expert" image with lectures, speeches, teaching, consulting, writing, and appearing on radio and television.

Word of Mouth Defined

Word of mouth means taking care of business. When you're doing your job well, people tell their friends, and you get referrals. Word of mouth referrals are the result of building a good reputation. If you have "good word of mouth," this means that you've done right by your clients.

To be sure, word of mouth may be your best form of marketing. Word of mouth, however, can be painfully slow, especially for a new venture. Good reputations take a long time to build. Advertising, publicity, direct marketing, and personal marketing are forms of promotion that can speed up word of mouth. The more people see and hear about you, the better. Promotion is a way to amplify word of mouth, to assist you in building that good reputation faster.

Promoting your service accelerates word of mouth.

Some people have the mistaken impression that word of mouth is the *opposite* of marketing. "I don't advertise because I get all my clients by word of mouth," they say. It's true that many businesses do not need promotion. Most businesses, however, will grow faster by using some form of promotion. One administrator told us, "My general experience is that 30% of business is generated by ads. The remaining 70% is word of mouth. This has been true with ad budgets of $10,000 to $200,000. Client satisfaction is everything. But ads get the ball rolling."

Psychological Barriers to Marketing

Why is there so much psychological resistance to marketing, especially among professionals? Why do some people think that marketing is unseemly or unethical? We believe that a good part of the problem is the language used by many marketers.

It's fashionable to compare business to war and marketing to combat. "Let's run it up the flagpole and see who salutes!" The image of the samurai businessman is colorful, but we question its accuracy.

On the cover of the best-seller *Marketing Warfare,* authors Al Ries and Jack Trout appear in combat helmets dispensing books from a military truck. War analogies run through every page. Niche marketing, for example, is defined as "reducing the size of the battleground in order to achieve a superiority of force." The book is a clever analysis of major advertising campaigns won and lost. The authors advise, "Most of America's 5 million corporations should be waging guerrilla warfare."

Appropriately, in *Guerrilla Marketing Attack,* Jay Conrad Levinson warns, "In the fight-to-the-death arena of marketing, you've got to think aggressively, spend aggressively, market aggressively. If your competitors don't hate you, at least they'd better fear you." In *How To Make Your Advertising Twice As Effective at Half the Cost,* Hershell Gordon Lewis also describes business in stark Darwinian terms: "You forget that you have any friends. You go out into the competitive arena and scratch and claw for your share of business." These are among the best marketing books around, practical and timely in their advice.

Many of us, however, want to succeed in business without having to "go to war." Escaping the rat race may have been one's initial motivation for abandoning a fast track corporate job, starting a home based business, or pursuing a career in teaching or the arts. Lilly Tomlin expressed this sentiment perfectly, "The trouble with the rat race is that it's the rats who win." Some professionals feel that it is undignified hustling to sell a service whose benefits should be obvious. A new mother operating a craft business in a spare bedroom doesn't want to become a guerrilla. Freelance photographers shoot with cameras, not guns.

We want to emphasize that you can be successful without donning psychological armor and putting your business on a wartime footing. We even considered titling this book *Gentle Marketing: A Dignified Approach* just to make this point. Good marketing does not mean selling fast and loose, or selling out your values. Michael Phillips and Salli Rasberry wrote *Honest Business* to show that high ethical standards actually have high survival value in business. Paul Hawken in *Growing a Business* underscores, "Being a good human being is good business."

The analogy between business and war is colorful but limited. Where warfare is destructive, building a business is a creative act. Warfare means beating your opponent; business means serving clients. Business does not have to be a zero sum game. Somebody doesn't have to lose for you to succeed. Hawken adds, "Remember that in business you are never trying to 'beat the competition.' You are trying to give your customer something other than what they are receiving from your competition. It is a waste of time and energy trying to beat the competition because the customer doesn't care about the rivalry."

Business thrives on cooperation and sharing.

The values of sharing and cooperation are at least as important as strategy and tactics. Honor and sincerity are vital, especially if you plan to be in business for the long run. At its best, marketing is a creative activity, one for artists, not just for soldiers. Even pacifists can win at this game!

Perhaps businesspeople would feel better about marketing if more marketers took the time to explain what they do. Marketing is a tool that is at your service. We believe that the whole point of marketing is to reaffirm your professional values, not to betray them. People in business who feel that they have to "sell out" to survive probably are in the wrong business to begin with. The proper goal of marketing is to help you find your audience, build the business you really want, and earn a good income doing it.

We must admit, however, that marketing sometimes fails. The marketplace does not always reward the good and noble. Worthy pursuits are not necessarily profitable. If you offer your service on the open market, you have to appeal to the values of those affluent enough to afford it. Sometimes we can humanize our professions, as with lawyers who work *pro bono publico* or doctors who volunteer time at free clinics. Some of us compromise, "doing well" on the job and "doing good" after hours. However, rather than seeing the limits of the marketplace as a barrier, consider it a challenge. Use marketing techniques to break past the limits, to inform and to educate, as well as to sell.

Mass Markets Versus Niche Markets

New lifestyles create niche markets.

One of your first marketing considerations is to determine the size and the duration of your prospective market. Marketers used to take it for granted that you'd try to sell almost every product to everybody. More recently, mass marketing has given way to targeting highly specialized niche markets.

As lifestyles have become more sophisticated and varied, many experts have analyzed the breakup of the mass market. In *Maximarketing*, Stan Rapp and Tom Collins note that loyalty to brand names has dropped precipitously. In 1975, 74% of the American population expressed loyalty to specific brand names. By 1984 loyalty was only 58% and still falling. Specialty products and services are arising to serve smaller and smaller segments of the market. Where there was once just Coca-Cola, there is now diet cola, cherry cola, caffeine-free cola, kosher cola, health food cola, the Uncola, and Perrier.

Harvard Business School's Theodore Levitt in *The Marketing Imagination* describes a "globalization of markets" that would seem to contradict this. He argues forcefully that the methods of production and distribution are becoming increasingly standardized. Companies face increasing competition in local markets from multinational competitors.

It seems to us that both trends are happening simultaneously: standardization for big business and diversity for smaller scale local markets. The message to business seems to be: Standardize globally; diversify locally.

The emerging new economy means displacement for some, opportunity for others. In *The Next Economy,* Paul Hawken shows how rising energy costs during the 1970's permanently altered the character of manufacturing. Because everything has become more expensive, people

MARKETING THE PROMISE:

"When prospective customers can't experience the product in advance, they are asked to buy what are essentially promises—promises of satisfaction. Even tangible, testable, feelable, smellable products are, before they're bought, largely just promises....

"The way the product is packaged (how the promise is presented in brochure, letter, design appearance), how it is personally presented, and by whom—all these become central to the product itself because they are elements of what the customer finally decides to buy or reject."

—Theodore Levitt
"Marketing Intangible Products and Product Intangibles"
Harvard Business Review
May-June 1981

make purchases more selectively. Hawken anticipates the end of the disposable economy and planned obsolescence. A person may spend more than ever for a performance automobile, but he expects that car to last longer and need fewer repairs.

Hawken's advice to all business is to emphasize "quality, courtesy, and service." Hawken asserts that the small operator can compete successfully against a corporate giant by responding more quickly to changing market conditions. His book shows how small businesses can compete against bigger competitors by emphasizing a commitment to personal service. The message is that the little guy has a better chance at succeeding than ever before.

Business benefits from 'quality, courtesy, and service.'

Products designed for mass appeal are marketed differently from specialty products. A Big Mac is a Big Mac throughout the world. The television spots and the newspaper ads look pretty much the same, even in foreign languages. Inexpensive fast food, a whistle clean atmosphere, happy times, and no bad surprises have a broad appeal. Mass marketing reaches just about everyone.

Specialty markets are different. If you want to sell healthy vegetarian Big Macro-burgers, you are appealing to a select audience. To broadcast your message throughout the major media could be a waste. A better approach might be to target your advertising to a health conscious audience. In this case, consider advertising on cable TV or in selected health and dining publications.

You can define products by objective performance specifications; services are more subjective. You know what to expect from your toaster or your cassette recorder. But what are the exact qualifications of a good doctor? Is it a prestigious degree, a short wait before appointments, or a particular bedside manner? Individual tastes and values play a big role in determining what constitutes good service.

Marketing specialty services requires ingenuity. This is especially true if your budget is tight. If you're marketing a product for mass consumption such as Coca Cola, you know where to advertise—the mass media. But how do you promote an advanced degree program? A well-known mass marketed product takes few words to describe. Everybody knows, "Coke is it!" But try to sell a Masters degree in three words: *"Hard to describe"*?

Specialized services require detailed explanations. It can take one thousand words to describe just one course in a Ph.D. program. The printed word handles such complexity better than television. Print is more portable. People follow at their own pace, not at a pace set by the monitor. People can repeat a passage if and when they choose. Thus you can promote a school program most effectively with catalogs, direct mail brochures, and selected print advertising. For any particular product or service, it takes a period of trial and error to find out what will work best.

Niche media serve niche markets.

Parallel to the decline of the mass market is the fragmenting of mass media. Television network audiences are starting to shrink as people are choosing cable and movie rental options. The urban daily newspaper now must compete with scores of independent advertisers and specialty publications for readership and revenues. To protect their markets, major newspapers soon might computerize their coverage, tailoring it to readers' individual interests and hobbies. For example, if you love sports, your home delivered edition might include expanded sports coverage. Your next door neighbor, a corporate executive, might receive expanded business coverage. Your purchases might be tracked, and this feedback could determine the content of future editions. If you like designer clothes, you'll love designer media. For better or worse, while you're watching TV, TV might be watching you.

Market Entry

A new provider in an established market might seem to be at a grave disadvantage against established competitors. Established providers have access to distribution, technology, experience, and capital. Using creative strategies, however, late entry can prove to be an advantage.

Late entrants can benefit from new technology, reducing operating costs and passing them on to consumers. Late entrants may find them-

PROMOTING SOMETHING NEW? INVEST IN EDUCATION:

When promoting something new in the marketplace, it takes an extra measure of education to get your message to the public. Therapeutic bodywork is a case in point.

Several years ago the distinction between therapeutic bodywork and sexual massage was poorly understood by the general public. A bodywork therapist who solicited business publicly was assumed to be a prostitute. People who practiced any form of touch therapy, including sex surrogates, had to "reposition" their profession in the public mind.

It took years to develop this awareness. The first mass media stories about bodywork made it appear "far out" or wacky. But articles in professional journals, community newspapers, and new age publications explored the benefits of bodywork. Interviews with bodywork practitioners and testimonies by clients pointed out specific health benefits. The popularity of bodywork led to mainstream media coverage.

Enterprising bodyworkers more recently have entered the corporate work place, giving back rubs to computer operators at work stations. Since *USA Today* and Cable News Network have reported on this phenomenon, therapeutic bodywork seems to have become widely accepted.

Still, some people continue to confuse the act of touching with the sex business. The situation tends to be worse for women in the field. A professional bodywork therapist has to choose her ad medium carefully to reach a sophisticated audience. Word of mouth, professional directories, new age publications, and networking usually work better than the daily paper or the telephone directory in this regard.

Much education remains to be done. A bodyworker always needs to emphasize the therapeutic or spiritual nature of her discipline. Sometimes she has to avoid phrases that can be taken as sexual puns, such as "totally release all tension," or "deep, penetrating strokes." Several disciplines—Rolfing, Feldenkrais, Trager, Polarity, Rosen, and others—have been trademarked to boost recognition and prestige. Clearly, marketing bodywork is not as simple as selling hamburgers.

Publicity creates new demands and opens new markets.

selves quickly accepted in an established market that incumbents originally took years to develop. Late entrants can be more responsive to changing market conditions, too. Incumbent organizations may have entrenched bureaucracies which stifle innovation. Late entrants may be more entrepreneurial and willing to take risks.

As a new provider, consider the following strategies. Identify a need and target an audience. Bicycles and Cadillacs travel the same roads, but with different riders representing different lifestyles. Quality and price help you to define your audience. Develop a market niche by focusing to a greater or lesser degree on economy or luxury, style or comfort. Develop promotional materials to reflect the values and lifestyle of your clientele.

Build your position by articulating how your service is special. Emphasize one or more unique aspects. How is it better, newer, higher quality, less expensive, more personalized, more convenient, friendlier, faster, longer lasting, stronger, prettier, or different? Make it clear why your service is the best choice.

Use price as a marketing tool.

Strategic pricing is a powerful tool in market entry. Price your service slightly less than your competition and emphasize bargain. Or price yourself higher and stress quality. A higher price increases profit margin. A lower price maximizes sales and market share. The psychology of pricing is interesting, too. Numerals ending in "4," "5," "7," and "9" sound lower and thus are more appealing than numbers ending in "00." It's no accident that most products are priced at $.99 rather than $1.00, or $15.95 rather than $16.00. In pricing seminars, for instance, we've discovered that $54 generally enrolls better than $50, and that $95 sounds much, much less expensive than $100. Above $99, consider pricing your service next at $104, $105, $109, $115, or even $124.

In a highly competitive market, many new entrants use lower prices as a strategic tactic, so there is a downward pressure on prices in general. However, once you have firmly established your market niche, you can slowly and steadily raise prices (and presumably profits) while maintaining or expanding your market share. Protect your market by diversifying, too. Diversify with a range of extra features and price options for prospective clients. "Keep a Cadillac on the lot in order to sell the Chevys."

Adopt strategies to overcome clients' doubts and fears. Attract attention with product demonstrations. Break down resistance with free introductions and special first-time discounts. Money-back guarantees remove the dread of being ripped-off. Where new clients may be hesitant, make their initial commitment small. Then increase their commitment incrementally. First get their mailing address. Then mail an invitation to a free demonstration. Consider offering a trial sample. When marketing big ticket items, give something away for free as an inducement to purchase. "A free radio with every test drive." "Learn investment basics at our free, no obligation seminar. We want to be your brokerage firm."

If you want to learn about whether a business is right for you, consider working for somebody else already established in that business. Learn about their successes; analyze their mistakes. This kind of "on the job training" will be invaluable once you venture out on your own. Also consider apprenticeships or volunteer work. Socialize with other established professionals. Do not pass up any opportunity to learn about your business.

When you start a new enterprise, don't give up your present job unless you really don't need the income. One of our friends quips, "Don't quit your day job." Allow yourself up to two years to become self-supporting in your new field. If you don't have to worry about the rent money, you'll be able to serve your clients better. One bodywork therapist told us that while developing his practice he kept working as a part-time administrator. This way he was able to grow at a comfortable rate. He could afford to turn away clients that he did not want to work with. In this way he built a solid track record of success.

Your Business Plan

When you're ready to build a business, it's time to prepare a formal business plan. This is where you put marketing principles into action.

Business consultant Paul Terry says a business plan is "most importantly a written document that allows the business to take advantage of opportunities and deal with problems by anticipating them in advance.... Each idea is thought through, tested, matched against the competition." A complete business plan contains information on organization, marketing, and financing. It's especially important in seeking outside funding with a lending institution. A business plan covers:

1.) The service or product defined.

2.) Research on the total market and prospective target markets.

3.) Management and employee requirements.

4.) The legal business structure–corporation, partnership, or sole proprietorship.

5.) Competition–current and anticipated.

6.) Sales and merchandising strategies.

A business plan will help you raise outside financing.

7.) Startup costs (up till the venture pays for itself).

8.) Income projections and cash-flow analysis for at least one year.

9.) Step-by-step action plan.

A business plan is especially important in acquiring outside assistance for your enterprise. Terry notes that a business plan enables you "to communicate to others—potential partners, investors, vendors or associates—about the nature and state of the business."

Your Marketing Plan

The core of your business plan involves marketing decisions. You may want to expand this into a separate marketing plan after you have taken care of the necessities of organization and startup capital. Your marketing plan should include answers to these questions:

1.) What is the size of the market—large and undifferentiated or small and specialized?

2.) Is there an ongoing market for my service or will it become obsolete at some point?

3.) Is my pricing low enough to attract new patrons, and high enough to make a profit?

4.) Do prospective clients already recognize the value of my service, or is this a new concept that requires educating the public?

Know your market before you start your business.

5.) What can I emphasize that is better than or different from other similar services?

6.) How do my price structure, hours of operation, method of delivery and location and style (formal or casual) compare with similar services?

7.) How do I gauge client satisfaction? What is policy for complaint and refunds?

8.) How do I measure the results of marketing efforts?

9.) Am I currently covering operating expenses? After two years can I recoup my investment and earn a living wage?

10.) Do I look forward to working or do I dread it? Will I still be having fun after two years?

Refer to your marketing plan in discussions with staff and associates, and revise it periodically.

Depending upon your budget, you might want to hire experts to help you on various aspects of marketing:

A *marketing expert* or consulting firm can collect demographic research, questionnaires, and client surveys to help you target your market and serve them more efficiently. Original research can be very expensive, but much data is available at the library from government and university

Marketing experts can help you reach your business goals.

SUGGESTIONS FOR STARTING A SMALL BUSINESS:

The Small Business Administration Answer Desk in Washington, D.C., lists these suggestions for starting a small business:

1.) Determine the type and nature of your business.

2.) Is there a need for your business?

3.) Is it the type of business you are suited for?

4.) Develop a business plan with written goals.

5.) Will you be the sole proprietor?

6.) Learn the legal requirements for your area, the licenses and permits you will need.

The key to successful business is being prepared. For more information, including free business publications, the Small Business Administration invites you to call them at 1-800-827-5722.

sources virtually for free.

Professional writing and editing services are offered by freelance consultants. These people generally are available at an hourly rate. Many work at home, keep their overhead low, and can pass these savings on to you.

A *booking agent* will arrange speaking engagements on the college and professional lecture circuits, cruises, resorts, and major hotels. Booking agents generally work on percentages. Most prefer to work with bankable speakers, known authors, or personalities who can command at least $500 per lecture.

A *publicist* specializes in garnering publicity for you or your service. He'll throw events, get your name in columns, and schedule news conferences and speaking tours. An independent publicist might charge by the hour, by the day, or at a flat rate for projects such as producing brochures or news releases.

An *advertising agency* will handle your promotion campaigns for you. They'll write and design ads for newspapers, radio, television, and can determine where to place them. Expect to pay a 15% commission (the industry standard) on all ads placed. You'll probably pay extra for design, production, and writing services. Expect to spend several thousand dollars with an advertising agency.

Public relations firm. A public relations firm can get you publicity on television and in the newspapers. The idea is to generate media coverage as an alternative to advertising. They can make you newsworthy. They can present you as a leading specialist in your field. A full service "PR" firm might charge as much as $5,000 per month, with a three month minimum, and no guarantees.

The price for any of these services varies along with what you need done and whether it is a one-time project or an ongoing contract. Since this easily involves thousands of dollars, it makes sense to do as much as you can "in house." If your budget is small, make a virtue out of necessity: Get good at marketing yourself.

As your business grows, you'll soon become immersed in a myriad of details. Just make sure that you're covering the basics. Listen very carefully to what your clients are saying. Their needs and wants determine what you have to do to make your business a success.

3

Organizing Your Business

How you organize your business reflects your personal style. Some professionals prefer to work alone or with a small staff, minimizing the responsibilities of management. An accountant friend of ours operates this way. He almost always has time to leave the office for an espresso break, and he vacations in Europe at least one month each year. Other people are more consumed by business. Entrepreneurial types love the excitement of "empire building," creating large organizations, branching out with several offices, possibly even franchising.

How do you want to spend your time? After earning enough for food and rent, all the rest is art.

Strategies for Independent Professionals

Freelancers and independent professionals frequently combine an income from two or more sources or "profit centers." There's the storefront lawyer with a sideline bodywork practice; the auto mechanic who teaches and writes about auto repair; and the theater actor who does commercial voice-overs and teaches vocal coaching. Some pursue specialized niches, such as the architect who develops co-op housing. People with multiple interests often seek to combine them and earn money in the process.

Sometimes it's difficult to integrate multiple careers. Consider our friend who is part carpenter, therapist, and yoga instructor. People who hire him for carpentry rarely have occasion to inquire about his therapy practice or his yoga classes. Our friend's advancement in any one of his specialties is slower than it might be because he is only a part-timer in each field.

The advantage of developing separate careers is that success in one area is not dependent upon success in the others. However, the disadvantage is that the markets are not mutually reinforcing.

There's more income potential when you build interactive markets. So consider developing your skills in ways that are mutually supportive. Rick, another fellow we know, started as an auto mechanic. He branched out by teaching about basic auto repair and maintenance. The personal interac-

Success in one market does not always mean success in other markets.

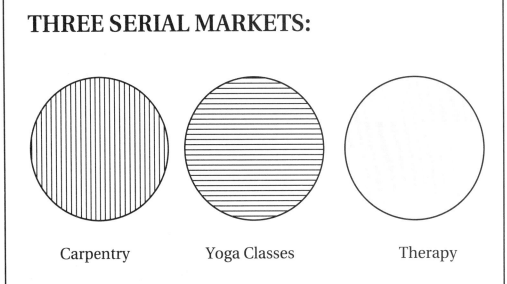

THREE SERIAL MARKETS:

Carpentry   Yoga Classes   Therapy

The serial markets represented here show three distinct profit centers, and that is good. But while there is strength in diversity, the disadvantage is that these three markets are not mutually reinforcing. Success in one area does little to foster success in other areas.

tion was rewarding and a real break from repair work. Having discovered how much students appreciated this led him to write books about auto care. After building his reputation as a teacher and author, Rick then branched out into other topics. Computers had been one of Rick's hobbies for many years. Now Rick earns money teaching and writing about computers.

Auto repair, teaching, and writing all are unique talents. Rick developed creatively by pursuing each of them. Rick's interactive market strategy enabled him to earn money while he was spreading his wings.

Like Rick, you can develop your talents and take advantage of interactive markets. Some examples:

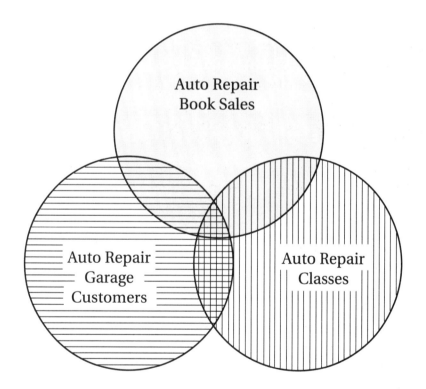

THREE INTERACTIVE MARKETS:

Auto Repair
Book Sales

Auto Repair
Garage
Customers

Auto Repair
Classes

The interactive markets represented here show three distinct profit centers. A particular advantage of interactive markets is that they are mutually reinforcing. Success in one area can help to build success in an aligned field.

Interactive profit centers reinforce each other.

Another way to develop niche markets is called "spoking." Popular lecturer and consultant Gordon Burgett develops this idea in depth in *Empire Building By Writing and Speaking.* Here's an example of spoking by topic: Start with a core topic such as weight control. Then develop specialty niches that branch out from the core. These specialties might include diet nutrition, anorexia in teens, psychological factors in obesity, and weight loss exercises.

As your business grows, continue to look for other ways to expand and diversify. John, the owner of a limousine service, was in danger of bankruptcy. He had relied almost exclusively on referrals from one local hotel.

Develop several specialties from a core skill.

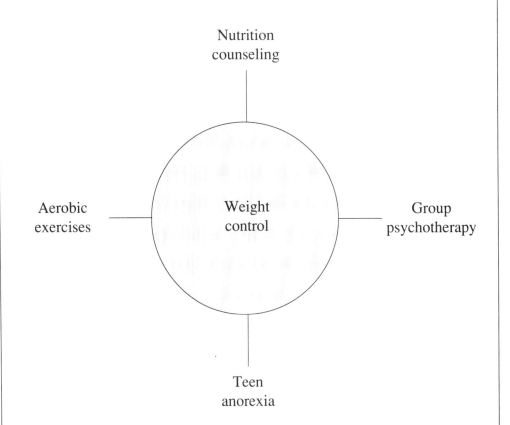

SPOKING FROM A CENTRAL SOURCE:

Nutrition counseling

Aerobic exercises

Weight control

Group psychotherapy

Teen anorexia

Start with a core topic such as weight control. Then develop specialty niches that branch out from the core. The number of possible spokes are limited only by the marketplace and your own imagination.

When hotel management purchased their own limousine, it nearly put John out of business. Too much reliance on one client, however lucrative, can lead to disaster. John saved his business by seeking contracts with several different hotels and building a private clientele. His future is now more secure, not dependent on the whim of a single client.

Startup Money

Starting or expanding your enterprise takes a combination of hard work and capital. The hard work is yours. Capital comes from savings, loans, or investments. Others may invest in your business because they believe in your goals or because they anticipate financial return. Some investors may want to become stockholders or influence corporate direction. How much responsibility and control you share is an important decision. At times your business may require a large infusion of capital. Sometimes, however, it's better to do without help if there are too many strings attached. If you're looking for money for startup or expansion, consider these sources:

A second job
Bank loans
Credit card advances
Credit from suppliers
Followers and supporters
Friends and family
Grants
Home mortgages
Personal savings
Reducing costs
Sweat equity
Venture capital

There are many sources of money besides banks.

A second job. Take on extra part-time work and earmark the savings for investing in your new business. Often this is easier than finding outside investors. A community fund-raiser once said to us, "We'd have been better ahead for our time spent if we'd all just taken second jobs as grocery checkers and pooled our savings."

Bank loans. Banks, credit unions, savings and loans, and brokerage houses frequently lend your own money back to you. Loan charges often make it a better deal simply to withdraw your savings. Up to $20,000, ask your banker to arrange a personal loan. To arrange a business loan, you, friends, or relatives probably will have to offer real estate or cash as collateral. Even as a business owner, you probably will have to sign personally and assume liability for the loan. Unsecured loans are an endangered species.

Credit card advances are a quick way to raise cash, but at relatively high interest rates. Most companies will raise your credit limit on request.

Credit from suppliers. Suppliers frequently will extend credit to a new enterprise to win the account. Negotiate for terms of up to 90 days or more to improve your cash flow.

Followers and supporters. Finance experts Michael Phillips and Roger Pritchard suggest throwing a get-together or potluck for all prospective lenders, investors, advisers, suppliers, and customers. With a good business plan and a strong presentation, you may be able to launch your venture amid good will and community support. If several people each contribute a few hundred dollars or more, this can create a sizable fund.

Friends and family. Who could be more supportive? Impress them with a detailed, professional business plan. Draw up a written loan agreement to avoid misunderstandings and protect everybody's interests. Specify whether the capital is a gift, loan, or investment. What is the repayment schedule? What is the interest charge? One guideline is to borrow at money market rates, which tend to be more than savings passbook accounts but less than what banks charge to borrowers. This way your loved ones can give you a "deal" and still come out ahead on their investment.

Grants. Corporate and government grants of all sorts are available, each with its own particular set of guidelines and requirements. Matthew Lesko has made a profession out of collecting this information. Lesko's book, *Getting Yours: The Complete Guide to Government Money,* should be available at your local bookstore or library.

Home mortgages are extensions of your personal credit. Borrowing against home equity usually is less expensive than consumer loans. This is because the loan is secured by the value of your property. Borrowing against your home often has favorable tax advantages, too.

Personal savings. Besides bank savings accounts, consider selling or borrowing against gold, silver, jewelry, or the equity in your life insurance policy. Maybe it's time to liquidate that collection of record albums, Lionel trains, or Barbie dolls.

Reducing costs. Some experts advise, "Don't buy if you can lease. Don't lease if you can rent. Don't rent if you can borrow." Consider joining local business barter clubs, but inquire about membership fees, restrictions, and potential tax liabilities. Barter directly, too. When negotiating private barters, it's helpful to specify the equivalent cash value and to write out the terms of the trade. Also negotiate a two to five percent discount by paying

Look into government grants before you borrow at bank rates.

suppliers in advance whenever possible.

Sweat equity. If you're just starting out, you probably have more time and energy than money. Consider substituting your own labor for money wherever you can. Instead of hiring janitors and office help, spend your money on advertising, business cards, the utilities bill! Hire lawyers, accountants, publicists, and other experts on a limited basis and learn to do many of their routine functions for yourself.

Venture capital. Private investors and firms are looking for a good return by investing in profitable businesses. These may be new ventures or established businesses primed for major expansion. Investors may become partners or stockholders in your enterprise. Make contacts through social clubs and business associations to find prospective venture capitalists. Also call established business brokers who specialize in networking with venture capitalists.

In the book *Start-Up Money,* Mick P. McKeever explains in detail how to create a business plan in order to obtain bank and private loans. Included are exercises which help you to decide if a prospective venture is financially viable. Joseph R. Mancuso's *How to Write A Winning Business Plan* is excellent, too. It includes original business plans that launched three successful medium sized corporations.

Of course, check with your accountant or tax attorney before you accept money from any second source. Make sure that your contract says what you expect it to say. A strategy that looks attractive may have hidden legal or tax consequences.

Explore creative ways to run your business with less money.

Are You Self-employed?

If you create your own job, you are self-employed. If you work as an independent contractor, you are self-employed. If you work for an organization that deducts taxes from your wages, you are not self-employed.

As a freelance teacher or consultant, you may be a self-employed independent contractor. The Internal Revenue Code says, "Self-employment includes more than regular full-time business activities. It also includes certain part-time work that you do at home or in addition to your regular job" (*Publication 17*).

You probably are an independent contractor if several or all of these conditions apply:

You are paid by the job and not at a set wage.
You set your own work schedule.
You provide materials or work space.
You are responsible for out-of-pocket expenses.

You contract with more than one person or business.
You advertise your services.

Being self-employed you have special tax obligations. A self-employed person who nets more than $400 per year must file a tax return. Social Security tax is more expensive for self-employed individuals than for people who are hired as employees. This is because the self-employed have to pay both the employee's and the employer's contribution to the Social Security system, about 15% of gross wages.

Fortunately, if you are self-employed you may benefit from some significant deductions. Pick up *Publication 17* and *Publication 334* from your local IRS office for details and provisions. Consult current publications to take advantage of the latest tax code revisions. In *Small Time Operator,* Bernard Kamoroff lists 112 typical business expenses that are tax deductible. "Any expense that meets the IRS's rules...if not specifically disallowed, should be taken whether it is on this list or not," says Kamoroff. The IRS requires that deductions be "reasonable,"..."ordinary and necessary." Our short list of normally allowable deductions includes:

The self-employed enjoy special tax advantages.

Accounting fees
Advertising
Business books (such as the one you're reading now)
Business lunches
Depreciation
Education
Employee benefits
Equipment rental
Interest
Legal fees
Occupancy
Payroll taxes
Pension plan contributions
Postage and shipping
Salaries and wages
Supplies
Telephone
Travel
Utilities

Consult a tax expert to make sure that the deductions you take are allowable. Rules that seem straightforward can get complicated in application. For example, if you're self-employed, the IRS may allow you to deduct home office expenses 'off the top,' whether or not you itemize deductions. If you're an employee, however, the IRS says "If you use part of your home regularly and exclusively for business purposes, you may deduct part of the operating and depreciation expenses on your home as an itemized deduction." If you use a spare bedroom exclusively as a home office, it is an allowable deduction. If you watch television at night in that room, it may not be allowable. A home office with a couch might be allowable, but if the couch contains a "hide-a-bed," the room may not be allowable. If you use your living room some evenings to teach a class, but other times to entertain guests, it probably is not allowable.

Overall, the tax laws function to encourage the formation of new products and services. Tax breaks encourage entrepreneurship. The expenses you incur starting up a new business may very well provide you with generous tax deductions off your present income. Pay by check whenever possible. Always ask for a receipt for *everything*. If you do nothing else, designate one desk drawer for receipts and keep them all together. When you finally sort them out for your accountant, they could be worth a gold mine in allowable deductions.

As your business grows, you'll find yourself hiring staff for bookkeeping, secretarial, janitorial, legal, and other support functions. You'll have to decide whether to hire employees or independent contractors. In general, hiring independent contractors creates less paperwork for you. However, independent contractors also are more independent and less under your direct supervision. It's a good idea to review this matter with your accountant when the time comes to decide which way to go.

Save all your receipts— many are allowable tax deductions.

Proprietorship, Partnership, or Corporation?

Businesses are organized in three distinct legal forms: proprietorships, partnerships, and corporations. The one right for you depends on the scale of your operation and your personal style. Proprietorships in essence are a form of self-employment. The owner, in effect, is the business. A fictitious business name statement is required in many states if a proprietor uses a business name. All profit is the proprietor's. The proprietor is liable for all debt, too. The proprietor also assumes full tax liability. Your business automatically is a proprietorship unless you make it a partnership or a corporation.

Partnerships are legal entities that divide profits and liabilities among two or more individuals. Partners share income and losses according to an agreed-upon ratio. There is a distinction between general partnerships and limited partnerships. In a general partnership, each partner has unlimited liability. If any partner cannot pay his or her share of debts, the other partner or partners are responsible. In a limited partnership, a general partner has unlimited liability. There are one or more limited partners who are liable only up to the limit of their investment.

Partnerships are like marriages. They require time and commitment, and they are legally binding. During startup, you may see more of your business partner than your roommate or spouse. When partnerships are first arranged, make specific provisions regarding who decides what, and how to divide assets and profits upon dissolution. If "prenuptial contracts" are a good idea for marriages, they are essential for partnerships. Set up a partnership with the assistance of a qualified business attorney.

See a tax adviser to determine whether or not to incorporate.

A corporation is a distinct legal entity. A corporation has an official name and birth date. It pays taxes unless specifically exempt. A corporation posts profits or losses in addition to the individuals who own or manage it. Because certain aspects of the tax codes favor corporations, one very good reason to establish a corporation is to shelter earnings. Another reason is to limit liability. Corporate managers normally are not personally liable for debts or lawsuits against the corporation. For instance, if a corporation goes bankrupt, an executive's personal assets and savings normally cannot be seized by creditors. However, a corporate employee may be personally liable if he is found guilty of gross negligence or criminal misconduct.

There are many corporate structures to consider. Private corporations may be "closely held" or family owned. Public corporations sell shares to investors and are traded on the stock market. This is a potential way to attract investors for additional business expansion. Smaller organizations may elect "S Corporation" status. For federal income tax purposes, the S Corporation is taxed in a manner similar to a partnership. Income, losses and tax liabilities flow through to stockholders. State laws vary as to how they treat S Corporations, so check the laws in your state. Another option is to form a non-profit corporation.

Should you incorporate or not? Choose incorporation for several reasons. Incorporate for prestige. Incorporate to secure credit from lending institutions. Incorporate to limit personal liability. High wage earners frequently incorporate for tax advantages, too. However, forming and maintaining a corporation involves extra time and paperwork. Unless your income is sufficiently high, you may be better off with a proprietorship or partnership. Again, consult with your attorney or accountant for details.

Non-profit Corporations

"Should we go non-profit?" is a question we're often asked. This quick run down should help you decide for yourself.

Non-profit corporations have distinct benefits and drawbacks compared with for-profit corporations. Non-profits, like for-profits, are distinct legal entities that provide officers and directors with limited personal liability. Non-profits pay little or no corporate taxes and can be excellent shelters of income. Non-profit tax-exempt status also may be an excellent way of raising contributions. Non-profits, however, are not attractive to institutional lenders or venture capitalists. Non-profits cannot be owned by private individuals or traded on the stock market.

The government encourages certain activities considered socially redeeming by making them tax exempt. (Being non-profit can get you extra publicity in the mass media, too.) If you engage in activities of a charitable (educational, scientific, or religious), social, or civic nature, you may qualify as non-profit. You must apply for tax-exempt status separately from federal and state governments. Contact the district office of the Internal Revenue Service for federal exemption. Contact your state capital for state tax exemption. The purpose of your corporation, your articles of incorporation and by-laws, will be reviewed for compliance with applicable laws. It may take several months to finalize approval at both the state and federal levels. Check with an accountant or attorney who is familiar with filing for tax-exempt status if you are not a "do-it-yourselfer."

Being non-profit does not mean taking a vow of poverty. You may compensate board members, administrators, and staff at rates comparable to the private sector, though not significantly greater. If you generate an operating surplus, save it or spend it according to your charter. As one accountant advises, "Just don't call it 'profit.'"

Non-profit status may confer property tax exemption, income and other federal tax exemption, tax-free savings accounts, discount postal rates, the ability to solicit tax-exempt contributions, and advantages obtaining publicity in the media.

However, there are specific limits on non-profit activities. Non-profits normally cannot engage in political campaigns, cannot be franchised, and cannot conduct significant activity outside their chartered purpose. This IRS restriction is highly interpretive, however. The IRS has found bingo acceptable for some churches but operating health clubs unacceptable for others. Finally, upon dissolution of a non-profit, assets cannot accrue to any individual member. Assets must remain dedicated to the original purposes expressed in the original articles of incorporation.

If you grow your business to a point where it is sufficiently large, you may find it advantageous to spin off into two or more corporations, one non-profit and the other for-profit. In this way you can enjoy the advantages of both types of incorporation. The most common situation we

'Non-profit' is a special tax category. It doesn't necessarily mean 'no money.'

encounter is a for-profit organization or center that wants to organize a non-profit arm to conduct classes and educational trainings. When you're ready for this, it's best to employ the services of a fairly sophisticated corporate attorney.

Your Board of Directors

A corporation is managed by its directors. Family members may serve on the board of a closely held family corporation. The board of directors of a non-profit corporation generally cannot include a majority of members who are related by blood or marriage. A corporation that offers public stock may include shareholders, employees, or other community members.

A board of directors serves several functions. Officers of the board may participate in the day-to-day management of the corporation, or they may serve a more advisory role.

Inviting a lawyer, an accountant, a publicist, or other experienced people to serve on the board can be a source of inexpensive professional assistance. One school in Kansas has a newspaper publisher on its board. After each directors' meeting there is a rash of new articles in the local daily. The board can represent a community constituency. For example, the board of an emergency switchboard includes telephone volunteers, directors of other social service agencies, and interested private citizens.

Board members may represent the living embodiment of the values of the corporation. Consider asking prominent community members and corporate executives to lend their names. If you're non-profit and seek grants, this adds credibility to funding drives and looks impressive on the letterhead.

Smaller boards make decisions more quickly.

A board functions best when members share a clearly articulated vision and agreed-upon strategies to attain that vision. A larger board with distinguished members can encourage community involvement and aid fund-raising. However, the advantages of a smaller board are quicker decision-making and less politics. It becomes a parttime job just to stay in touch with and assemble a board of 20 or more members.

Our own non-profit corporation has a small board of five people who know each other. The Executive Director manages the corporation, sets meeting agendas, and files the required paperwork. Board members are re-elected to successive terms over long periods. Quorums are easy to raise and politics are kept to a minimum. The business part of meetings typically is less than one hour per year. We're not sure if this is a *Guiness Book* record, but it's close.

Bookkeeping and Accounting

Good record keeping is vital to your business. At some point you'll probably want to get outside assistance with bookkeeping and accounting. Hire a bookkeeper to work with accounts payable and receivable, employee wages, and balancing the checkbook. Hire an accountant, preferably a Certified Public Accountant, to create a general ledger and to help you with tax planning.

You can design a very basic chart of accounts for your business by extrapolating from your federal tax forms. These include categories for income, expenses, assets, and liabilities. However, you'll probably need to modify and expand certain categories to fit the particular needs of your enterprise. For instance, federal tax forms require only one account for "postage" expenses. In our case, as publishers, we divided this into three accounts. This isn't required legally, but it's useful for us to know how much we're spending on first class letters, third class catalogs, and fourth class books.

Work with an accountant to devise a chart of accounts which conforms to tax requirements as well as helping you to understand your business. Paying taxes is only one part of good accounting. Helping you to be more efficient and profitable is what the best accountants are all about.

You may find it useful to get professional accounting and tax assistance in these areas as well:

Billing
Budgeting
Capital requirements
Deferred income
Employee productivity
Inventory
Management planning
Product costs
Profit areas
Projections

Bookkeeping is the scorecard of business.

Depending on the economics of scale, ask your accountant about computerizing payroll, inventory, or other areas. Once you've developed a good accounting system, you or an in-house bookkeeper should be able do most of the rest. You can hire a full service accounting firm to handle all day-to-day record keeping, but you're likely to pay a premium for the convenience.

Income and Loss Analysis

Many businesses expect to be profitable within two years, if not before. Of course, this timetable can vary greatly, depending upon the amount of initial capital investment, the anticipated return, executive salaries, and any other variable costs. The figures we're about to mention refer to real growth and do not include the impact of inflation.

How much income to expect varies widely. A new company may be expected to grow at 40% to 80% annually just to satisfy the demands of capital investors. Family owned businesses are under far less pressure to support this kind of growth. For a mature, privately owned business, keeping pace with inflation and supporting the lifestyle of the owner or chief executive officer may be all that's expected.

For non-profit organizations, a 5% surplus over and above wages and expenses is good; 10% is very good; and 15% or better is excellent. It is good policy to review and revise financial projections at least annually, if not more often. Too many non-profits seem to be victims of "crisis management." We heard that one non-profit failed, not for lack of support, but because the proposal writer couldn't keep up with grant proposal deadlines.

If you work as an independent professional, budget your income to allow for vacations and burn-out. Figure that nine or ten months of income has to pay for twelve months worth of expenses. To repeat the adage: "Make a dollar; save a dime." This will help you survive that inevitable slow month, a prolonged case of the flu, or two weeks on the beach when you absolutely have to get away.

Budget for vacations and emergencies.

Here is the ultimate secret to long term survival: Whatever your budget, learn to live slightly below your means. Make it a habit to save a certain percentage of your earnings. When you pay the monthly bills, pay yourself, too. Write out a check and put it directly into a savings account.

Surviving A Recession

Whether recessions are inevitable or simply the result of bad government planning, you'll probably experience several during your career in business.

The federal government defines recession as a period of two consecutive quarters of declining gross national product, or GNP. However, by the time the government gets around to admitting that we're in a recession, usually we've been in one for several months.

Recessions typically last 18 to 24 months, although they can extend much longer. The Carter presidency was plagued for years by "stagflation," slow growth accompanied by high inflation. The worst period in living memory, the Great Depression of 1929, lasted over 10 years. The economy never fully recovered until the early 1940's, just before industry mobilized for entry into World War II. (Mobilization may bring full employment, but manufacturing armaments does not improve the general standard of living. War is hell, not to mention a complete waste of resources.)

The difference between a "mild" recession, a "deep" recession, and a depression is open to interpretation. If your neighbor is out of a job, it's a recession. If you're out of a job, it's a depression. Actually, this isn't as flip as it sounds. A recession isn't some monolithic monster that affects everyone equally. Different parts of the country are affected to different degrees. High home heating oil prices are lousy for New Englanders but good news for Texans. Some industries are counter-cyclical and actually prosper during hard times. Bart's parents ran an auto parts store for over 35 years, through good times and bad. When people couldn't afford new cars, they'd spend more money keeping the old ones running. A recession offers opportunities for those in a position to take advantage of them.

Generally, the white collar service industries suffer fewer layoffs than manufacturing during a recession. People may put off major purchases such as appliances and automobiles. Universities often grow during a recession. Students who can't find work stay in school, and displaced workers go back to school to retrain for new jobs. The entertainment industry booms because people are looking for relief and escape. Expensive restaurants may lose patrons, but fast food places and grocery stores are much less affected. After all, people have to eat something. Similarly, people may scale down vacation travel plans. That European vacation may become a family outing closer to home, actually keeping more money circulating in the local economy. Elective surgery may be postponed, but necessary medical procedures are less interrupted. Tax lawyers may handle fewer mergers but more bankruptcy cases.

Recessions create panic for some, opportunity for others.

An important key to surviving a recession is to understand recession psychology. Recessions make people more uncertain about the future. They postpone spending, which further slows the economy. Don't retreat in fear when a recession is predicted. If a recession seems eminent, try to gauge its severity. Find out from peers and associates how it's likely to affect your particular business. In most cases you'll find that there is no need to panic or quit your business. There are rare exceptions, however. One fellow we know operated a home moving business. He calculated that the combination of a predicted recession and deregulation of the moving industry meant that his business would become unprofitable. Anticipating rough times ahead, he closed his doors and paid off all accounts in full. That showed real class. It also kept his credit rating as good as gold.

*The best
antidote for
recession is
to maintain
good will with
your clients.*

Show empathy with the recession mentality. The best antidote for recession fears is to maintain stability and consistency. Avoid raising your prices at the onset of a recession, even if your own costs are rising. This creates good will and protects your client base. If cash becomes tight, offer alternative payment options to your clients. Extend credit terms. Accept smaller monthly payments, but insist on a regular payment schedule. Paying on time is a good habit to keep. If you are having trouble paying your own bills, re-negotiate with creditors. Again, continue to make regular payments, even if you have to reduce the amount. Be cheery! A recession tends to be depressing to people in business.

Most businesses find it natural to grow but difficult to deal with contraction. If your cash flow is contracting during a recession, there are several options available to you. These include:

Borrowing
Cutting back advertising
Cutting employee training
Cutting expense accounts
Cutting salaries
Deferring equipment maintenance
Delaying salary increases
Delaying the introduction of new service lines
Extending credit from suppliers
Moving to less expensive offices
Postponing equipment upgrades
Renegotiating loans
Replacing salaried staff with contractors
Working harder or longer hours

Don't make matters worse during a recession by slashing your marketing budget beyond reason. Rather, try to make cuts in several areas. Businesses that continue to market and promote through a recession often come out with a larger market share than at the beginning of the recession. So, don't abandon your market simply to save a few dollars in the short run. If you market consistently, you're likely to survive a recession stronger than you went into it.

Since we started our educational newspaper *Open Exchange,* we have survived two major recessions. As we edit this text, we also have to decide our business strategy for the 1991 recession. Our previous track record is a strong indication of what we can expect. In most years our business has grown 5% to 20% annually, but we have experienced periods of two or three consecutive declining months during recessions. We consider cer-

SURVIVING THE COMPETITION:

The high minded talk about every individual's "unique selling position" pales when somebody steals your concept and competes directly for your clients. As publishers of a professional directory, we have had to field this complaint from advertisers: "My ad was working great, and then somebody copied my idea with a similar ad. Now I'm losing business to them. What do I do?"

We answer that question with the following story. During the late 1970's hypnosis had a small but constant following, and we offered just two classes teaching self-hypnosis. Next came major media coverage and a burgeoning interest in hypnosis for therapy and consciousness-raising. At the high point we were offering as many as 40 hypnosis listings—classes, private consultations, past-life regressions, weight and habit control clinics, and certification trainings.

Unfortunately for some providers, 40 listings were more than the market could accommodate, and there was the inevitable shake-out. The people who entered the field late or expected quick financial rewards seemed to drop out first. Those who were more committed to the discipline—who truly loved their work—stayed with it. By the early 1980's the number of providers in our publication leveled out to between 15 and 20.

We learned several lessons from this experience. The hypnosis "fad" brought many competitors into the market. This raised performance expectations by consumers, which hurt some of the less competent or less efficient providers. Even after the fad peaked, the audience for hypnosis was several times larger. The providers who dropped out often did not recoup their business investment. Those who were good and persevered through the lean times, however, ultimately benefitted from everybody else's advertising.

We've seen this story repeated a dozen times. It could just as easily apply to accounting, dance, auto repair, professional fashion design, or psychotherapy. Chances are it applies to you, too.

If you love your business, you will probably outlast the opportunists and late comers.

Plan for the likelihood of recession.

tain costs "fixed," and not negotiable. These include office rent, utilities, newspaper circulation (100,000 copies per quarter) and distribution. Other costs are "variable" and subject to economic conditions. For example, we will defer upgrading our computer system and cost of living wage increases until the economy turns around. Even though this is an inflationary recession and our own costs are increasing, we will defer raising our advertising rates in order to protect our market share. Also, we will extend credit terms to regular advertisers to keep them as clients and to help them protect their market shares. If the recession is mild, this may be all that's necessary. If the recession is severe, we'll take stronger medicine, including administrative salary cuts. The point is to do what you must to survive.

We have contingency plans that enable us to continue operating reasonably intact with a 25% decline in revenues. We recommend that you develop your own contingency plans to weather inevitable economic storms. Growth rates rarely remain stable, predictable, or uninterrupted over any length of time.

Managing Growth

Managing growth presents a special challenge to entrepreneurs and independent professionals. Business consultant Claude Whitmyer notes that many enterprises have been derailed by their inability to handle the rapid growth that marketing efforts sometimes generate. You must be able to delegate responsibilities, have a good bookkeeping system, make sure your communications systems are working smoothly, and be ready to fill orders or serve clients in a timely, responsible fashion. During the personal computer boom in the 1980's, several hardware companies nearly went out of business because they could not handle increased demands for their products. Phone lines were not covered, repairs were delayed, and shipments to suppliers were late. Markets may be lost forever if financing for expansion is not available when needed. Timing is critical!

Even slow, steady growth presents its special challenges. Feldenkrais bodywork practitioner Richard Adelman had built a successful practice over several years. Using directory advertising, posters, free demonstration evenings, and direct mail solicitations, Richard was filling over 30 hours a week with private clients. Running groups, managing his business, and marketing took up much of the rest of his time. Richard's success led him to ask us, "Where do I go from here?" We told Richard that he had several options: He could cut back on his advertising and increase his profit margins. He could increase advertising and contract with assistants to help handle the growing case load. He could raise his hourly rates and begin to take his market "upscale." He could explore new markets, perhaps designing stress reduction and pain relief programs for corporations. Finally, he might consider writing articles, eventually writing a book to popularize his particular style of body therapy. The question for Richard is: "Where do you want to go?" It's a question we all need to ask.

Building a business often requires a major investment of your time. As your enterprise grows bigger, you'll spend more time managing business affairs and less in direct contact with clients. Consider carefully how big you want your business to grow. One school administrator told us, "I cut back the size of my business in order to spend more time teaching my own classes. It's teaching that I really love, not administration." Once your business is stable and profitable, you may be able to hire managers and minimize your own day-to-day involvement in administration. However, many corporate executives and small business owners find that they have to put in 60 hour weeks just to keep the competitive edge.

Sometimes staying smaller is better. *Running A One-Person Business* is a practical book that covers how to operate a micro-business profitably while you maintain emotional well-being. Authors Claude Whitmyer and Salli Rasberry examine real life decisions: setting office hours, organizing work space, selecting office equipment, methods of accounting, calendar planners, childcare, and more. If you're setting up shop on your own, you'll find this book to be a comforting companion as well as a font of expert advice.

Business Ethics

In the movie *Wall Street,* Michael Douglas portrayed a sleazy corporate raider who declares, "Greed is good." What's wrong with business and how to right it has been a topic of conversation ever since the Golden Rule was written.

Since the 1970's advocates of "good work," and "right livelihood" have articulated the nobler aspects to earning a living. Writers such as E. F. Schumacher, Paul Hawken, Michael Phillips, and Marsha Sinetar have provided a broader vision of success that enriches the spirit as well as the wallet. Their writings variously address issues of respect, creativity, love of work, employee participation, ecological awareness, and having fun.

What is ethical business? We believe that good communication is the cornerstone. When the contract between client and provider is clear, problems are minimal. Reprinted here is our Code of Ethics. We developed the Code for businesses and independent professionals who list in our San Francisco Bay Area resource directory, *Open Exchange.* We use the following as general guidelines, not hard rules:

OPEN EXCHANGE Code of Ethics

The following statement is printed in every edition of OPEN EXCHANGE, Bay Area's largest circulation independent directory of classes and services. The theme of the statement is to encourage good communication between providers and clients, teachers and students:

OPEN EXCHANGE stands for quality, integrity, and service to the community. We strongly urge all who list services here to adopt the following guidelines for professional conduct. While we cannot control or assume responsibility for what is offered, it is our editorial prerogative to publish listings only where we believe these standards are upheld. We encourage your active participation and feedback in determining future offerings.

- Products will work as advertised.

- Services will be rendered as described.

- Personal qualifications will be truthful and accurate.

- Fees and materials costs will be described in advance of services rendered. This is to include establishing payment schedules and explicit provisions for refunds, where applicable.

- Scheduled events will take place at published dates, days, times, and locations. Conveners will notify participants in advance regarding changes in schedule, costs, or substitute teachers.

- Partial or complete refunds will be offered where listers break their commitments to participants. However, listers are not obligated by participants' schedule changes or absences.

- Listers afford OPEN EXCHANGE staff the right to visit or inspect their products or services.

4

Your Client Profile

WHO ARE YOUR CLIENTS? How big is your potential market? How do you target the most likely prospects? In this chapter we look at several ways to create a client profile: demographics, lifestyle marketing, surveys, and tracking purchases. We also discuss how to make contact with likely prospects, and how to keep current clients happy as well.

Analyzing Your Market

Demographics is the statistical analysis of human populations. Experts divide populations into subgroups for many purposes. A population may be divided by age, income, career, geographical distribution, home ownership, political preference, or any other useful category. Government census takers gather information helpful in public planning. Businesses collect information for marketing and merchandising. Every individual is unique, but taken as a group, people act in predictable ways. For example, because non-smokers and vegetarians live longer and are healthier, some insurance companies offer these groups reduced rates.

Demographic studies may confirm the obvious or help you discover new, previously hidden correlations. Sample populations are polled about product preferences before the product is marketed widely. You can read collected public demographic reports, commission experts to do original research, or conduct your own surveys.

The traditional demographic categories of age, income, and geography are helpful references, but they are not the whole story. The decision to purchase a service also involves consideration of motives, values, and lifestyles. Demographic analysis is not foolproof. People's marketing choices also reflect their dreams and ideals. Surveys cannot always calibrate the depth of these feelings. Experts don't always know the right questions to ask, either.

Coca-Cola is the most successfully marketed product in the world, but its marketers are not infallible. In 1985 the Coca-Cola Company abandoned it's one hundred year old formula to introduce "New Coke." Thousands of people preferred the new, sweeter formula in sample taste tests. This preference was especially strong with younger drinkers, a prime share of the soft drink market. However, immediately after the announcement of a formula change, the American public raised a furor over losing an old tradition, the original "real thing." The company cleverly rebounded by offering the public both formulas, old and new.

Some accused Coke of having planned the dual marketing strategy from the start. It did result in increasing Coke's allotment of valuable display space in stores. However, nobody could have anticipated the intensity of public outcry—headline news articles, television debates, picketing, and "Coke dumping" by indignant consumers! It seemed that Coke executives had been caught off guard by the fierce public reaction. Insensitive executives were tampering with an American institution. Had they been misled by inadequate product research?

Thus the "experts" are not always right. If you have strong convictions about a particular product or service, your instincts may be ahead of conventional wisdom. Don't ignore the numbers, but remember that they do not tell the whole story. If you are marketing a new specialty service you may be entering uncharted territory. You may be on the cutting edge of a brand new market niche.

Now, the most direct way to target a market is to track actual purchase behavior. If you are new to a particular business, gather as much data as possible about established competitors and their clients. As your business matures, you can poll your own clients. When we needed to know which of two locations was preferable to hold a business party, we "polled"

Numbers don't tell everything. Trust your instincts, too.

several of the expected guests. Not rigorously scientific, perhaps, but sometimes an informal survey is all you need.

What people actually do is often more telling than what they say in response to a poll. When we analyzed class enrollments at our school, we found that people were much more likely to travel West, toward San Francisco rather than East to any other city. Evening classes were better attended in neighborhoods considered "safe" and well lit. Business classes were better attended when held close to the San Francisco financial center. But students will travel for hundreds of miles to experience a favorite guru. Patterns such as these may not show up in surveys because you don't necessarily know in advance what questions to ask.

Thus, there are several ways to look at populations and profile clients. You can count heads, interpret lifestyles, survey target populations, and track purchase patterns. Throughout this chapter we do a little of each.

The Baby Boomers

If you are offering a service on the open market, the baby boom generation is your most likely audience. It is not only the largest demographic group but also the most educated and affluent. Baby boomers are in their prime years for earning and raising families. Let's take a closer look at who they are.

The "baby boom" started when soldiers returned after World War II, married their sweethearts, and settled down to live the American Dream. The 76 million Americans born between 1946 and 1964 belong to the baby boom generation. This is about 45% of all adults. By their sheer numbers alone, baby boomers have rocked the economy at every stage of their growth. From the explosion in diaper sales to the anticipated bankruptcy of Social Security, baby boomers cannot be ignored.

Baby boomers lead different lives from their parents. Baby boomers are better educated, more health conscious, and have more investment savvy. They shop for quality. They pursue diverse leisure activities with a special passion. Here are some of the numbers provided by a *People* magazine survey published in *The Experts' Guide to the Baby Boomers:*

> 90% are high school graduates
> 57% are college graduates
> 51% professional/managerial
> 58% married
> 54% dual income households

Baby boomers are the best educated generation ever. They were

45% of all adults are baby boomers.

reared during the economic boom of the 1950's and early 60's, so they have high personal expectations. Despite the crowded job markets, boomers expect to get ahead. To do this they have learned to plan and save. Boomers are more likely to be home owners than their parents. They want their first homes to be as nice as their parents' second or third homes. Many of them have succeeded.

In order to live as well as or better than their parents, many baby boomers are willing to make sacrifices. Many are two career couples. They marry later and have smaller families, usually only one or two children. There is more equality in sex roles, with men assuming somewhat more responsibility for household chores and parenting. More boomers have chosen to remain single, too. Although communication skills are better, there is more divorce and remarriage. Nothing seems as permanent to baby boomers as it did to their parents.

Baby boomers are quality-conscious consumers.

Boomers are more travel and leisure oriented than their parents. This is possible because their median income is higher and fewer are poor. They have more disposable income, so they spend more freely on themselves. Where their parents burned the mortgage as soon as they managed to pay it off, boomers extend payments for perceived tax advantages. They thrive on the credit economy. They know how to spend as well as how to save. They participate more in sports and outdoor activities. They are health conscious and expect to live active, sexual lives well past middle age. They eat their bran, watch their fats, time their aerobic workouts, and do not expect to die of a heart attack at 50.

Boomers as a whole are liberal on social issues, but they are fiscal conservatives who are wary of big government. They are entrepreneurial. Such individualism is partly a carry over from the youth rebellion. If an employer does not reward or appreciate him, a boomer is likely to go out and start his own company. Many boomers are torn between differing world views: competition versus community; getting ahead versus finding oneself; doing well or doing socially responsible work; political nihilism versus new age idealism. They expect equal opportunity. They demand clean air, clean water, and open parks. But they also like the fruits of technology–stereos, performance cars, and Rolex watches.

Baby boomers believe in themselves and live with a special intensity. They grew up with the understanding that they could consciously choose where and how they lived and worked. They were raised in an era of change and have learned to adapt to it. They are future oriented and innovative. They embrace new ideas and experimental lifestyles. They want spiritual fulfillment, material security, and many traditional goals, too. They want it all, and they live intensely to get it. Baby boomers are special because they believe that they are special.

When marketing to baby boomers, recognize that they are media savvy. Boomers are the first generation to grow up with television. They understand surveys, ratings, promotion campaigns, marketing strategies and the bottom line. They are amused but not deceived by technological tricks. It's harder to fool them. They can read between the lines and assess the motives of a corporate campaign. They are tolerant of ambition but impatient with deception, especially if they are the target.

Baby boomers are quality conscious and discriminating consumers. They were raised with high expectations. They will save up and sacrifice for something they really want. A boomer will outfit a ten year old auto with a first rate stereo that costs as much as the car itself! Craftsmanship has experienced a revival thanks to boomers.

Baby boomers come in all political stripes and colors. The older baby boomers were deeply affected by the civil rights struggles and youth rebellion of the 1960's. They believed in Camelot and the Summer of Love, if only in their youth. Many remain idealistic and community minded. Vietnam-era youth believed that their protest stopped the war. However, the younger baby boomers did not experience this cultural clash. They came into the job market after their older sisters and brothers filled many of the best positions. This subgroup tends to be more cynical, competitive, and materialistic.

Broad characterizations do not fully account for the variety of values and lifestyles held by this generation. Trend watchers note that many boomers are rediscovering family values and religion, even as others glorify the singles lifestyle and career independence. Threatened by AIDS and other consequences of casual sex, many boomers have paired off and live stay-at-home lives, sometimes called "cocooning." Still, older singles are leading a more active social lifestyle than ever before. While "sex, drugs, and rock and roll" was the motto of the 60's boomers, "safe sex and light rock" may become the motto of boomers well into their 60's.

The pampered children of baby boomers are causing new cultural ripples. Aging boomers have married later, are having fewer children, but are spending more to give them the best of everything. "They are shelling out millions for educational toys, videos, and tutoring services" (*Business Week*, "Those Aging Boomers," May 20, 1991). Boomer kids constitute a new demographic "boomlet" which is responsible for exploding sales of designer kids' clothes, electronic toys, childcare, and specialty services. Boomlet kids, raised more permissively than their parents, are making many of their own purchasing decisions at a much earlier age. From their choice of foods and clothes to their interest in Teenage Mutant Ninja Turtles, boomlet kids are exercising a new economic clout, and marketers are responding happily.

Baby boomers are entering middle age.

Throughout the 1990's and into the next century, baby boomers will be enjoying their peak earning years. Boomers as a group may never earn quite as much as their parents, but their sheer numbers and active career and lifestyles will make them the primary arbiters of culture. Educated and affluent, the boomers will continue to be the primary consumer market for an increasingly diverse range of products and services. In *100 Predictions for the Baby Boom,* Cheryl Russell concludes, "The result will be more of everything–more technology in the home, more imported goods and exotic foods, more ways of buying things, and more things to buy. Consumers will demand choice, and the successful businesses of the future will deliver it. The baby boom will dictate its wants and needs to businesses for the next five decades."

Aging Americans

More older Americans are staying active and healthy.

The market of people over 50 years old is another important demographic group to consider. The percentage of the population in this category is growing, too. After 1996 the first baby boomers will be entering this group. By the late 1990's the over 50 market will be a larger segment than that of the baby boomers. Notes Jeff Ostroff in the introduction to *Successful Marketing to the 50+ Consumer,* "More than 60 million Americans are now at least a half-century old. And every day, some 6,000 others join them. To truly appreciate how amazing those numbers are, consider the fact that at the turn of this century *life expectancy* itself wasn't even 50!"

The stereotypes about aging are quickly crumbling. Mature Americans, as a group, tend to be affluent, not impoverished. They continue to enjoy companionship, sex, and sports well into later life. They have diverse interests and are willing to try new activities, including foods, relationships, and careers. Many seniors are re-entering the work force after retirement, not just for money but because they don't want to stagnate. As the oldest baby boomers approach 50, they are helping to redefine what it means to grow "old." Boomers expect to stay youth oriented and active well through middle age, according to psychologist Ross Goldstein (*USA Today,* May 10, 1991, p. 4D).

Older Americans want acknowledgment and respect for their maturity and wisdom. However, they don't feel "old." As a group they are living decades longer than in the last century. And they are living generally with a minimal decline in mental and physical prowess. The American Association of Retired Persons (AARP) has used the term "youth creep" to define these feelings. People are feeling young far later in life than they used to. "Old" is at least ten years from whatever age you happen to be at the time.

Looking at the numbers closer you can see what a large and diverse group this is. Demographers have identified several subgroups:

Prime lifers, ages 50-64
The young old, ages 60-74
The old, ages 75-84
The oldest old, ages 85+

The *prime lifers* share much in common with younger Americans. Thanks to youth creep, they're generally better educated, wealthier, and healthier than the other mature subgroups. More of them live with their spouses, and more of them are still active in their careers. The *young old* are the most affluent of the subgroups, and many of them are healthy enough to enjoy their abundant leisure time. There is a noticeable loss of health and vigor among the *old* which limits their decision making and consumer options. Among the *oldest old,* issues of declining health and the necessities of primary care frequently take precedence.

The sons and daughters of older seniors have been called the "sandwich generation." They are trapped between caring for their aging parents on one side and raising their children on the other. This has robbed them of leisure time and strapped them financially, too. The sandwich generation has to spend their money on basics, because they have little extra money to spend on leisure products and services.

Older Americans have become more savvy consumers.

Products and services with special appeal to seniors include health care, finance, vacation, sports, and recreation. Consider seniors' special circumstances and needs when designing products and services for this group. Customer service is a priority, often over price. Issues of safety, security, and convenience are important. Seniors have become more savvy consumers, too. AARP has proven to be an effective lobby organization in securing rights and privileges. Seniors are more outspoken, assertive, and knowledgeable as a result.

The lifestyle of older Americans includes home based products and services. These include microwaves, computer controlled appliances, mail-order shopping, housekeeping, landscaping, special transportation, home companions, and physician house calls. Target seniors for special financial instruments, such as reverse mortgages. As the baby boomers age, there is an increasing number of seniors living in single person households. Singles oriented events and vacations, already popular among the boomers, are growing increasingly popular among seniors.

Market to seniors by emphasizing the attractive parts of aging, more time, wisdom, accomplishments, and the desire to give of oneself. Older Americans generally feel good about who they are. They are proud and do not want to deny their age. As Art Linkletter has said, "Old age is not for sissies." Reinforcing these positive feelings in your own promotional materials is a good strategy.

Soft sells can work well, especially because older Americans have been bombarded by high pressure sales and many now have a core of skepticism. Older people generally don't want to be categorized. Some disdain terms like "senior citizen," but there is no clear consensus here. Showing older people in ads works well, as do testimonials. However, segregating seniors usually is a mistake. Seniors do not want to feel isolated or caricatured. Copy that reads, "People of all ages...," or words to that effect, makes the point. Photos of seniors, adults, and children together also is a good strategy. Finally, seniors prefer larger typefaces which are easier to read.

Each new generation feels it must redefine itself.

The Baby Bust Generation

In the shadow of the baby boomers is the "baby bust" generation. These are the 48 million young Americans born between 1961 and 1972. The last few years of the baby boom are swept into this category because the habits and attitudes of late boomers make them more similar to their younger cousins.

This "twentysomething generation" has been ignored by demographers and marketers because it is a smaller, quieter group. But this generation is now coming of age. "They are finally out there, saying 'Pay attention to us,' but I've never heard them think of a single thing that defines them," says Martha Farnsworth Riche, national editor of *American Demographics* magazine (*Time*, July 16, 1990, p. 58).

The baby busters came of age in the late 70's and 80's, a time of cultural blandness compared with the turmoil of the 60's. Busters romanticize the past, when the civil rights movement and the Vietnam War encouraged commitment and heroics. Busters feel that there is no art or music they can truly call their own. Where boomers had the fiery musings of the Beatles and Dylan, busters have been offered the Bee Gees and Michael Jackson. Art itself has been co-opted by corporate values. Michael Jackson sings for Pepsi. Rolling Stone concerts are sponsored by Budweiser. In response, some busters have turned to nostalgia or new wave.

Busters would like to make a contribution to the culture but feel powerless to act. Rejecting both the utopian notions of the hippies and the empty materialism of the yuppies, busters are adrift and sometimes cynical. The biggest problems—pollution, famine, and war—all seem too complex to solve. Individual effort, it seems, no longer counts for much in a world of multinational businesses. Busters care, but they lack the driving motivation of boomers who thought that they could "change the world."

Coming of age has always been difficult. Jonathan Alter addresses this curious mixture of cynicism and idealism in busters: "The Sixties Generation legitimized hypocrisy. Better to aspire to do what's right and fall short than not to try at all…. For the Nowhere Generation, irony is compatible with small *i* idealism, in which saving the world is replaced by saving a few homeless people down the street—or at least saving cans and bottles." (*Esquire,* May 1991, p. 100.)

Marketers find that there is "less passion for prestige" purchasing among the busters. The hippies wore jeans as a badge of rebellion. Yuppies disdained jeans for their lowly status. Busters, however, wear jeans for their durability and practicality. However, expensive designer labels are out.

Having grown up in a stagnant economy, busters are more cautious in their purchases. They know that they'll have to work harder than previous generations for their share of the American Dream, home ownership and the good life. Busters, however, are not sure that they want to work that hard.

Marketing to this generation is difficult because no distinct consumption patterns seem to apply. Busters "have been known to turn down big promotions or to quickly acquire clout and then give it all up for leisure…. It's hard to figure out what they think is most important" (*Fortune,* August 27, 1990, p. 42). To their elders, busters seem disengaged, lacking in passion and commitment. Are we witnessing something new here, or is this merely an update of James Dean's "rebel without a cause"? Time will tell.

Lifestyle Marketing

Traditional demographic categories don't seem sufficient to explain why some people respond to a particular advertising inducement but others ignore it. Values and lifestyles affect patterns of consumption as much as age, occupation, and income.

Market to values, not simply to income levels.

People with similar backgrounds can have very diverse interests. Jim spends his vacation gambling in Las Vegas. Sue would rather meditate at a Tibetan ashram. The Tibetan vacation may seem less materialistic, more spiritual, but it may actually cost more. The psychology behind these preferences is the focus of lifestyle marketing.

During the turbulent 1960's many young people were forsaking the American Dream. The work ethic was openly attacked. Some people were turning introspective, seeking ultimate truth in Eastern religions or psychological encounter groups. Others dropped out to travel, play, and avoid what seemed like a pointless resignation to a "plastic" workplace. A rising ecological awareness spurred a back-to-nature movement that challenged the status-quo. Voluntary simplicity meant resisting the inducements of Madison Avenue advertising. What heresy!

Psychographic profiles were developed in the 1970's to track changing cultural patterns. Stanford Research Institute's Values and Lifestyles (VALS) Study revealed a double hierarchy, a dual pattern of values and consumption. For traditional *outer directeds,* a house in the suburbs, Sunday barbecues, and the corporate career track were the ultimate success. However, for the unconventional *inner directeds,* the quest for authenticity, to "find oneself," was predominant. Inner directeds then numbered only 10%, but were projected to swell to over 25% by the year 2000.

Inner directed consumers resist traditional advertising approaches.

Stanford Research Institute's Arnold Mitchell expands this theme and identifies several distinct consumption patterns in *The Nine American Lifestyles.* At the bottom rungs of society are *survivors* and *sustainers,* people who are need driven and economically marginal. Other groups wield more buying power. Traditional outer directed sub-groups include *belongers* (somewhat older, more patriotic, often blue collar); *emulators* (easily impressed by the trappings of success, e.g., using the right cologne, driving the right car); and *achievers* (traditional, success-oriented, and big ticket consumers). Inner directed sub-groups include the *I-Am-Me's* (searching for selfhood); the *experientials* (motivated by the quest for new experiences, from hang gliding to meditation); and the *societally conscious.* Then, there is a group of *integrateds,* individuals who possess both inner and outer directed qualities. By the early 1980's VALS population percentages looked like this:

Integrated: 2%
Inner Directed: 20%
Outer Directed: 67%
Need Driven: 20%

Inner directeds tend to be idealistic, politically aware, and well educated. Inner directeds possess a high degree of self-awareness and a resistance to traditional appeals. They tune out mindless approaches and resist overt manipulation. Inner directeds don't believe that two beautiful people fall in love only because of a certain perfume. This kind of commercial is so insulting that some inner directeds make a conscious decision *not to buy* the product. They are more resistant to celebrity endorsements. They judge a product according to their own value systems, not advertising inducements.

Since advertising agencies are staffed with outer directed achievers and emulators, marketing to this newly identified group of inner directeds was at first a mystery. Early attempts to reach the inner directed market were heavy handed. The Honda car company once hired philosopher and geodesic dome builder Buckminster Fuller to be their ad pitchman. Hard to swallow, but there was old Bucky on TV, standing next to a Honda car parked in front of a dome home. Could that visionary futurologist really be praising the internal combustion engine, the ultimate symbol of ecological waste and obsolescence? What next, Zen flavored mouthwash?

Marketers quickly improved their pitch to both inner directeds and outer directeds. Psychographic research has helped to sell everything, from electronic thermometers to beer to designer homes. By the late 1970's, even the Army was using lifestyle marketing in its recruiting campaigns. "Be all that you can be. Join the Army!" This was a clear appeal to youthful inner directeds seeking selfhood. It was quite a change from the conventional patriotic appeals such as, "Join the Navy and see the world."

Market the same service differently to inner directeds versus outer directeds. An outer directed marketing appeal for aerobic workouts is that it makes a person look great. An inner directed appeal is that you'll have a great experience. An outer directed appeal to play tennis is to beat the competition. An inner directed appeal is to appreciate its metaphysical dimension, à la *Zen and the Art of Archery.* An outer directed vacation is jetting to Atlantic City to test one's luck at gambling. An inner directed vacation might be a guided tour of Egyptian pyramids to experience the majesty of an ancient civilization. Making money is outer directed. Finding fulfillment is inner directed. Getting results is outer directed. Experiencing the process is inner directed.

It would be an oversimplification to define outer directeds as practical and inner directeds as unworldly. It turns out that inner directeds, especially the societally conscious, are as affluent as traditional achievers. Jay Ogilvy of SRI notes that societally conscious inner directed women are more career oriented, more entrepreneurial, and earn more than their outer directed counterparts who adopted the conventional housewife role. According to Ogilvy, these inner directed women were not deterred by traditional cultural restrictions (KCBS Radio *Newsmagazine,* February 6, 1987).

Inner directeds are affluent and selective.

Inner directeds spend their money in novel ways, too. Their furniture, for example, may be hand crafted burl instead of Queen Ann. The societally conscious consume selectively, and they like to justify using Earth's finite resources. One SRI researcher, a self-proclaimed inner directed, put it this way: "I log over 100,000 miles a year by air. I justify the use of this much fossil fuel in terms of the important work I am doing."

With lifestyle marketing, it is critical to understand the values and aspirations of the consumer, and to communicate this understanding in clear words and images. For example, offer a Stop Smoking program to the general public and you might emphasize the health and beauty benefits. Offer the same program to corporate executives for their employees, and you would emphasize reduced health care costs, greater employee productivity, and higher profits. The point is to identify the values of the purchaser and frame your message accordingly.

A dual marketing strategy can combine both inner and outer directed appeals in varying degrees. This is a way to reach the coveted market of the *integrateds*. The integrateds have managed to combine inner and outer directed characteristics—material success, social conscience, and self-confidence. Almost everybody who thinks about it either is integrated or aspires to be integrated. Don't *you* want success, fame, contentment, a clean environment, and world peace? Be it sincere or be it cynical, the pitch to aspiring integrateds is: "You *can* have it all."

Yuppies, New Collars, New Agers, and Unicorns

There is no consensus on how to segment a market.

There is no consensus as to the best way to segment a market. Some experts believe that lifestyle marketing is overrated. Comments Bert Metter of the advertising agency J. Walter Thompson, "You have to keep in mind...people are all individuals with individual differences" (*USA Today*, July 29, 1985). Metter was reacting to the failure of yuppie lifestyle marketing.

The Young Upwardly-mobile Professional, or yuppie, (1980-1989 R.I.P.) was a mythical creation of marketing experts. The opposite of hippies, these supposed trend setters were characterized as self-absorbed, materialistic, and conspicuous consumers. But the yuppie model did not inspire mass imitation. "If you're selling BMW's the yuppie market is still a good one to go after. But I think one of the problems was they represented such a tiny segment," says Jeffrey Zeller of Cadwell Davis Partners, a New York advertising firm (*USA Today*, July 29, 1985). Too many merchants were chasing too few yuppies.

It's not just that there were too few yuppies. People with enough money to live the supposed yuppie lifestyle were not responding to the inducements of advertisers. "Yuppie" had quickly become a joke or an insult, a paean to mindless materialism. Almost nobody wanted to be called a yuppie.

Undeterred, market watchers continue to look for alternative psychographic models. For example, N. W. Ayer (*Target Marketing*, August 1986) divides the baby boomers into four distinct subgroups:

Satisfied selves: 34% well-educated, professional managers, optimistic, risk-taking, goal oriented, well traveled.

Contented traditionalists: 31%, home and family oriented, socially conservative.

Worried traditionalists: 23%, anticipate major disaster and hold traditional values.

60's in the 80's (90's?): 10%, aimless, unfulfilled, nostalgic and undirected in life.

Satisfied selves respond to programs offering professional advancement, new ideas, travel, health and leisure. *Traditionalists* mostly are interested in products and services involving family and home. Finally, the *60's* group will purchase products with nostalgia value, if the ongoing popularity of Grateful Dead concerts is any indication.

Similar to Ayer's *contented traditionalists* are the "family oriented." The pitch is to family and community tradition. Bill Cosby's television character is typical of this group. Dr. Huxtable is a successful professional man who is nevertheless quite comfortable wearing jeans around the house. He is not overly self-indulgent. He is not compelled to impress his neighbors, but he indulges his family and can be induced to make purchases on this basis.

Another prospective group is the "new collars," the sons and daughters of blue-collar America, the new middle class. These are the "workhorses of the service community: secretaries, nurses, teachers, insurance agents, keypunch operators, and clerks." They're young and hip, having grown up with television, the sexual revolution, Vietnam, and urban sprawl. However, they're not as affluent as yuppies or as introspective as the societally conscious. Their tastes run middle-brow and include Bruce Springsteen and David Letterman. They will shop bargains at K-Mart and Sears, and they appreciate the economy and reliability of Hondas and Toyotas. They are more likely to drink beer than vintage wine. New collars earn less than yuppies and cannot afford to be as showy. New collars, however, outnumber yuppies perhaps as much as ten to one.

Interest in the "New Age" defines yet another group. New age advocates are hungry for "social transformation," "enlightenment," "planetary healing," "new paradigms," "peace and ecology." The readers of the nationally circulated *New Age Journal* are affluent and college educated baby boomers. New agers purchase products and services which further their quest for higher consciousness. They're into natural foods, meditation, environmental music, crystal jewelry, psychic development, and self-awareness books, tapes, and seminars. How large is this group? According to a 1990 Gallop poll, 11% of the general population believe in trance mediumship or "channeling," 2% have visited a channeler, and 3% use crystals for healing.

New agers are searching for meaning and self-knowledge with the same intensity that other people crave wealth or fame. New agers are misunderstood by some and abused by others. Some marketers pander to them slavishly. One book publisher asked an author to claim that his

'New agers' search for self-awareness and social transformation.

material had been "channeled" by a spirit guide. Trance channeled entities apparently sell better than living gurus. Eric Utne is founder of *New
Age Journal* and current publisher of the *Utne Reader,* a kind of *Reader's
Digest* of the alternative press. Utne says that he's "concerned about all
the hocus-pocus" attending the new age movement. However, he notes
among new agers a salutary "parallel interest in social activism" (*American Demographics,* September 1988, p. 36). Publisher and political satirist
Paul Krassner comments, "There are many new agers who don't take
crystals or channelers seriously, either. I'm very hard up for mystical
experiences myself" (*Free Inquiry,* Summer 1990, p. 35).

Other groups to target include "socially conscious," "aging, affluent
professionals," and "youthful retirees." There's also the "dink," which
stands for "double income, no kids." Dink couples supposedly have lots
of money to spend on luxuries (*San Francisco Chronicle,* February 15,
1987, "Sunday Punch," p. 1). Then there's the "muppie," which stands for
maturing urban professional and the "guppie," or gay urban professional. Our production assistant Maija Vinerts believes that all this is
sounding slightly "dippie." What's that? A double income hippie, with lots
of money to spend on designer tie-dye shirts and the *Complete Beatles
Collection* on compact disk?

The attempt to define a dominant new lifestyle category is looking like
the quest for the mythical unicorn. We doubt that any single group will
prevail in the near future, despite the efforts of some Madison Avenue
marketers. All categories are arbitrary anyway. There's probably a little bit
of the hippie in the most upwardly-mobile yuppie, and vice versa.

Psychographic categories fluctuate with social and economic conditions. Sustained high economic growth might rekindle yuppie hedonism
and shrink the number of societally conscious. Environmental degrada-
tion seems to be reviving social conscience. Many baby boomers, after all,
were activists in their youth. Their idealism lies dormant, waiting to be
tapped. However, protracted economic stagnation could make people
suspicious of alternative lifestyles and reinforce conservative values.
Another great depression could stifle all social experimentation. Or it

**Lifestyles
change with
social
conditions.**

could be a catalyst to the insights of 60's inner directeds: voluntary
simplicity and new age transformation. Demographers, like economists,
seem to be better at tracking changes than predicting them in advance.

Lifestyle marketing, or psychographics, has certain advantages over
traditional demographics. It can differentiate between populations with
similar incomes but different values and lifestyle preferences. However,
psychographics is not a foolproof predictor of purchase patterns. It can
tell you what people believe, but not necessarily how they will act as
ultimate consumers.

Targeting, Mining, and Spelunking

The whole point of demographic studies and other surveys is to target likely clients. Targeting is like prospecting for high grade ore. You need to identify, describe, locate, and—ultimately—to contact prime prospects. Mining means digging even deeper, perhaps with follow up solicitations, special offers to established clients, or deep discounts to large spenders. Digging the deepest, one marketer calls it "spelunking," which means cave exploring. How deep is deep? Spelunk with computer database analyses, selected mailing lists, coded coupons to track respondents, letters of introduction, telephone queries, and business visits.

How targeted should you get? That depends largely on how specialized your product or service is. If you offer a professional service on the open market, target baby boomers. You can reach them by advertising in the mass media or local newspapers. You can target them according to special interests (sports, computers, home decorating, etc.) with specialty publications and direct mail. Seniors constitute the next largest demographic group. The more youthful seniors between 50 and 75 years old are affluent and active, too. There are more and more periodicals being published specifically for seniors. If you want to focus more narrowly on any particular age range or sub-group, look into radio and direct mail. If your target market is small, emphasize client calls. If you are a corporate consultant, for example, obtain the names and phone numbers of decision makers. Then arrange to make on-site presentations.

Create your own database of likely prospects. Let's say that you are developing a condominium retirement community adjacent to a golf course in Arizona. First you would want to identify seniors who can afford the purchase price. Seniors who are home owners would be a good lead here. Research property records for names or rent compiled mailing lists from independent companies. Obtain subscriber lists from "home and garden" type magazines. Digging deeper, you might want to select for active seniors who golf. Country club membership rosters might be a lead. Subdividing further, you would want to identify seniors who live near your site or who would be willing to relocate. Ads in local papers might also attract hot leads.

Create your own database of prospects.

As you are targeting clients, keep in mind the limits of the marketplace. Some audiences are almost impossible to serve unless your program is subsidized with outside funding. Groups that have little or no discretionary income include the oldest old, immigrants, the disadvantaged, and the homeless. Many of these people have difficulty affording even basic necessities. Most independent programs find it difficult to market services to these groups. Government or private funding is necessary here.

A market based service has to distinguish itself from funded government or "community" programs. At one time we were offering independent adult auto repair classes in "competition" with the local community college. Our classes were $25 for four weeks. Theirs were free and lasted over four months. In the community college classes, students had to sit through lecture after lecture. Why wait months to find out what was wrong with your car? Students in our classes got under the hood the first night. We actually had students drop out of the community college classes and pay to attend ours. We ended up targeting a more "upscale" clientele, more affluent and professional, who valued their time and could afford our classes. We marketed our program successfully by emphasizing exceptional quality, practicality, and very small class sizes.

If your business is new, identify who is spending money for similar or related services. If already in business, consider adding a questionnaire or feedback form as an extension to your sales receipt. As your business grows, develop a profile from your existing client base. As the business becomes more established and your client base grows, your client profile will become increasingly detailed. Consider updating your client profile periodically to make sure that you are on track.

Keep polling current clients.

As your business matures, you may want to extend or change your client base. Here is an example: One computer consultant had clients who were home users. They were spending about $200 each for her services. She was making money, but lining up each prospect was time consuming. She had her eyes on a more lucrative market, small business computer consulting. Here each client spends, perhaps, $2,000 for assistance. The consultant asked some basic marketing questions: How do the demands of small business owners compare with private users? How must I change my service to meet these demands? What are the best promotional media? A survey questionnaire for the projected market gave her many answers. Personal client calls, in depth interviews, and focus group sessions also helped to fine-tune her solicitations and sales presentations.

Once you develop a client profile, match this information with a prospective advertising medium. Most newspaper, radio, and television advertising departments make their own extensive audience surveys available to prospective advertisers upon request. Compare their demographic information with your own client profile. If the match is close, your advertising is more likely to get results.

Once you have an established client base and other interested leads, keep mining them. Offer free or low fee introductions to new clients. Offer special discounts, volume purchases, or payment options to established clients. Reward established clients who refer others to your service. Design parties, open houses, and "graduate" or advanced trainings to allow past and present clients to continue participating. Concentrate a large part of your marketing and promotion efforts on current clients. Ask current clients what they like best about your service. Put this in the form of a testimonial and use it in your promotional materials. Recommendations from happy clients may well be more important than any other efforts you make to build your business.

Seven Tips for Happy Clients

Knowing about your clients is only the beginning. Keeping them happy is the rest. Satisfying your clients is vital to surviving in business. It's good word of mouth and it also means lower operating costs. For example, in marketing classes to adults, it costs six times as much money to get a new customer as it does to keep an existing one happy. Here is our list of tips for keeping clients:

Screen prospects in advance
Stress service
Encourage client loyalty
Reassure clients
Follow through on promises
Act on complaints
Have fun

Screen prospects in advance. Screen prospects by phone or at a "no risk" first meeting. Make sure that prospective clients will benefit, have the ability or authority to pay, and are sincerely interested in your service. Build your track record by accepting clients where you can produce the most dramatic results. Consider preparing a set of questions to help both you and the prospective client determine if the fit is right. Refer a client if you can't help them.

Stress service. AT&T says that 68% of all customers switch brand allegiances because they feel that they were ignored. How is every customer treated by every clerk? Make your clients feel special and they'll think of your service as pretty special.

Encourage client loyalty. Project confidence and encourage clients to make a commitment. If offering services on an hourly basis, specify how many hours are needed for completion of the service. If the service is open-ended, such as psychotherapy or bodywork, try to create a structure in which the client can pace his progress. Put your commitment to the client in writing. Give clients a contract which specifies their own financial obligations, payment schedules, and the like.

Encourage client loyalty.

Reassure clients. Reassure your clients at every stage that their needs will be met. Once a client is committed, congratulate him on making the right decision. Remind him of any explicit provisions for refunds, or any redress for complaints. This helps to reassure them and alleviate "buyer remorse." Product warranties often begin, "Congratulations! You have just purchased the finest personal stereo on the market today...." More informally, use a phrase such as, "I believe that we're going to develop a productive working relationship."

Follow through on promises. Convey a "can do" attitude. Build trust with a track record of performance. Deliver a little more than you promise, and deliver it a little ahead of schedule. If you get in over your head, have the courage to admit it to yourself. Be open to calling for help. Use your referral network to find assistance. Call in advisers or additional consultants. Split fees if necessary. Once you've accepted a job, make sure that your client's needs are met.

Act on complaints. Survey clients about your performance. Feedback forms, telephone surveys, and suggestion boxes show clients that you care. Soliciting feedback also helps you to improve your service. Beyond that, negotiate solutions when clients are dissatisfied. As publishers, we're continually fielding questions and complaints by advertisers. We once credited an advertiser $100 because we published a sentence with "of" instead of "for." It was a silly little error, but it did alter the meaning of the sentence and diminished the effectiveness of the ad. "What do you think is fair?" is one of our opening lines in dealing with complaints. "Here's what we usually do..." or "We'll meet you more than half way..." are two of our follow ups. Take a non-adversarial approach. Focus on solutions, not on who's to blame.

Have fun. A positive, upbeat attitude is infectious. If you project goodwill, your clients are more likely to enjoy their experience as well. If you don't feel comfortable working with a client for any reason, refer him elsewhere. You'll be doing a favor for the client, the referral, and yourself. Don't let yourself get financially strapped so that you're desperate to take any job that comes along, whether or not you really want it.

To summarize, service is all. As entrepreneur Paul Hawken explains *(San Francisco Chronicle,* July 31, 1985): "All business is service, regardless of whether it manufactures, produces, or distributes." Every business is essentially a service business. Consumers expect products to be "serviced" after the purchase. Hawken recommends identifying with the customer, always trying to satisfy, taking as much time as the customer wants, making it "feel right," and always asking for feedback. He adds, "Our most fiercely loyal customers, the ones who create the most word-of-mouth business, are ones who had a problem we solved."

5

Researching
Your
Market

ABUSINESS CONSULTANT WE KNOW is fond of saying, "No matter what business you think you're in, during the first two years your business is market research." Market research helps to reach the right audience with the appropriate message. You can obtain market research from one or more of these sources:

Published books and articles
Government and university research
Private research
Your own research

By the end of this chapter you should know which of these options will work for you.

Published Books and Articles

If you want to survey existing research, start at the largest library in your immediate area. If you live in a big city, your options probably include the main public library, a business library, and several university libraries. If you live in a small town, you may need to journey to a bigger city to do your market research.

First, read pertinent articles in trade publications, newspapers, and magazines. The main advantages of these articles are that they are short, timely, and usually reflect the consensus of several experts.

Before you get too serious about market research, check out some recent back issues of *American Demographics* magazine. *American Demographics* is the lazy person's guide to market research. Your work is done for you! This magazine runs features which interpret current demographic trends for businesspeople and marketers. Samples: "Demographics on vacation—gray travel, gay travel, and touring teens....lucrative markets for the vacation industry." "The independent elderly...new choices about retirement." Here are most of the concise, predigested insights you'll probably need.

Locate specific magazine articles by consulting one or more reference works. The reference desk of the local library probably should be your first stop. The general indexes are the best place to start your basic research. Ask for *The Reader's Guide to Periodical Literature*. This source cross references subjects with periodicals, including the issue, date, and page numbers for quick access.

Newspaper indexes (like the one for the *New York Times*) are also helpful. The *Business Periodicals Index* and the *PAIS Bulletin (Public Affairs Information Service Bulletin)*, similar to the *Reader's Guide,* are good resources, too. Once you locate the reference, however, your library may not carry it. You may have to check at another library or check directly with the publisher.

The Reader's Guide to Periodical Literature is an excellent reference source.

Also, see if your library's reference department has the *Research Centers Directory,* a two volume index published by Gale Research Inc. It's a guide to thousands of university-related and other non-profit research organizations that carry on continuing research in all areas, from business to religion. For example, organizations listed include the Stepfamily Foundation and the Western Illinois University Center for Business and Economic Research. Check the subject index for quick reference. Contact an organization in your field to see if they can help you with any information.

Sales and Marketing Magazine publishes the *Survey of Buying Power Data Service.* This survey has state and regional summaries of metropolitan market rankings, TV market rankings, retail sales by store group, and by merchandise line. Also, there are state and regional summaries of population by age and sex, number of households, income distributions, and more. Ask at the nearest large business library if they have this survey available.

Small Business–An Information Sourcebook, edited by Cynthia C. Rinse and Paul Wassermann (published by Oryx Press, 1987), is a wonderful reference book on different literature helpful to small businesses. Listings include everything from accounting to warehousing to women in business.

Finally, if you are computer literate, consult the library computer to find periodicals and books on your subject. (If you are not computer literate, here is a good place to start. Ask a reference librarian for assistance at the keyboard.) Enter a word like "marketing," and all the references that appear on screen may amaze you.

Government Research

Public research is free or cheap.

Visit the reference desk of your public library and ask for any publications with current surveys, polls, or census materials. As with most reference books, you generally can't check anything out to take home. You can always buy the publications, but that can get quite expensive. If you don't want to spend the money, allow yourself at least two half days at the library. Government materials can deluge you with data, so the challenge will be to figure out what's useful and how to interpret it.

Consider visiting the closest university library. Some universities also have specialized survey research centers or data libraries on or near campus. See if there's an Institute of Governmental Affairs (or something like that) affiliated with your local university. Ask if the public has access to data and survey results. If the university library requires student enrollment, hire a student to collect research for you. (That is, unless you plan to enroll in school again.) A good student will be very familiar with using library resources, a tremendous asset to you in collecting research.

For convenience, telephone the U.S. Government Printing Office and order *The Statistical Abstract of The United States.* In it there are over 1400 statistical tables which you can use to target your market and make your promotional materials more persuasive. Call (202) 738-3238 and order your copy for about $25. Call this number to inquire about any other government publication, also.

Another excellent source of data is *The Consumer Expenditure Survey* from the Department of Labor Bureau's Labor Statistics. The Department compiles annual data on household expenditures and demographics for the entire nation.

The Census Department publishes several large reference books. For example, the *U.S. Census of Service Industries* highlights different geographic areas, usually by state. The *U.S. Census of Manufacturers* references different subjects such as "metalworking operations," etc. The *U.S. Census of County Business Patterns* is printed nationally and for each state. It includes employment and payrolls, number, and size of establishments by industry.

We found three excellent indexes published by the Congressional Information Service. The *American Statistics Index* is a comprehensive guide to the statistical publications of the U.S. government. The *Statistical Reference Index* is the same kind of index, except this one is a guide to American statistical publications from state governments, private businesses, and university research centers. And the *Index to International Statistics* lists statistical publications of major international inter-government organizations such as the UN and the European Economic Community.

These Congressional Information indexes are published annually and also as cumulative source books. Each includes a user guide and comes in two volumes, one being the index and the other containing the abstracts. You look up what you need in the index volume and find a title and reference number. Then you look up the reference number in the abstracts volume. The abstracts volume includes short summaries and the accession numbers for different publications. The books explain how to acquire the documents, either by request or through purchase. Further suggestions for making information searches also are given. These reference books contain many indexes, including geographic, economic by commodity, income, industry or occupation, and demographic. The demographic breakdowns include age, educational attainment, marital status, race, ethnic group, sex, and more.

Many libraries also subscribe to several indexes on microfiche. If your local library doesn't carry a particular government publication, ask your librarian to direct you to the nearest U.S. Government Document Depository library for more information. You also can buy government publications at Government Printing Office bookstores located in several major cities. Direct telephone inquiries to (202) 783-3238.

We've also listed a sampling of additional government resources in our Books and Resources chapter at the back of this book.

Private Research

Larger corporations spend vast sums of money on customized market studies. If you have a large budget, consider hiring a private firm to

Contact the Government Printing Office for research leads.

conduct primary research. Consult the Yellow Pages under "survey reports" and then call a company and explain your needs. You'll have to determine what kind of information you want, how many interviews or questionnaires you'll need, how in-depth your study will be, and how long the project will take. Even the least expensive survey probably will cost you a couple thousand dollars.

Many companies specialize in conducting market research for corporations. About 90% of the work the Field Institute in San Francisco does is commercial marketing research, and their prices start at about $20,000. Some ongoing market research projects that last at least a year can cost up to $100,000 or more, depending upon your needs.

Private research firms sell syndicated research to all interested parties who can afford to pay. A single report from Stanford Research Institute International, for example, can cost hundreds, if not thousands of dollars. Their Values and Lifestyles Studies (VALS) pioneered psychographic (lifestyle) marketing. Write for information to Stanford Research Institute International, Values and Lifestyles Program, 333 Ravenswood Avenue, Menlo Park, CA 94025.

Some firms, notably Gallup and Field, conduct custom surveys and make available some of their results for the general public. These may not be specific enough for your needs, however. They are not technically market studies, because they usually contain only an analysis of the results of the survey and little or no general information about the industry. However, if your main interest is the end-user market and you can't afford a custom survey, then they may be valuable.

The Gallup Poll–Public Opinion by George Gallup, Jr. is a book that has annual series from 1971 to the present (as well as a 1935-1971 edition) and publishes political, social, and economic trends. An international version is also available. The *Gallup Report* or *Gallup Opinion Index* may also be available from your library. Look under "surveys" or "statistics." The book is published annually by Scholarly Resources, Inc.,104 Greenhill Ave., Wilmington, Delaware 19805-1897.

The Field Institute, affiliated with the Field Research Corporation in San Francisco, conducts public opinion and attitude surveys on social and political issues, especially in California. According to the *Research Centers Directory*, the Institute publishes the California Opinion Index (eight times annually), and they maintain all California Poll surveys from 1956 to the present. The results of the Field's Poll are available at survey research centers or data libraries at large universities. For instance, The Field Institute in San Francisco archives the California Poll and other surveys at the University of California Berkeley library. However, Field mainly conducts survey reports for companies. (They also sponsor the

Custom surveys are the best—and the most expensive.

annual Field Institute Workshop, which is open to the public.)

You can also purchase the results of private surveys from *FINDEX–The Directory of Market Research Reports, Studies and Surveys.* This book is published annually and it gives industry reports with abstract description, publisher (U.S. and international), publication date, pages, report ID number, and price. The book includes addresses, telephone and FAX numbers of all publishers and a contact person's name as well. A subject index, geographic index, and company index are also in the back. The research reports tend to be very expensive, in the range of $2000. However, they are very specific and could be exactly what you need if you can afford it. The address for the main office is Cambridge Information Group Directories, Inc., 7200 Wisconsin Ave., Bethesda, MD 20814. Or phone (1-800-227-3052 or 1-301-961-6750 in MD).

Maija's Library Adventure

What will happen when you go to the library with real life questions about marketing a new business? We commissioned our crack staffer and production assistant, Maija Vinerts, to do just that. What follows is her own story, in her own words:

"I started using a fictitious 'business idea.' I pretended that I was looking into the possibilities of opening a vitamin or health food store in a town of 50,000 people. How would this store compare with other such stores? Who would stock it? What would I stock? Who would I want to sell products to? I tried to acquire specific information while I was checking out the basic reference materials at several local libraries.

Start at the main branch of your local library.

"It's not that easy to do personal research on something very specific, at least not quickly. You can count on spending a long time looking through different indexes and periodicals to find exactly what you want. You have to be patient and not afraid to ask questions. Most of the librarians I encountered were understanding and knowledgeable. The more I learned, the more focused my questions became, and the more they were able to help me find what I wanted.

"I had some advantages in doing research because I live next to a large university with specific libraries. I also have experience doing academic research. Of course I had some disadvantages as well. I had to do my research rather quickly. And I always had to explain what I was doing to every librarian. But I kept at it.

"The very first place I started at was the largest and most complete library I could think of, the main library on the university campus. I sat down at the computer and punched in all kinds of key words, from 'vitamins' to 'health,' for the computer to bring up book titles. My research was rather specific, and most books about vitamins tend to be too general. I figured that if I was hoping to open a vitamin store I would already know enough basic information about vitamins. So I knew that I had to look in recent magazine and newspaper articles for specific numbers, survey results, etc. I looked in the "#1 source," the *Reader's Guide to Periodical Literature.* There I found references to some relevant articles.

"From the main library I was directed to other smaller, more specific libraries. I checked in the Government Documents library on campus, where I found government publications that quoted general statistics and that included addresses of business contacts, also.

"The Business/Social Science library on campus was where I hit the jackpot on reference materials. Here I could really research specific questions.

"There were manuals available for new small business owners in California where I could find addresses of other agencies and companies to contact for support and information. There were many indexes that I could use to look up the topic of vitamins and then find specific magazine articles. I could get a general idea of what the population was for a certain region, what the age and sex breakdowns were for that region, how much money people in that region spend in general and specifically on health-related products.

"Contacting business consultants or others in this field might help me to decide how much to invest in the business, and how much money I could hope to earn. Articles and data printed in health magazines like *Prevention* would lead me to specific answers such as which vitamins are taken the most, which brands sell the best, and how to market them. For example, I found a reference to an article about the popularity of comic figure-shaped children's vitamins.

"As a last step I went to the main branch of the city public library. The *Reader's Guide* and other indexes were available, including newspaper indexes that the business library on campus didn't have. In many ways the reference room at the public library was not quite as well-stocked as the specific business library, but it still would have been a good place to start research.

"After several hours of personal research for my make-believe vitamin business I stopped. I didn't have all the specific data in hand, but I had many leads to go on, including addresses and phone numbers, articles and books to read. My next step would have been to obtain as many of the relevant articles and publications as were available. I would have written to other companies and asked for information from them, contacted associations that deal with health care products or foods, and asked them if they had information. I would also have written to the government for

Ask the librarian at the reference desk to help you conduct research.

free (or cheap) publications.

"From my research I discovered that the answers to my basic questions were readily available from public records. However, the more specific my questions got, the more I had to research. I also had to keep my patience and not get frustrated when a librarian would say, 'Well, I don't think we have *Amicus* magazine in stock here....'

"What you'll find is that personal research takes a lot of time, patience, and determination. You have to ask a lot of questions and seek out helpful librarians. Even if the only sources you have access to are the *Reader's Guide* and newspaper indexes, you could still find out a lot about your subject. Eventually your research will most likely include government-published materials, which not all libraries will have in reference because of their expense. Again, a public library main branch, a business library, or a university library are your best bets."

Your Own Research

In addition to reviewing government statistics, consider doing your own "primary" research. Collecting your own data in-house is far less expensive than hiring private research companies to do it. Fortunately, doing your own research isn't that difficult, either. Consider the possibilities:

Canvassing
Communications with established "competitors"
Feedback forms
Focus groups
In-depth personal interviews with targeted prospects
Telephone surveys

Conduct your own in-house surveys

Your own small scale surveys are the most immediate and cost effective way to gather information. Let's say *you* want to open a vitamin store. Design a questionnaire for prospective customers. You could type up a list of questions on one page, leaving room for people to write answers. Make copies at your local copy store and hand your questionnaire to friends, relatives, and maybe to people at the local mall near where you might want to open your store. Also, consider conducting a telephone survey.

Questions for prospective customers might include: Do you use vitamin supplements? If married, does your spouse use vitamins? If you have children, do they use vitamins? What are your favorite brands of vitamins? Where do you now buy vitamins? Would you shop for vitamins in a store nearby? What other products do you buy when you shop for vitamins?

Don't be shy about examining the prospective "competition." The point here is not to copy slavishly what they do, but to find out what they're *not* doing or what could be done better. Make a physical inspection of their stock. Talk to store owners. What are their worst problems? Their greatest joys? Were their income projections on target? If the business were for sale, how much would they want for it? Chat with employees. What do they like the most about their job? What would they change? Ask yourself: Is this kind of business really for you?

If your business already is established, ask current clients to rate your performance. To develop a good set of questions, you need to see the world from the client's prospective. In one sense, you have to become a client of your own business. As a client, are your needs being met? Do you enjoy the interaction? Is the service prompt and reliable? Are the personnel attentive? Do they genuinely seem to enjoy serving clients, or do they seem bothered and rude?

The best questions allow clients to sound off as well as helping you to improve your service. Avoid getting more specific than you need, especially regarding age and income. Avoid redundancy. If a person gives their name, you probably know their sex. If they agree to be on your mailing list, you have their address. You need at least thirty or more responses to get reasonably reliable data.

If your business is established, gear your survey toward client feedback and keep blank forms available for clients at your office. This is a great way to let clients know you care about them. And it gives you the information you need continually to improve your operation.

As few as 30 responses can give you statistically useful data.

Focus groups are useful at almost any stage of development. Bring together groups of prospective or current clients. Give them a detailed description of your service and ask them for feedback and comments. Poll them for specific preferences relating to price, quality, duration, etc. Also, allow for open-ended commentary on what they like and what could be improved.

If your business is still on the drawing board, avoid conducting a random mail survey. It's expensive, and your return rate will be only around one percent.

If your budget is small, a telephone survey makes good sense. Find numbers in the white pages and call people at random. The phone company sells a "reverse directory" that lists people by address, so you can target a specific neighborhood if you like. Alternately, telephone friends, professional associates, or anyone who may be a client or who may be in a position to refer a client to you. This is a great way to begin to target your market and build your practice as well. If you reach just eight people each hour, you can collect a respectable sample in about half a day's calling.

Adapt this sample questionnaire to your own business needs. Poll in person, by phone, or by mail.

CLIENT QUESTIONNAIRE:

Help us improve our service. Please take just a moment to answer these questions:

1.) Have you ever used a service like ours?

2.) Would you use this kind of service in the future?

3.) What is a fair price for this kind of service?

4.) Would you like to be on our mailing list?

5.) Would you like to put a friend on our mailing list?

6.) Give our service an overall rating:
    (Choose one: excellent; good; fair; poor.)

7.) Rate our service on performance quality:
    (Choose one: excellent; good; fair; poor.)

8.) Were our staff people prompt and courteous?
    (Choose one: excellent; good; fair; poor.)

So that we can serve you better, please tell us a little about yourself. All answers will be kept confidential:

1.) What is your occupation? (Choose one: professional; retail; manufacturing; student; unemployed; retired).

2.) What is your age? (Choose one: under 20 years; 20–29 years; 30–39 years; 40–55 years; over 55).

3.) What are your favorite recreational activities?

4.) What is your educational background? (Choose one: postgraduate; other professional degree; bachelors; some college; high school).

Here is an easy format for a telephone survey. First state your name and business affiliation. Then proceed: "We are conducting a survey and would like to get your opinions about our service. There is nothing to buy. Do you have just two minutes?" Make sure that you can complete your survey within whatever amount of time you specify. We have conducted telephone surveys with this opening and have rarely encountered a rude reply. In fact, most people are delighted that somebody genuinely wants their opinion. They volunteer to spend extra time on the line giving advice and feedback!

Keep your survey focused by asking questions that require specific "yes," "no," or reasonably short answers. But if a survey participant seems motivated and helpful, ask open ended questions to draw him out further. Some examples: "What do you think of our management?" "How could we improve our service?" You might be surprised at what you learn. On one survey we found out that one of our receptionists had a real split personality, polite to us but mean and surly to our clients!

Up to now we've been focusing on gathering data which lends itself to straightforward interpretation without statistical analysis. For most small businesses and independent professionals, this is all you'll ever really need. Beyond this stage, you may want to chart sales forecasts, inventory control, market-share analysis, product life cycles, pricing analysis, and any number of correlations. If you're serious about learning the technical aspects of marketing, you may want to take a college course in this area. Brian R. Smith's *Successful Marketing for Small Business* is a very readable summary of marketing analysis. If you want to do the arithmetic and set up your own graphs and pie charts, this book is a good place to start.

Trends last longer than fads.

Fads and Trends

Collecting research is an ongoing process. Once you've identified a market, you'll want to chart its evolution. Some markets are ongoing; others become quickly obsolete. It is not always possible to tell the difference, but there are cues.

Business consultant John Naisbitt in his best selling *Megatrends* draws a distinction between long term trends and short lived fads. A fad is created from the top down, initiated consciously by a small number of people. A trend, however, is a ground swell with a grassroots origin. A fad arrives and disappears rather quickly, whereas a trend builds slowly and makes a lasting impact. Marketing to a trend is quite different from marketing to a fad.

The way to take advantage of a fad is to get in early and get out before the wave has crested. Immediately after John Travolta glamorized disco dancing in the movie *Saturday Night Fever,* savvy dance instructors updated their old ballroom routines to include disco. Two years later John Travolta starred in *Urban Cowboy.* Those very same instructors donned Stetson hats and boots and taught the same dance steps to Western tunes. There's much money to be made with fads if you get in early and don't invest too heavily. However, beware of getting stuck, like the unfortunate investors who opened disco clubs just when country music was taking over. Marketing to fads is never a sure thing—just ask the producers of three unprofitable Lambada movies.

Marketing to trends, as opposed to fads, is more of a long distance run than a sprint. To market to trends you have to look beyond the headlines and find more enduring themes and values. For instance, one ongoing trend is health consciousness. What started in the 1960's as an interest in health foods has continued with jogging, aerobic exercise, dieting, body building, and food supplements. The trend has matured with the population. Consider the popularity of life extension books and Jane Fonda's over-40 exercise videos.

We've tracked trends as they affected enrollment in our own non-credit adult classes. Our method was to analyze purchase behavior. If a class on a particular topic enrolled well, we'd offer more of the same. If it failed to enroll, we'd try to fix it or, finally, drop it. During the 1960's, the youthful baby boomers participated actively in social and political inquiry. Studying business was definitely unpopular. During the 1970's the market shifted to an interpersonal and metaphysical emphasis. At first yoga was the preferred method of body conditioning. Jogging replaced yoga, which in turn was superseded by aerobic workouts. During the 1980's the thirtyish baby boomers took a decidedly practical bent. Former meditators may still reserve moments for quiet contemplation, but they tend now to focus on career building. As a former admitted encounter group junkie said to us, "Oh, I did EST in the 70's. I've got *it.* What I need now is a good business class."

Our *Open Exchange* San Francisco Bay Area survey (opposite page) shows many diverse interests among our readers. A wide variety of topics each had their constituency: arts and crafts, business, health and fitness, travel and leisure, spiritual and psychic, sports and bodywork, camping, computers, meditation, and meeting new people.

What future trends are on the horizon? Here's our view of the big picture in two words: More diversity.

Environmental necessities increasingly will shape consumption patterns. Aging baby boomers, their youthful idealism not entirely extinguished, will hold the reigns of power in business and government. They'll be strident in their demands for clean air, clean water, and protected

Environmental concerns are likely to dominate marketing in the 21st century.

wilderness. They envision a sustainable future and they'll have the political will to make the changes necessary.

Driven by environmental concerns, new efficient technologies will help to standardize large scale production. There may be severe economic upheavals in local economies that are overly dependent on aging technologies which must be abandoncd. Even so, change will produce opportunity. Niche markets will continue to diversify, spurred by the eclectic tastes and sophistication of maturing baby boomers.

Quality based service industries will continue to thrive. Innovation will be rewarded in companies large and small. Experienced workers will be valued since there will be insufficient numbers of skilled younger workers to replace them. There will be continuing career opportunities for people of all ages and backgrounds with good interpersonal skills who also can handle the increasing pace of change.

READERSHIP SURVEY:

Impact of OPEN EXCHANGE Magazine:
92% actively use the listings and respond to advertisers
49% for individual consulting or counseling
46% for group instruction
33% for mail order services and products

Sex:
53% temale; 47% male

Age:
5% 18-24 years old; 75% 25-44 years old; 20% 45 years and over

Occupation:
46% professional/managerial; 37% white-collar services
08% retail/sales; 06% student
02% retired/unemployed; 01% blue-collar

Education:
95% attended college; 61% bachelors degree or better
30% masters, doctoral, or other professional degree

Credit Cards
83% have major credit cards

Reading Habits:
76% buy 12-120 books per year; 28% buy 48-120 books per year
10% buy 120 or more books per year

TopTwelve General Interests:
61% health and fitness
48% meeting new people
47% business and career
46% arts and crafts
46% camping and sports
44% counseling and psychology
42% travel and leisure
37% computers
37% massage
34% meditation
32% spiritual and psychic
14% certification and degrees

Geographic Distribution:
50% San Francisco and Marin; 50% East Bay and Contra Costa
(1/3 million Bay Area readers; 100,000 copies per quarter)

Summary:
OPEN EXCHANGE readers are highly active, well educated people with stable employment in business and the professions. They are inquiring and have a diverse range of interests, from computers to yoga, business to bodywork.

Francis Brewster is a speech therapist in private practice. Breaking into a new field can be difficult, but Francis found a winning strategy. Running ads in community newspapers and a minority business directory, Francis offered tutoring to people with foreign accents and regional dialects. Immigrants and regional transplants were more interested in how Francis could help them than her number of years in practice. Francis persevered and her client base grew steadily. She was hired by an automobile repair shop to conduct trainings for its employees, many of whom were foreign born. Now Francis is shifting her emphasis toward corporate consulting. The financial rewards will be better, with new opportunities to grow professionally. Francis explains her work:

"Each of us wants to be viewed in a positive way by others. Often this is difficult to achieve if we lack skill and confidence in our verbal expression. I provide a speech training service which helps individuals change speech patterns or habits.

"My work has evolved from an early interest in language and psychology and how the two interplay in establishing our identity as individuals and as members of a group—family or business.

" I provide a nurturing environment for persons with foreign accents or regional dialect not only to change their speech, but also to build their confidence and self-esteem. I have found this to be the key in a client maintaining motivation and making changes in his or her life. The relationship which develops between myself and the client helps to enrich the learning experience. We support each other, and you can see satisfactory results of the training almost from the start.

"Most of my professional work experience has been in environments lending support to those in transition. In my work with clients, I rely on my counseling background. It allows me to see the clients' needs more clearly and organize these needs into a realistic goal-oriented program.

"Language and speech are culture-bound. Individuals do not seek my service to change or lose their cultural identity. Rather it is an active choice to integrate into their lives speech skills which complement their cultural backgrounds.

"I believe that we each must choose for ourselves work which connects us to others in a sharing way. My work does this for me."

—Francis Brewster

6

Your Promotion Campaign

WHEN WORD OF MOUTH is too slow, promote your business to help it grow faster. A well-executed promotion campaign can be money in the bank. However, there are no guarantees. All marketing involves taking risks. Here we'll show you how to minimize your risks. Develop your promotion campaign step-by-step:

1.) State your goals.
2.) Interpret market research.
3.) Explore 121+ marketing options.
4.) Establish your initial budget.
5.) Implement a test campaign.
6.) Evaluate test campaign results.
7.) Change and expand your campaign.

1.) State Your Goals

If you're working in a group, meet with the policy makers to draft a set of goals and priorities. If you're working on your own, it's still worthwhile to write out your plans. If a business or marketing plan already exists, review it now. Answer these questions for yourself as specifically as possible:

What market are we now serving?
What is our position, or market identity, in the public's mind?
Is there a continuing need for what we offer?
How do we protect or expand our market share?
Do we develop new product lines or profit centers?
Are we heading in the direction we really want to go?

Much of goal setting has to do with self-knowledge. Start with a greater vision of what you want to do in business. What unique contribution do you want to make to the community? A personal goal statement may include beliefs, desires, skills, likes, and dislikes. You might have wide ranging talents but choose to pursue one path in particular. For example, we know a multi-talented psychotherapist who decided to specialize in working with adult children of alcoholics. She did this, in part, because her own father was an alcoholic.

Once you have established long term goals, concentrate on short term strategies.

After you have established long term goals, focus on strategies and tactics. If your budget is limited, concentrate on the immediate situation. A classic mistake is to worry about image and ignore the basics. "Oh, that ad never brings me any business. But I run it just to keep my name before the public." This kind of thinking is a good way to go bankrupt. To quote psychologist Fritz Perls, "Be here now!" Stay focused in the present. For the private practitioner, "being here" might mean securing five new clients in order to pay the rent.

We call "being here" the Warm Body Rule. The Warm Body Rule means taking care of business. If you need to fill a workshop in the next four weeks, don't get sidetracked designing a new business card or giving a magazine interview. Focus on the immediate goal. Spend your efforts calling prospective workshop participants. Place calendar announcements for the workshop in the daily and weekly papers. Mail an announcement of the workshop to your warm leads. Talk about the workshop at parties and business networking socials. Obsess yourself with finding warm bodies for that workshop!

Setting goals also means setting priorities. If your operation is not yet at "break even," then generating cash is probably your top priority. Most businesses expect income to equal expenses within the first year or two. If your income projections are already on target, then it's time to work on longer term goals. These might include preserving market share, building corporate image, getting known as an expert, developing new product lines, or public recognition for community service.

2.) Interpret Market Research

Who is your audience? Where do they live? What are their ages, incomes, values, and lifestyles? How do they spend money? Your promotion campaign is a real test, in dollars and cents, of any market research you've been gathering and conducting.

Collect information about your market from several sources if possible. Get published demographic profiles at the local library. Conduct your own telephone and mail surveys of current clients or test audiences. A limited test campaign is also a form of market research. Use networking to gather information, too. Attend associate and professional meetings and conferences. Lunch with friendly "competitors." Share stories about what's working and what's not.

You already may have a client profile. Modify it based on any test campaigns you conduct. One program discovered that its enrollees came mainly from two small but affluent communities. Promotional efforts outside these communities had been a waste. There was no sense advertising to audiences that were unresponsive. Their efforts, in fact, were bankrupting the program! The administrators concluded that it was better to succeed with a smaller program than to fail trying to build a larger one.

Examine the promotional materials of the programs similar to yours that have been around for at least two years. Take note of their advertising and publicity in newspapers and on radio and television. Start saving "junk mail" letters, coupons, and catalogs. Collect business cards. Learn from the survivors. Their marketing techniques have worked. Apply their methods to your program.

Learn from your predecessors and competitors.

3.) Explore 121+ Marketing Options

Your marketing options include the print media, broadcast media, direct mail, telemarketing, planned events, novelties, and whatever else you can imagine. Just about every option that we can imagine is on our Marketing Options List (see next page). If we failed to include a favorite of yours, drop us a line in care of the publisher.

The way we organized the Marketing Options List is somewhat arbitrary. Some options are used several ways. For example, we listed "open house" under "planned events." However, an open house also may be publicized in print or broadcast media.

Whether you use words, pictures, or moving images, become knowledgeable about your chosen medium. Recognize its limitations, too. Professional services deserve a more sophisticated and subtle approach

MARKETING OPTIONS LIST

All services do not benefit from all marketing options. Find what works best for you.

Broadcast Media:

Radio, AM and FM
Television–cable
Television–network

BROADCAST PUBLICITY:
Community calendars
Feature stories
Free speech messages
Independent productions
News conferences
News releases
Public service announcements
Talk shows

BROADCAST ADVERTISING:
Commercial spots
"Infomercials"

Print Media:

Catalogs
Corporate publications
Directories
Magazines
Newsletters
Newspapers
School publications
Special interest publications
Trade journals

PRINT PUBLICITY:
Columnists
Community calendars
Feature stories
Guest editorials
Letters to the editor
News stories
Press releases

PRINT ADVERTISING:
Advertising inserts
Classified advertising
Directory listings
Display advertising

MARKETING OPTIONS LIST, continued...

Direct Marketing:

PRINTED MATERIALS:
Acknowledgments and "thanks"
Announcements
Banners
Books
Brochures
Business cards
Catalogs
Circulars
Coupons
Flyers
Gift certificates
Handbills
Holiday greeting cards
In-house organs
Invitations
Newsletters
Order forms
Packaging
Pamphlets
Posters
Signs
Solicitation letters
Surveys and questionnaires
Testimonials

ELECTRONIC:
800-numbers
900-numbers
Answering machines
Audio cassettes
Computer bulletin boards
FAX
Computerized telemarketing
Video cassettes
Voice mail services

PLANNED EVENTS:
Bake sales
Benefits
Board meetings
Book signings
Breakfasts
Celebrations
Client calls
Canvassing
Conferences
Contests
Dinners
Discount sales
Expos and fairs
Flea markets
Grand openings
Lectures
Lunches
Networking events
Open houses
Parties
Press conferences
Public speaking
Raffles and prizes
Receptions
Retreats
Reunions
Seminars
Shows
Surveys
Sweepstakes
Trainings
Workshops
_____
_____

A personal marketing approach stresses personal contacts or professional accomplishments.

MARKETING OPTIONS LIST, continued…

Novelties (with your logo, address, phone):

Backpacks
Bags
Balloons
Booklets (from company prospectuses to coloring books)
Bumper stickers
Buttons
Calendars
Flags
Hats
Holiday gifts
Lighters and Matches
Pens and Stationery
Tee shirts
_____(Look under "Novelties" in your phone directory.)

Miscellaneous:

Auctions (offer your service as auction prize at your local public
           television auction, church or club auction, etc.
Billboards (on highways, buildings, busses, in transit stations, etc.)
Booths
Bus stop benches
Free samples
Painted cars
Refreshments (from wine and cheese to printed gumballs)
Referral networks
Sandwich boards
Searchlights
Shopping cart signs
Sky writing
Store front displays
Transit advertising
Window displays

_____

Mix and match options from several marketing categories. For example, publicize an open house in the local newspaper.

than mass marketed products. It's no accident that psychotherapists don't advertise on highway billboards with snappy slogans such as, "If you're blue call Dr. Blume." Billboards highlight identifiable drive-by images, which make them more suited to selling motor oil, soda pop, and the occasional optician. Psychotherapists, on the other hand, promote themselves more appropriately through public speaking, media interviews, and more lengthy catalog and directory listings. These formats reach more targeted audiences and carry more complex messages.

Professionals usually benefit from a soft sell approach.

We can't state categorically which marketing options will work best in your specific case. If 121+ options are too many and you don't know where to begin, here are some general guidelines. Use these only as starting points, and don't limit yourself:

Community organizations—use mass media publicity, open houses, planned events and, if budget permits, direct mail brochures and newsletters, display advertising, and telephone book ads.

Independent teachers—try posters, classified ads in community papers, directory listings, flyers, networking events, direct mail to targeted lists, telephone calls to targeted prospects, radio and newspaper interviews.

Private consultants—develop business and institutional contacts with business cards, brochures, introduction letters, telephone calls, office visits, published articles, public speaking, joining clubs and associations, and advertising selectively in trade journals.

Retail businesses and services—use newspaper advertising, novelty items, coupon books, discount sales, telephone book ads, and direct mail.

Therapists and independent professionals—reach the general public through networking events, directory listings, introductory classes, public speaking, classified newspaper ads, newsletters, radio and newspaper interviews, brochures, and writing popular articles.

The marketing options that work best for you depend partly on how comfortable you are using them. We know a business consultant who makes a wonderful impression in person, but who is stiff and inarticulate on television interviews. Some people are shy about "selling" themselves and do not like to talk in groups. Others really shine in front of an audience. Some people cringe at handing out business cards. They would rather use direct mail solicitations. Still others dislike brochures and prefer to talk with clients at the office or over the telephone. Finally, some professionals really love to write and build their reputations through published articles and books. A particular marketing option always seems to work better if you enjoy using it.

At first, use the marketing options that you're most comfortable with. As you build a track record of success, you'll naturally gain more confidence. When you're ready to spread your wings, explore new marketing options and see what works for you.

4.) Establish Your Initial Budget

Budget both dollars and time for your promotion campaign.

How much of your time and money should go into promotion? That depends on the nature and the scale of your enterprise. Large and medium sized corporations typically budget 2% to 5% of their gross revenues for promotion. "Guerrilla marketing" expert Jay Conrad Levinson recommends 10%, a strong, aggressive strategy. If you're offering non-credit classes on the open market, put perhaps a third of your time and money into promotion. Home based services with no inventory and little overhead may spend 25% to 50% of their gross on promotion. If you're starting a home based service business, promotional efforts may account for most of your initial start up costs. Make your biggest push during your first year of operation. As your business matures you'll need to spend proportionately less time and money on promotion. If you're an independent professional with a solid client base and good word of mouth, your business may sustain itself. After a few years, you may not need to do any promotion.

Promotional costs to enter a market are almost always higher at first. In the first year of practice, an independent professional may purchase new stationery and business cards, mail announcements to colleagues and prospective clients, and saturate local newspapers with advertising. The proportion of the budget for promotion generally declines as the business matures. Many of the established professionals we know—artists, business consultants, therapists, dancers and musicians—do little other than an occasional directory listing. Some independent professionals—particularly accountants, medical doctors, lawyers, and the most established therapists—rely exclusively on referrals after the first couple years. However, you may expand your budget if your business is growing, adding partners, or franchising.

Evaluate your budget both in dollar costs and staff time. Divide your efforts between capital intensive marketing and labor intensive marketing. Advertising is capital intensive. You can spend lots of money quickly with advertising. Getting publicity is labor intensive. Publicity is free, but it takes time to arrange.

How would you rather spend your afternoon—being interviewed on radio or stapling posters on telephone poles and kiosks? We once chose postering. Why? We decided that postering was more productive. The radio program's audience was not in our prime demographic market. It's always fun to be interviewed on radio, but postering was bringing us business.

Before you choose one marketing option over another, consider the scale of your enterprise. For example, if you're looking to recruit participants for a lunch-hour exercise class, you may not need to advertise in the daily newspaper. A few handbills at or near the dance studio probably will do the trick. On the other hand, if you're responsible for marketing a franchised fitness program of fourteen classes located throughout the city, think big. Consider large display ads in the daily papers, direct mail, radio and television. Highlight your fourteen convenient locations.

5.) Implement A Test Campaign

Here's an exercise that we give to marketing clients and students. From the Marketing Options List, select five options that have worked for you in the past. If you have no personal experience, select five options that businesses similar to yours are using. Or simply choose five options that you're comfortable with and would like to try. Write down your five choices. Decide how much money and how much time you can commit to each during the next three months. This is your test campaign.

Test market before you commit your full resources.

Keep your expenses minimal in your initial tests. Trial-and-error is an acceptable scientific approach. You can afford to make many mistakes if you make cheap mistakes. This advice applies whether you use direct mail, advertising, or any other marketing option. So hedge your bets. For example, place several small ads in different newspapers rather than one large ad in just one paper. Repeat or enlarge the ads that at least pay for themselves. Rewrite the ones that show promise, or at least get some nibbles. Experiment with rewriting an ad until it brings in several times its cost. Drop the ads that don't seem to work after you've given them several chances.

Everybody makes mistakes. The trick is to make cheap mistakes. In fact, we want you to make *lots and lots* of mistakes! The more you experiment, the better your chances of discovering something that really works. Once you've hit on a formula for your particular business, *then* pull out the stops.

Finally, timing is critical. The worst mistake that a novice makes is not scheduling advertising and publicity far enough in advance. We're always receiving announcements in the mail for events already past. What a waste! Allow at least four weeks, possibly more, to promote an event. Mark your calendar and keep to your schedule. Each task will take you longer than you think. The artist will get sick. The printing will be delayed. The radio station will "misplace" your press release. So start early. Leave yourself enough time to do each task over again if necessary.

6.) Evaluate Test Campaign Results

Evaluate your campaign according to both short term and long term goals. If you're organizing a seminar or group event, track your responses. Be ready to count heads. Find out what drew each participant to your event. Ask participants when they register or have them fill out feedback forms. For longer term goals such as name recognition or corporate image building, counting heads is not enough. You may need to conduct in depth surveys to evaluate subtle changes in public opinion or name recognition.

There may be reasons for continuing a promotion campaign that is not getting immediate response. There is "hidden response," where you are building name recognition which will boost sales at some time in the future. There is a synergistic effect to promotion, where using one marketing option indirectly helps to make other promotion more effective. For example, your newspaper advertising could make your telephone directory listing more effective. Finally, direct response may not even be your primary goal. For example, you may want to advertise in a publication to identify with its editorial policy or to support it financially. Advertising in a union paper says, "I support your goals."

Tracking responses is not a perfect science. Some promotion takes time and repetition to achieve a desired response. Respondents will tend to mention your most recent campaign and forget about the others. Your surveys are bound to turn up some confusing, offbeat, even contradictory replies. For example, people will say that they saw your ad in a paper that you've never been in. We usually file such replies under "miscellaneous." The larger your database grows, the more accurate it becomes. So keep polling.

A successful test campaign can pay for itself.

Our own experience suggests that one dollar of promotion should be worth at least three dollars at the door. The promotion costs in a direct mail campaign, for example, might include mailing lists, printing, labeling, postage, and staff resources. If you spend $1,000 and it results in $3,000 worth of orders, the cost to benefit ratio is 1:3. If the benefits fall below this ratio, you may need to try something else.

Many businesses expect a minimum return of 1:4 or 1:5 on advertising and direct marketing campaigns in order to justify their costs. Now, if benefits exceed 1:5, that is, a $5 return for every dollar spent, the campaign is working extremely well. However, if the cost to benefit ratio is much greater than 1:5, it may mean that not enough money is being spent on campaigns which could greatly expand the business.

Start small scale before you go big. Profit from failure as well from success. If a particular marketing option isn't working, revise your copy or

TRACKING RESPONSES BY CODING

Telephone responses—Ask each respondent how they found out about your service when they call. Or use this shortcut: If your telephone number appears in more than one media source, use three different telephone extensions. For example, in each of three places list your number as "555-9999 (extension–1)," "555-9999 (x–2)," and "555-9999 (x–3)." It doesn't matter that you have only one telephone line. When callers name the extension, you'll automatically know what ad brought them to you.

Mail-in responses—Code reply forms in various ways. Code reply forms distributed in different districts with different letters, numbers, or colors. If placing ads in three successive newspapers, vary your address with "Department A," "Department B," and "Department C," or "Suite 1," "Suite 2," and "Suite 3," even if all mail goes to the same office. Put expiration dates on promotional materials whether or not the actual expiration date is important to your sales strategy. Know where and when your response is coming from.

drop it after a few good trials. It's better to fail in a cheap test than in an expensive full-scale campaign. Consider this case: People running a children's math program wanted to expand their market. They spent thousands of dollars mailing flyers to every home in their area, without regard to whether the residents had any interest or need for their program. They got virtually no response. Their mistake was classic. Random "occupant" mailing lists almost never work to market a highly specialized service such as math tutoring. Of course, their program might have been an exception—after all, the "experts" can be wrong. Their mistake was in failing to test market first. They would have saved thousands of dollars if they had first mailed to a few hundred addresses rather than several thousand.

Try several tests to determine what works best for you.

This story has a happy ending. After analyzing the situation, our math friends switched from direct mail to personal marketing. They experimented with giving their flyers to high school teachers who handed them out at class. It worked well! The kids passed the literature on to their parents. Motivated parents responded to the flyers, and the program enrolled quite well. The moral of the story is: Experiment. Evaluate. Experiment. Evaluate. And keep the experiments *cheap*.

7.) Change and Expand Your Campaign

Don't expect all your efforts to be winners. Many, in fact, will not bear repeating. But if a promotion breaks even, that is, if it brings in as much money as it cost you, keep repeating it for a while. Edit and rewrite promotion that is getting inquiries but not leading to enough "warm bodies." However, don't repeat costly promotional efforts indefinitely if you don't see any results. Keep experimenting with new and different media options. Eventually you'll hit on a few that work really well.

Stretch your campaign budget over several months, perhaps a year.

Develop your campaign, not just in terms of money spent, but also in terms of staff time and effort. Use marketing options appropriate to your budget. One client told us that she had rented a classroom space for six months because it was cheaper than the day rate. However, this was before she had taught even one class or attracted one student. She counted on advertising to fill her classes right away, but it didn't. She was stuck with an empty class space and no money left for other promotion. Her plan to build her practice was delayed several months because of this one costly mistake.

Realize that many marketing options require time to build. For example, newspaper or directory advertising may require at least three or more insertions before you know if it's successful. You have to hang in there long enough to build momentum. "My ads drew calls four months after I stopped offering my service," is an ironic complaint we sometimes hear. One business consultant told us that it takes up to two years to get replies from business cards. Plan to stay in business long enough to see your marketing pay off!

If your messages are generating inquiries but not committed customers, ask yourself the following: Are you targeting a specific need and offering a unique solution? Does your copy highlight one or two specific benefits? If your copy is vague, you may get inquiries but no committed

---

BONUS TIP: INVOLVE THE MEDIA!

Offer to give a reporter, interviewer, or talk show producer a "free sample" of your service, product, class, or event. Invite members of the media to your open houses and networking parties. Interest them with something free, fun, and engaging!

clients. When clients call or visit the office, are their needs being recognized? Is your staff doing its job to "close the sale"?

If you can afford the luxury of repetition, by all means do it. The conventional wisdom is that you need to repeat an announcment 16 or more times to achieve market penetration. Repetition makes people comfortable with your service. It usually improves client response. However, if results start to decline, it is a signal that you may have reached saturation. It may be time for a new campaign, possibly in different media.

Promotion can be cumulative, and some people won't respond until they've seen your materials several times in many places. Here's an example of the cumulative effects of ongoing promotion, the "second source" factor. We were consulting for a science program at a local university. We had been conducting a promotion campaign and had obtained some dramatic results. One applicant, upon hearing our radio publicity, nearly ran her car off the road trying desperately to write down the telephone number of the program. The radio spot was credited with bringing her into the program. Actually, she had heard and read about the program for years. The radio announcement was only the final spur.

Change the message and change the medium.

If people aren't responding to your message, follow these steps:

1.) *Give your message time to work.*
A promotion campaign takes several weeks, if not months, to prove effective. We've even had clients tell us, "I've been meaning to call you for *years*. I'm finally ready now."

2.) *Repeat your message.*
Most people need to see your announcement more than once before they respond. Your ads become more believable with repetition.

3.) *Rewrite your message.*
Highlight a different benefit for your prospective client. Come on with a stronger promise, a free introduction, or a money-back guarantee.

4.) *Follow-up inquiries.*
Contact everyone who has made a recent inquiry about your service. Find out if they intend to become clients and if not, why not. Is there a problem with marketing, sales, or the service itself?

5.) *Change the medium.*
Select another set of marketing options and try something new.

6.) *Change the message entirely.*
Consider a new audience, a new geographical area, or a fundamental change in the nature of your service.

You can get great results even on a limited budget.

Our experience with the science program demonstrates what you can accomplish on a limited budget. Their marketing department already had spent several thousand dollars when we came in. We were allotted about $2,500 to produce a newsletter, place ads in several high school newspapers, obtain publicity spots on a few local radio stations. We also tracked the effectiveness of other marketing approaches already in progress. The program enrolled about 50 students, each paying several thousand dollars in tuition. Several of these enrollments came from our special efforts. We surveyed the current crop of students to find out exactly where they came from. We printed the results in the inset titled "Science Program—Campaign Analysis."

SCIENCE PROGRAM— CAMPAIGN ANALYSIS:

Our survey indicated that word of mouth, which cost nothing extra, accounted for 35% of new students, the largest single source. It's nice to know that your reputation has preceded you.

Ongoing advertising in the metropolitan daily newspaper consumed about half of the promotion budget and netted about 24% of the students. The daily newspaper was working well, but the ads were expensive for the results achieved. In subsequent campaigns the ads were made smaller and less expensive.

The graduate program's own newsletter, which cost perhaps only 10% of the budget to produce, was garnering about 20% of the student response. Subsequently the newsletter was expanded and circulation beefed up.

The radio public service announcements cost less than 3% of the budget and netted about 10% of the response. In future campaigns the school made greater use of a combination of paid radio commercials and public service spots.

Advertising in various weekly and high school newspapers cost 10% of the budget and netted less than 5% of the responses. This option was not worth the time and expense involved and was dropped in subsequent campaigns.

The catalog cost perhaps 10% of the marketing budget, accounted for perhaps 7% of the student response, and was left unchanged.

Miscellaneous and "don't know" accounted for the remaining 5% or 6%.

As a result of our efforts, future campaigns for the science program focused on publishing the newsletter, advertising and publicity on radio and in the daily newspaper.

The results of any promotion campaign can't be guaranteed. However, good planning, careful polling, and a judicious analysis of initial results can build an increasingly effective promotion campaign. Once you know what works for you, expand your campaign.

A Promotion Campaign for "Your Program"

Now, let's conduct a hypothetical promotion campaign for Your Program. Your Program is a small scale local service with a limited initial budget. Your long term goals are to build a much larger organization. For now, your immediate goal is to generate cash flow, and that means warm bodies. Preliminary market analysis suggests that Your Program appeals to young professionals and working people who respond to reasoned promotional appeals. Your Program, in other words, targets baby boomers. Other similar services have used newspapers, direct mail, and postering.

Your Program is already off the ground. You have already run a test campaign for $50 cash and several days of your valuable time, concentrating on public speaking, free publicity, classified advertising, distributing business cards, and postering. Let's make your budget for this campaign

PROMOTING "YOUR PROGRAM":

MARKETING OPTIONS	EXPENSE	INCOME	#CLIENTS
word of mouth	free	$200	2
newspaper display advertising	$400	$600	6
directory listing	$ 85	$400	4
radio interview (travel costs)	$ 10	$200	2
direct mail announcement	$200	$600	6
newspaper interview (query letter)	$ 5	none	0
postering	$100	$400	4
TOTALS:	$800	$2,400	24

Some promotion requires more time than money.

$800, which is what you are comfortable risking right now. Let's say that these are your results after three months:

Now let's analyze the results:

Total expenses of promotion: $800
Number of clients from promotion: 24
Average amount spent by each client: $100
Total income from promotion: $2,400
Return on investment: 300%

Careful record keeping produced useful data. A total of twenty-four clients each spent $100. As they telephoned or visited your office, you were careful to ask each client how they found out about Your Program. These clients purchased a total of $2,400 in services, a return of $3 for every dollar spent on promotion. For starters this is very good. You've made money on your first large campaign, and Your Program shows great potential.

Word of mouth was your best deal. It cost you no extra time or money and generated $200. Thanks to referrals, Your Program will continue to grow. Word of mouth alone, however, may be too slow.

Telephone surveys are easy and inexpensive.

"YOUR PROGRAM'S" TELEPHONE PAD SURVEY:

(Poll respondents when they call.)
Q: "How did you first find out about our Program?"

word of mouth	2
newspaper display advertising	6
professional directory listing	4
radio interview (travel costs)	2
direct mail announcement	6
newspaper interview (query letter)	0
postering	4
TOTALS:	24

Display advertising in the daily newspaper cost $400, half of the entire $800 budget. The ad resulted in lots of query calls, but more quantity than quality. In terms of money generated, it barely paid for itself. Maybe you can rewrite the ad to work better. Maybe the weekly entertainment newspaper with a younger readership would be more effective. Maybe you should reduce the newspaper ad budget in favor of other options. This is a judgment call that depends upon your budget and whether other sources can give you a better return on your investment.

The professional directory listing brought in almost five times as much as it cost. This listing is worth continuing and possibly enlarging in future editions of the directory. Consider trying other private directories in future campaigns.

The radio interview was fun and resulted in a couple of new clients. Moreover, the personal contacts with media people seemed promising for coverage in the future. The interview, however, took much time to arrange. Moreover, there were travel costs. The newspaper interview never happened, but it might be worth contacting other papers in future campaigns. Getting publicity turned out to be time consuming, better suited to long term than short term goals. This experience, incidentally, is not uncommon. Publicity gives you exposure but does not necessarily generate warm bodies.

The direct mail announcement generated three times its costs. This shows promise, but there is room for improvement. Maybe the brochure needs polishing. Maybe you need a better mailing list. Enlarge your mailing list over time or consider renting lists from private sources.

Postering brought in four times its costs, but it was a nuisance to put flyers all over town week after week. Hiring an extra staffer or the local postering service to do the stapling will increase costs but may be worth the expense.

You took care to collect polling responses, but there is still uncertainty in the statistics. Some of the respondents didn't remember how they found out about Your Program and didn't answer the question. Some of them probably heard about Your Program from several sources but only mentioned one. Keep polling clients and your data will grow increasingly accurate. New promotion campaigns should prove more and more profitable.

Of course, this is only a hypothetical promotion campaign for Your Program. When you conduct a real campaign, your choice of media options will be different. So will the results.

Find out what works for you. Pour a generous share of the money you make back into promotion that's working. Then, watch your business grow.

PROMOTION CAMPAIGN PLANNER:

Copy this form. Choose five to ten marketing options from the over 121+ listed in this chapter. Establish an initial budget of time and money to conduct a test campaign. Keep careful track of your responses, and expand your budget for whatever marketing options that work well for you.

Use a calendar or an organizer to keep track of print deadlines, interview dates, follow-up calls, and other commitments.

Marketing Option	Time Investment	Money	Notes
1.)			
2.)			
3.)			
4.)			
5.)			
6.)			
7.)			
8.)			
9.)			
10.)			

Start with marketing options familiar to you.

JANUARY

*BART'S PLANNER. PLEASE DON'T REMOVE FROM DESK.

Sun.	Mon.	Tues.	Wed.	Thurs.	Fri.	Sat.
1 *Happy holidays! Call Mom.*	2 *Review ad copy for Feb. edition of the Monthly Review. Deadline Jan 10.*	3	4 *Rewrite press releases for the Weekly Guardian, due Fri. for following Thurs. edition.*	5	6	7
8	9	10 *Turn in ad copy for February edition of the Monthly Review.*	11 *Rewrite press releases for the Weekly Guardian, due Fri. for following Thurs. edition.*	12	13	14
15	16	17	18 *Rewrite press releases for the Weekly Guardian, due Fri. for following Thurs. edition.*	19 *Prepare for radio interview with Fred Kelley on KBUS, 11am Fri.*	20 *11AM, interview with Fred Kelley on KBUS, 2000 Market Plaza, room 503.*	21
21	22	23	24 *Rewrite press releases for the Weekly Guardian, due Fri. for following Thurs. edition.*	25 *8pm, meet Joan at the Last Thursday Business Club. Have brochures ready to hand out.*	26	27
28	29	30			*Next month— While showering, think about speech to give at the Last Thursday Business Club.*	

FEBRUARY

Sun.	Mon.	Tues.	Wed.	Thurs.	Fri.	Sat.
			1 *Rewrite press releases for the Weekly Guardian, due Fri. for following Thurs. edition.*	2	3	4
5	6 *Review ad copy for March edition of the Monthly Review. Deadline Feb. 10.*	7 *Turn in ad copy for March edition of the Monthly Review.*	8 *Rewrite press releases for the Weekly Guardian, due Fri. for following Thurs. edition.*	9	10	11
12	13 *Rewrite copy on brochures— needed ready by the 23rd.*	14 *Turn in brochure copy to typesetter (deadline the 23rd.)*	15 *Rewrite press releases for the Weekly Guardian, due Fri. for following Thurs. edition.*	16	17 *Pick up and proof typeset copy for brochure (deadline the 23rd)*	18
19	20 *Final corrections and paste-up for brochure copy (deadline the 23rd)*	21	22 *Rewrite press releases for the Weekly Guardian, due Fri. for following Thurs. edition.*	23 *4pm, pick up brochures ready from printer 8pm, Speak at the Last Thursday Business Club. Have brochures ready to hand out.*	24	25
26	27	28				*Next month— Start to schedule book tour. Interview new designer for new ad campaign.*

Calendar planners can be simple or fancy. You can obtain expensive organizers, even computerize your schedule with elaborate software database managers. A simple solution works for us. We mark up a 12 month calendar just for campaign planning and public speaking.

Bruce Tessler is founder of the San Francisco School of Art, one of the Bay Area's most prominent independent art schools. Here Bruce gives a sense of the vision and perseverance it takes to build an institution from the ground up:

"As a student at two of the three major art schools in the Bay Area and an instructor at one of them, I saw firsthand a need for a different direction in the fine arts education. Classes were typically short on technical and academic information. They did not offer personal instruction or they offered information which was detrimental to student development. As a graduate art student, as assistant to the head of the Fine Arts Department, I had the opportunity to learn about how to run—and how not to run—an art school.

"Having a lack of faith in the political structure where I was studying and teaching, I started offering drawing classes at my own studio. The experiment was successful and, in January 1982, with ten regular students, I rented a 1000 square foot storefront. I spent the next month installing lights, distributing flyers, and painting the walls until the wee hours of the morning.

"At the end of the first year, 30 students were enrolled. By 1985, our two-year Certificate of Fine Arts program was authorized by the State of California. A school library was started. We began to offer specialized workshops and held our first faculty show. In 1988 we doubled our space, added more classes, and established a gallery. Then the October 17, 1989 earthquake struck. The next eight weeks were spent furiously looking for a new location. With help from students, we quickly moved most of our equipment to our new space at 667 Mission Street. Even in the midst of confusion we continued to provide the best education we could.

"The little red schoolhouse I started in 1982 has grown beyond my original conception. There is always more work to be done. With the time and energy it takes to run an art-related business, personal life and personal work as an artist are often set aside.

"Why do I keep going? There are always those few students, working just as hard as I am...watching and nurturing their growth makes the struggle worth it. When you have a 'mission,' you don't let anything stop you, not even an earthquake."

—Bruce Tessler

7

Personal Marketing

PERSONAL MARKETING MEANS promoting yourself. It means becoming known for your unique contribution to the community. Clients tend to purchase more from people that they know.

The key to personal marketing is being visible, accessible, and active. Personal marketing doesn't necessarily mean high pressure selling. It does mean putting yourself in front of the public. Here are some guidelines:

Talk about your work. Allow your work to be a topic of casual conversation without necessarily "selling." Let people know how important your profession is to you.

Build networks. Join associations and attend business mixers. Make allies out of potential competitors by swapping information and referrals. Build an executive network of advisers, a personal think-tank.

Cultivate a personal style. Find a style that works best for you and fits the demands of your profession. One accountant we know never wears a tie except when he testifies in tax court.

Become an authority. Develop a unique database of information. Become a recognized expert in your particular field.

Branch out. Become known and reach new clients by developing new profit centers. Consider the arenas of public speaking, corporate consulting, writing, and teaching.

Your Business Introduction

Most of us find it easy to talk about our work with friends. It's often much harder with strangers. Because first impressions are so important (how else do you get to second impressions?), it helps to be ready with a brief introduction.

Here's a little test. You are about to enter a social gathering of friendly, interested strangers, some who may be excellent professional contacts or client prospects. Are you prepared right now to describe, in twenty-five words or less, your line of work, your specialty, and your target market? Many of us freeze up at the simple question, "What do you do?" However, the answer doesn't have to be complicated. Here are some examples:

> *I am a chiropractor specializing in working with people with sports injuries.*

> *I am a psychologist in general practice. Commonly recurring issues that arise include loneliness, anger, alcohol and cocaine abuse.*

> *I am the admissions officer for Nova University's computer training program. The curriculum includes evening and weekend classes geared to the needs of working professionals and business people.*

We confess that the last description is twenty-seven words, two words over our self-imposed limit. The point is that you should have something ready to say. We call this the "box top rule." Your introduction should be as pithy as a prize winning contest slogan written on a cereal box top.

Practice saying your introduction until it becomes second nature. A close friend should be able to awaken you in the middle of a deep sleep and your introduction should roll off your tongue. This introduction will serve you especially well if you are interviewed on radio or television. One or two sentence answers are the rule. At parties a quick introduction will get your message across before your new acquaintance gets distracted and makes a beeline for the punch bowl.

Be real. Some professionals, overly immersed in their specialty, describe themselves with jargon-laden terms that nobody else understands.

Have a business introduction ready for any occasion.

Others get very convoluted with their introductions. They talk about saving humanity, offer deep metaphysical insights, or speculate about how successful they expect to be in two years. Keep it brief. Share something about yourself. Look for permission from the listener to continue.

The point is to make yourself accessible for further contact. If the situation permits, hand out something printed, a business card, brochure or flyer. Exchange telephone numbers. Make contacts.

Talk about your work with others so that they can share a sense of how important it is to you. Professionals work for many reasons besides making money. Sharing your sense of purpose and dedication tells others something about the real you. A bodyworker tells us that she entered the profession to help break down the artificial barriers to touching imposed by our Western culture. A real estate broker specializes in negotiating low down payment purchases for first time buyers because he enjoys seeing people get their slice of the economic pie. A mask making art instructor wants to help participants release personal demons and uncover psychic archetypes.

Talk about your work when the opportunity presents itself.

Networking

Networking is socializing with a purpose. Community business experts encourage the formation of interactive networks, extensions of family, social clubs, and professional gatherings. Right livelihood consultant Claude Whitmyer encourages cultivating planning buddies, business support groups, advisers, and business advisory boards in his book *Running A One-Person Business.*

Back in the radical 1960's, "networking" first described progressive organizations that shared information on interrelated themes such as peace and ecology. By the 1980's the term had grown so popular that AT&T was using it in their commercials to encourage businesspeople to phone more often. By 1989, *Webster's Ninth New Collegiate Dictionary* defined networking as "the exchange of information or services among individuals, groups, or institutions." Networking is a great way to establish trust and build relationships. This makes it an ideal tool for personal marketing.

There are different kinds of networks. Employee functions, professional networks, and social mixers all present different business opportunities. If you work for a large corporation, you know the obvious political and social value of attending employee functions. Independent professionals and small business operators do not have a built-in community of peers and associates as do corporate employees. Professional and trade organizations make up for this to some degree. Participate at conferences to keep abreast of new developments in your profession. Attend community events and mixers to combat isolation and make new client contacts.

Peer networks usually are not a good source for client prospects. One psychologist told us about a gathering she attended with fifty other therapists, each eyeing the other hungrily in search of new patients. Unfortunately, she was in a room where everybody was selling and nobody was buying. Peer networks are great to build alliances, trade mailing lists, find office partners, or initiate political lobbying efforts. However, don't expect to increase your client load from associates or "competitors." Peer groups aren't your client market.

General admission events, on the other hand, do provide marketing opportunities. Church or social clubs, chamber of commerce meetings, business luncheons, and hobby groups may prove fertile ground for personal promotion. One fellow who specializes in conducting mixed business socials talks about "miracles" that occur almost every evening when two people find that they have complementary skills and needs. A computer expert needs a therapeutic massage. A massage therapist needs his records computerized. People trade services. Sometimes partnerships are born. People generally come away feeling less isolated. There's also the chance to gossip, share business news, and find out firsthand what's working and what isn't.

Group activities provide marketing opportunities.

The best events we've attended have three main features. First, a guest speaker or resident expert provides a topic for discussion. Secondly, there's an opportunity for people to introduce themselves to the whole group, make announcements, hand out cards or flyers. Thirdly, there's food and drink. The informal socializing at the chow line or bar allows for follow ups to introductions, and perhaps even the chance for lasting intimacy.

Attending open business networks is especially good to combat loneliness, feel more connected with the community, and gather marketing information. It's easy to make friends at business socials. Here are two good opening lines: "What did you think of the main speaker?" "Is this your first meeting?" What you accomplish at networking events really depends upon your personal and professional agenda.

Your Executive Network

Your executive network is your personal brain trust, your personal "board of advisers." Every person in business has to wear many hats—know something about law, accounting, publicity, insurance, and more. It's almost impossible, however, to become a real expert in more than one or two of these areas. For this reason, you'll want to develop a relationship with experts in many fields. Often these will be freelancers who will serve as your consultants or "gurus" as the need arises. If you work in a larger organization, you may handle several of these functions in-house:

Accounting
Banking
Catering
Coaching
Confidence
Graphics
Healthcare
Insurance
Legal
Photography
Printing
Publicity
Therapy
Travel
Writing

> *Develop your own informal "board of advisers."*

Tailor your own executive network to your personal needs. You might also want to add a team of marketing professionals such as:

Advertising agency
Booking agent
Marketing expert
Public relations firm
Publicist

Line up your executive network before an emergency arises. Look in the Yellow Pages for initial leads, or get referrals from your associates. It can be frightening to have to hunt for a lawyer after you've been sued. Build your executive network by soliciting qualified referrals. An unqualified referral such as, "He's the greatest lawyer in the world!" is of little value. However, "He's the world's greatest authority on the legal responsibility of tour guides!" is an excellent qualifier, especially if you're a tour guide looking for a lawyer.

Discuss philosophy, expertise, and methods of payment at your first meeting. Most professionals offer low cost or introductory initial appointments. The advisers in your executive network may be available hourly, on a fixed retainer, or on call as the need arises. The method of payment may depend upon how often you make use of a particular specialist. Don't put an expert on a monthly retainer until you know you're going to need him on a regular basis.

The people we've chosen for our own executive network tend to reflect our personal philosophy of doing business. Since we do our own book-keeping and tax accounting in-house, we've developed a working relationship with a tax accountant who helps us do these things ourselves. We only contact him when we can't figure out a portion of the tax code on our own. We only pay him once a year or so. We work with him by phone. We've never been to our accountant's office, and he's been to ours just once many years ago.

Find professionals who complement your own style of doing business. Work with experts who understand your needs, keep costs within an agreed upon budget, and can explain what they do in plain English. Avoid experts who leave you feeling confused or mystified. Hire those who help you to feel confident and enhance your ability to make smart decisions. You are, after all, paying the bills.

Cultivating A Personal Style

Choose a style of interaction appropriate to your service.

Your business style colors your client's experiences. The Disneyland management takes great care to immerse every visitor in a total environment. All new Disneyland employees are encouraged from the outset to think of themselves as "performers." Even the uniforms of the street sweepers are "costumes." Park guests are the "audience." The idea here is to create the perfect illusion, a seamless experience with memories to last a lifetime.

Different services raise different client expectations. Maybe a visit to the orthodontist is no trip to Disneyland. The challenge is to find out what the client expects and prefers. Should the room be lighted brightly or softly? Should there be magazines or music? These and other important considerations may be discovered through more extensive market research or polling your customers.

Your personal style of relating to customers also affects their experience. We've identified three distinct (but not mutually exclusive) styles of performance: expert, facilitator, and entertainer:

EXPERT, information based:
Participants are initially receptive, later active when they use what they've learned.

FACILITATOR, process oriented:
Participants are active as they share feelings, contacts, and information. The focus is away from the leader.

ENTERTAINER, diversion or inspiration:
With spotlight on center stage, participants are passive as
they are being amused or enlightened.

An expert is the bearer of specialized information. The participants are
receptive while they're learning what the expert knows. Participants
usually expect to act later on the knowledge they've gained. A facilitator
provides an opportunity for participants to be active in the present. A
facilitator will rarely assume the center of attention. An entertainer provides amusement, diversion, or inspiration. An entertainer's audience
typically is receptive. Sometimes audiences become active participants in
question and answer sessions. At this point the entertainer becomes a
facilitator or expert.

Whether you are an expert, a facilitator, or an entertainer depends
upon the nature of your service and your personal style. These categories
are not exclusive, so you can be a little of each. For example, we know a
dentist who is part expert and part entertainer. He amuses young patients
with a hokey impression of Dracula and an unreal four foot syringe. Such
diversions are pure entertainment, clearly outside the role of expert. But
they put the kids at ease.

Modify your role to fit client expectations.

Most occupations tend to emphasize one role above the others. But
feel free to improvise the way our dentist friend does. Sometimes an
expert needs to change roles. Lawyers and accountants tell us that part of
their job includes playing the therapist. Comforting and consoling their
clients, they take on the role of facilitator.

Determining which role you should emphasize often depends on
client expectations. We once employed a business teacher, a graduate
from the prestigious Wharton School, who wanted to conduct a values-
oriented business class. Unfortunately, this approach was turning off his
practical minded students. People who sign up to learn how to start a
small business don't want very much philosophy. They want hard facts
and access to resources. In other words, they want an expert, not a
facilitator. Students complained and enrollment fell.

Fortunately, we caught the problem in time. We had been gathering
feedback on student evaluation forms. Students were asking for practical
information on zoning, permits, startup capital, and bank loans. After we
confronted the instructor, he was savvy enough to modify his approach
and provide students the information they were seeking. Feedback evalu-
ations went from poor to excellent. We gave the class extra publicity and
enrollment swelled. The teacher had changed to a style more suited to
student expectations, not his own ego. The ultimate result was many
more satisfied students, grateful administrators, and a happy teacher.

You, the World's Greatest Authority

Discover your potential to become the World's Greatest Authority! Of course, this sounds incredible, and it would appear rudely immodest printed on any business card. It is nonetheless absolutely true. You can become the World's Greatest Authority.

The trick to becoming the World's Greatest Authority on any particular subject is to narrow your focus. For example, we know a business consultant who is expert in finding alternatives to bank financing. He also knows the applicable local laws regarding home-based businesses. So, in our city this fellow undoubtedly is the World's Greatest Authority on starting home-based businesses. In your area somebody else may know the local laws best and be your own World's Greatest.

World's Greatest Authorities are in demand in the media, on the lecture circuit, and to author articles and books. Kate, who operates a one-person service specializing in organizing desks and closets, has appeared several times on television and radio to share her expertise. Sue, a psychotherapist who has worked with the special problems of aging hippies, frequently speaks to groups on this and related topics. Jim, a massage therapist with a doctorate degree, lectures and trains all over the globe.

Your own unique combination of training, hobbies, and local knowledge gives you the potential to become "the world's greatest authority." Here are some steps you can take to enhance this potential:

Do your homework to qualify as an expert.

Subscribe to periodicals in your field.
Compile your own reference library.
Correspond and visit with other experts.
Write down or record your original thoughts.
Collect pertinent local names and contacts.
Join business or professional associations.
Attend professional development seminars.
Obtain and update appropriate certificates and degrees.

Being the World's Greatest Authority is really all about building your reputation as an expert. It doesn't advance your career to be a great authority unless others recognize it. We confess, it's a bit forward to promote yourself as "World's Greatest." It's up to others to judge whether you are the World's Greatest or merely a top contender. False modesty, however, is every bit as unprofessional. Don't trap yourself with mediocrity. If you unconsciously project the belief that you're not very good or only average, others won't take you seriously as an authority. So do your homework and become "great." Then make it known to peers and the public that you have staked out a particular specialty.

Once you feel pretty confident about your authority status, consider listing in the *Yearbook of Experts*. The mass media regularly consults this resource guide for leads. You'll be contacted for interviews on television, radio, and newspapers often by phone, without leaving your own home. A basic listing costs at least $225. People tell us that their listings generally pay for themselves, especially if you have a book published or a lecture tour upcoming. For information contact the *Yearbook of Experts*, 2233 Wisconsin, N.W., Washington, D.C. 20007. Phone (202) 333-4904.

Public Speaking

Public speaking helps to build your authority image.

Public speaking is the way to educate, to enhance your reputation as an authority, and to develop client prospects most effectively. It can be financially rewarding as well. Having hired and evaluated thousands of teachers and public speakers, we have a working background in this field. Here are our best tips.

Would you rather die than speak in front of a group? Polls say that fear of public speaking is the number one fear, even ahead of fear of dying. About half of all Americans are afraid to make a speech. If you're afraid, you're in very good company. Sir Laurence Olivier, perhaps the greatest actor in the history of the theater, admitted that stage fright plagued him recurrently at the height of his career.

Practice and preparation are the best (but not perfect) cures for stage fright. It's reassuring to know that your internal experience of nervousness doesn't show at all. In a college experiment audience members were asked to identify which speakers were frightened and which weren't. They couldn't tell! Don't announce it, either. Confessing nervousness may make the audience uncomfortable. Learn to channel the energy. Experienced speakers actually come to enjoy the adrenaline rush they get before speaking. They say the edge improves performance.

There's less pressure on you than you think. As a professional in business, remember that you are selling yourself, not "performing" as such. You don't have to be anything that you're not. If you are organized, thoughtful, and confident of your material, these qualities will show. As a businessperson or authority, you will not be held to the same standards as a professional actor. In fact, any occasional slips or stutters will make you all the more human, more accessible to your audience.

If you're new to public speaking, practice your speech in front of the mirror, your roommate, children, or the pet cat—wherever the risks of embarrassment are minimal. Start by giving shorter speeches to small

Make time for audience participation after a speech.

groups and work up. Attend classes, not necessarily speech classes, and make a point to participate. Consider joining Toastmasters, a national organization dedicated to helping anyone learn impromptu speaking.

We recommend preparing speeches in two basic lengths, ten minutes and 30 minutes. Your shorter speech, ideally, should be as pithy as a Johnny Carson monologue. First, develop your ten minute speech. A ten minute monologue can be a lot of time to fill on stage. Get your material from real life experiences. Describe what you do in a few sentences. Then list five to ten questions that clients most often ask you about your work. Jot down some short answers. Work these into a conversational presentation. Once you have ten minutes of interesting material you can work on expanding this presentation.

Your longer speech can go into more detail about your topic or your work. You'll rarely need to speak for longer than 30 minutes. If there's more time to fill, add a question and answer period. (Making time for audience participation is recommended in any case.) Your audience will appreciate it, and you'll find it to be valuable feedback. We like to think of audience questions as a kind of marketing research to find out what people really want to know!

Start your speech with a pertinent statistic, a human interest story, or a quick joke. There are probably more professional joke writers working for businesspeople and politicians than there are writing for comedians. Less expensively, you can find quips and quotes in several good reference books. If you write your own jokes, be careful. Avoid offensive or "politically incorrect" humor. Avoid long-winded stories which fail to build to the anticipated belly laugh. Self-disparaging humor is the safest, because it helps people identify with you. Consider sharing a personal anecdote. It can be a story about one of your most successful, saddest, most heart warming, or most frustrating experiences with a client. Again, play it safe. Use a story that you've told several times already with predictable results.

Throughout your speech, keep your message simple, honed down to one or two important themes. Sometimes it's appropriate to have a catchy slant or topic. Bart occasionally gives a well-attended presentation billed as "The Two Minute Marketing Analysis." He starts with the disclaimer that a two-minute marketing analysis really isn't worth much, but then the audience hadn't paid much either. The opening remark lowers expectations, commands attention, and raises chuckles at the same time.

Keep your speech lively. Even non-experts should find your speech entertaining to listen to. Remember, unless you're giving grades or speaking at a prison, you do *not* have a captive audience. They're free to talk among themselves, fall asleep, or even leave! Their attention will flag if food or drink is present. Avoid jargon, long sentences, and tortuous logic.

Above all else, avoid being boring. Err on the side of brevity. If the audience says, "He should have spoken longer," then you've given a great speech.

Learn your material well enough so that you can look out at your audience at least half of the time during your presentation. Scan the room from one side to the other gazing directly into people's eyes. If you are naturally shy, scan foreheads at first. Make eye contact as you build confidence. Avoid just looking at one or two people, playing favorites. Try working from notes on index cards. Don't worry if you forget part of your speech because it all wasn't scripted. The audience will never know what you forgot to say. They'll only know if they enjoyed what you did say.

Let people know something about the real you. The person who introduces you will list your professional qualifications. You want to get known, not just for being knowledgeable, but for being an accessible expert. You do not necessarily need to be funny or witty. You don't have to be a know-it-all. Simply be approachable and sincere in your desire to be helpful. Don't worry about not being liked. No matter what you do, most people will like you and a few won't. That's their problem, anyway. Just be yourself, and enjoy the limelight!

Always have brochures or business cards available at the end of a presentation so that members of the audience can make follow-up contact. After all, isn't that the point of giving the speech?

Have brochures available to hand out after your speech.

If you enjoy public speaking, consider developing your own local lecture circuit. Almost every club, business, or professional organization that holds regular meetings is hungry for guest speakers. Make a list of local groups you belong to or know about. Get additional leads from your chamber of commerce. Ask your reference librarian to see any local directories of associations and businesses which may be available. Also draw up a list of the major corporations in your community which are likely to have meeting rooms, company newsletters (to announce your engagement), and lunch halls.

Once you have made your list, send a query letter to the meeting planner of a particular group and offer to speak. Include your business card, brochure, and local references, if available. Place a follow-up phone call about a week or two after your mailing. (It may be more impressive to delegate this part to a secretary, publicist, or friend.) When a group wants you to speak, it's time to talk money. Ask what they usually pay speakers. Tell them that your usual speaking fee, based on your normal hourly rate of compensation, is (let's say) $200, but that you're open to negotiation. Many community groups do not pay for speakers, although the better financed ones at least will offer you an honorarium. However, even without compensation, local speaking engagements provide excellent exposure and a chance to hone your oratorical abilities in real life situations. Before the deal is final, inquire gently about the possibility of travel expenses, meals, lodging, and publicity in the company or club newsletter. Also ask if the person who introduces you at the event can plug your service, sell your books or tapes, mention your next seminar date, etc.

Once you're an articulate and polished speaker, you may want to break into the professional lecture circuit. When starting out, drum up your own speaking engagements. Notes Gordon Burgett in *Speaking for Money* (p.204), "For non-celebrity speakers, 95% of our business will come from our own marketing effort!" He advises beginners to "focus your marketing on your own home state." Take an entrepreneurial attitude. For example, motivate hotel or club owners by offering them a finder's fee or commission to arrange your engagement.

Once you're commanding over $500 per speech, you may want to contract with a booking agent. Booking agencies hire marketable speakers for engagements before clubs, conventions, hotels, cruises, resorts, on college campuses, and independently in every major city. Major celebrities, politicians, entertainers, sports figures, writers, and others, earn over $25,000 per engagement. Very few agencies will book relative unknowns. Booking agencies generally offer guaranteed advance fees and/or a percentage of the proceeds, typically 25-35%. Go slowly if an agency asks you for a large advance fee, because here you're assuming the financial risk. If you're a marketable speaker, it shouldn't cost you money to secure bookings.

A very good source for booking agents and lecture bureaus is *Speakers and Lecturers: How to Find Them*, a two-volume reference book at your local library. See the Books and References chapter for this and several other excellent resources on public speaking.

Sideline Teaching

Sideline teaching can help build your reputation as an accessible expert.

Sideline teaching is a great way to build prestige in the community. Lawyers, accountants, Realtors, doctors, musicians, artists, and psychologists all find that teaching helps to build their practices. If you have a storefront business or service, offering classes can boost sales and improve public relations. Teaching classes can become a lucrative adjunct to your business—an additional "profit center," too.

There are many benefits to teaching in addition to any money you might earn. First and foremost, teaching itself can be fun, a real ego boost. When you have to review and explain a topic, you come to know it better than ever. Sharing this information with fresh minds helps you to appreciate it anew, also.

The teaching marketplace is wide open, and no single provider dominates. Non-credit learning is not one mass market, but an almost endless number of tightly focused niche markets. Identify prospective students by vocation, hobby, special interest, geographic area, and lifestyle. Target your promotional materials to reach your audience.

You don't need lots of money. You don't necessarily need formal credentials, either. You can turn almost any life experience into a rewarding career teaching freelance or parttime. You can customize the length of your class, the price, location, and number of participants. You don't even have to be affiliated with a sponsoring organization. You can go right out and advertise non-credit classes in your local newspaper or entertainment tabloid.

Whether you're interested in volunteer teaching, paid employment, or want to design your own class, you'll find a myriad of possibilities at:

Adult schools
Community centers
Community colleges
Corporate training programs
Extension schools
Independent marketing
Lecture circuits
Open universities
Parks and recreation departments
Specialty markets
Storefront businesses
Trade schools

Class catalogs are a valuable source of publicity.

If you want to teach at a particular institution, read their school catalog closely before proposing your own class. Then contact the person responsible for hiring. If you propose to offer a class, make it topical, practical, and fun. Be flexible and willing to teach whatever the administrator needs, at least at first. If you help him out here, he'll be more willing to experiment with the course that you'd like to try later.

Different institutions pay in different ways. Some schools pay on an hourly basis, usually $8 to $25 or more per class-hour. Others negotiate a fee split and pay teachers a percentage of the gross, usually 20% to 50%. A teacher with a popular course can negotiate a higher percentage and a share in the profits. Some institutions hire teachers as independent contractors and expect you to participate more actively in organizing, marketing, and publicity. If the pay is low, teaching still may be worth the intrinsic rewards. In some cases, it can also be a publicity bonanza.

If you participate in writing your own class description for a major

COURSE DESCRIPTION FORMAT:

Here are the main elements of a course description. Customize them to your particular needs:

1.)   Title identifies topic:

2.)   Who should attend (part of title or subtitle):

3.)   Stress benefits (consider using testimonials):

4.)   Topics covered:

5.)   Format, i.e., lecture, discussion, multimedia equipment, exercises, class size, etc.:

6.)   Prerequisites and commitment required:

7.)   What is provided, including books, tapes, lunch, parking, accommodations, etc.:

8.)   What participants need to bring:

9.)   Teacher qualifications, relevant degrees, professional background, insider's information, references to your institutional affiliation, private practice, book tour, etc.:

10.) Day, date, and times:

11.) Place:

12.) Cost, including early-bird or group discounts, billing, credit cards accepted:

13.) Ways to enroll, including billing, credit cards, preregistration (Invite inquiries; design an easy to use registration form if appropriate):

14.) Registrar's contact phone, address, FAX, etc.:

A short class description should at least identify the topic and stress a benefit. "Learn piano the fun way! Call 555-KEYS. Ask for Mark."

STARTUP MONEY FOR FREELANCE TEACHING:

SMALL SCALE (Under $100)—Freelancers, depending on the kind of class and materials involved, you can frequently launch a class for less than $100 startup costs. Keep costs down by teaching out of your home and recruiting students with flyers, postering, telemarketing, your own public speaking, directory advertising, and inexpensive classified advertising. Often you can arrange to pay for advertising on a payment schedule, deferring out-of-pocket expenses to almost nothing.

MEDIUM SCALE ($100–$1,000)—You can make more money with larger attendance, but you have to invest more, too. That means a higher minimum enrollment to "break-even" on your investment. Consider classified and display advertising in weekly entertainment papers, directory ads, and, possibly major daily papers. Experiment with direct mail campaigns, mailing flyers, brochures, or newsletters to prospective students.

LARGE SCALE ($1,000 and up)—Appropriate if you have a series of classes or are a small school administrator, etc. Make more extensive use of display advertising. Publish your own catalog and distribute it by direct mail, as an advertising insert, or directly into stores. Also consider local radio spots and Yellow Pages advertising.

INVESTING YOUR TIME, TOO—Budget time for networking, i.e., talking about your classes in public. That means speeches, interviews, circulating at parties, and attending professional gatherings. Check out media possibilities, too. Publicity is a valuable tool that costs time, not money. It may take several hours worth of phone calls to local newspapers and television stations to net one interview. Publicity lends prestige and credibility to your efforts, but it may or may not result in "warm bodies" at class. Will it be worth your time? Experiment!

If new to teaching, do not cancel low enrollment classes. Teach for the experience and collect feedback.

Market professional services with low cost, introductory classes.

institution, realize that the catalog is widely circulated throughout the community. Big city adult school catalogs commonly reach hundreds of thousands of local residents, in some cases almost as many readers as the daily papers. Course descriptions, in effect, become a great way to build your authority image. Add pertinent promotional information to your catalog course description if school administrators allow it. For example, a psychotherapist who is offering a class on interpersonal communications might add, "Sarah is a psychotherapist in private practice, with an office in downtown Boston. Private sessions are available upon request." It is not uncommon for a teacher to mention his institutional affiliation or plug his new book in many class catalogs. Your classes will be filled with prospective clients or customers, too.

If you decide to market your own classes independently, you become, in effect, the dean of your own mini-school. You are responsible for everything, from registration to refunds, from lesson plans to janitorial. There's more financial risk, more administration, but much greater profit potential, too.

Students value expert information and will pay a premium for topical information taught by a knowledgeable expert. Generally you can charge each student between $5 and $150 for 2 to 10 hours of instruction. Expect enrollments of between 5 and 50 when starting out. Poll registrants to find out what they want most, and rewrite your promotional materials accordingly. Then watch your enrollments grow!

You can structure classes for one day (usually on a weekend) or over several evenings. Drop-ins or ongoing enrollments may be appropriate if your course content does not necessarily build sequentially from class to class. Consider offering free or low cost introductory classes as samples or "loss leaders." Many healthcare professionals and business consultants, for example, build their businesses by holding free lecture demos and then selling their services directly to interested prospects.

Non-credit classes are a year-round activity, but different classes have their seasons. Avoid scheduling on or around major holidays unless you can make a connection with the holiday theme. "Vegetarian Singles Thanksgiving" might work. "Christmas Eve Bookkeeping" certainly would not, unless your students all are named Scrooge. Early April also is slow because so many people are obsessed with tax returns at this time.

The best way to promote a class is to write an enticing course description. Publish course descriptions in catalogs, and on flyers, and brochures. Also use calendar announcements, classified, and display advertising in newspapers and magazines. If you get serious about offering classes, you'll want to make use of the entire range of marketing approaches offered throughout this book.

Distribute your flyers and brochures by direct mail or in stores and community centers where free literature is displayed. Usually it takes between 30 and 150 copies of a course description to net one "warm body" in class. Target your audience for maximum results. For example, offer a backpacking class by putting brochures in all the local sports and outdoors stores. Offer children's ballet by postering at grade schools and in community centers where children play. Offer computing classes through specialty publications and in the business section of your local newspaper.

We have written a book all about freelance and sideline teaching, *The Teaching Marketplace.* This book covers everything you need to organize classes, find sponsoring organizations, or market your own classes independently. We include sample class descriptions, registration forms, flyers, and ads. Find *The Teaching Marketplace* at your library, request that your bookstore order you a copy, or obtain it directly from the publisher at (510) 525-9663.

Corporate Consulting

Many independent professionals prefer marketing to corporations rather than the general public. One consultant told us, "I spend 80% of my time working in the community, but I earn 80% of my money from corporate contracts. I enjoy community work more, but corporations really pay much better." Corporate consulting pays between $200 and $5,000 or more per day, gross wages.

Corporations pay top dollar for gifted trainers and speakers.

Jane, another consultant, offers individual speech and video coaching to the public, but corporate consulting is her bread and butter. "It's just as easy to sell a company on a $1000 program as it is an individual on a $150 program." Jane builds her professional image and gets corporate leads by speaking before business groups such as the Rotary. She's a member of the National Speakers' Association and advertises in their directory. She also goes after publicity in order to "position myself as an expert." A major article in a local paper resulted in only one corporate engagement. However, Jane photocopied the article and made it part of the press kit she mails to corporate prospects.

When offering services to corporations, first identify what market you are serving. Chief executive officers (CEO's) have different needs from middle managers or employees. Specify what you have to offer, whether it's advice to executives or training programs for personnel.

Corporate executive officers are looking for ways to improve profits, tax and investment strategies, employee relations, retirement planning, and new ways to unwind. When marketing services to CEO's, approach them directly whenever possible. Join clubs and civic organizations like the Kiwanis, and build personal contacts. Your brochures and solicitation material need to be first class, using rich paper and several colors. If you hire artists or copy writers, find ones who understand this market.

Corporations regularly provide training programs for middle managers on topics that include sales, communication, negotiation, productivity, computer applications, time management, and handling stress. "Seminars and workshops are almost an industry by themselves," stresses Herman Holtz in *Advice, A High Profit Business.* Always emphasize the bottom line: increased profits. Generally, you need to charge at least $1,000 for in-house corporate trainings. Price your services for less and you may not be considered good enough to hire.

Programs of interests to employees include health and fitness, habit control, upgrading job skills, travel tours, hobbies, and social events. Advertise in company newsletters. Get permission to make lunch hour presentations in company meeting rooms and cafeterias. Make a personal contact in upper management or go through the personnel department with your initial idea. Companies such as Levi Strauss, Kaiser, Clorox, and Bank of America have allowed individuals we know to set up classes for their employees using company facilities.

Your previous work experience in a particular field is your first and best entree into consulting. It helps to specialize. Specialization doesn't limit you, because you can always develop additional specialties, or "extend your product line," as marketing experts say.

Be aware of the corporate chain of command. Make contact at the level appropriate to your services. If your intent is to market advice to executives, don't start by offering a seminar to employees. It's optimal, though not always possible, to contact executives first. Try to start at the top and work your way down.

There are several good resources for aspiring corporate consultants. You can contact established consultants through the *McLean Consultants and Consulting Organizations Directory* and also *Dun's Consultants Directory*, one or both of which should be at your library reference desk. Howard L. Shenson's *The Contract and Fee-Setting Guide for Consultants and Professionals* is a very detailed guide for pricing your services.

> *Writing solidifies your position as an authority.*

Writing Articles

Writing articles is a great way to position yourself as an authority. You don't have to be a professional writer or journalist, either. There are over 66,000 newspapers, magazines, and journals published regularly in the United States and Canada. And there are over 48,000 more professional associations that publish newsletters and membership organs. They're looking for interesting articles from people like you!

A published article can live forever. Make copies of the article, including the publication's masthead and date of issue. Include it in any promotional materials that you send to prospective clients. Put it into the press kit that you send to major newspapers, radio and television interviewers. Send your first published article to other magazine editors when you propose your second article.

If you want to write and get paid for it, too, follow a few simple guidelines. Write what editors are looking for. There's a relatively large market for non-fiction. Fiction, humor, and greeting cards are more difficult to sell. Poetry, television and movie scripts are the hardest to sell. Script writing almost always requires obtaining an agent. It also means lots of unpublished practice writing.

Develop low risk strategies to improve your chances of being published. Send query letters to editors before you write your article. Submitting unsolicited articles is more risky and time consuming. Contact editors of smaller specialty publications to get into print faster. Don't be discouraged by initial rejections. Many popular writers started their careers with dozens of rejection letters. Learning to write query letters is an art in itself. You'll improve with practice!

Non-fiction writing is always in demand.

Your query letter should show that you have some understanding of the style of the publication, the values of the readers, and a very clear sense of what you want to say. Experts who can translate what they know into "plain English" are always in demand. Some publications will guarantee payment with receipt of your article. Others will accept writing from untried authors "on spec.," which means that they may reject your work and there is no obligation for them to pay.

Write from your immediate experience. Slant your topic in a way that everyone can identify with. Even if your field is technical, find a universal theme. As editors, we receive submitted articles all the time. We're always telling prospective authors, "Give us an article that someone will want to read even if they know nothing about your profession. Even if they'll never call you for a consultation. Even if they'll never want to take a class from you." Discover something new about your topic. Here are some examples: "New Ways to Finance Your First Home;" "Are You An Entrepreneur? Take This Test..."; "10 Steps to Recovery From Drugs"; "Men and Women— Relationships in the 1990's"; "Biologist Paul Ehrlich on Birth Control, Earth Day 2010, and Speech Writing for George Bush."

Will a published article generate new clients for your service? Not necessarily, but there are ways to improve your chances. When you submit an article for publication, write your own introduction. Write it in the third person, as if the editor had written it about you. Be sure to include your address, phone number, and institutional affiliation, if any. When you talk to the editor, ask if he will use the introduction you've written or, at least, include your address and telephone number so that readers can contact you directly for details. Also, more readers will respond if you encourage them. "Please call our center for more information. Our telephone number is...."

When you start looking for a publisher, there are several excellent references. The *Standard Periodical Directory* lists over 66,000 periodicals published in the United States and Canada. *The Magazine Industry Market Place* is a comprehensive directory of magazines that also lists specific names and titles of decision makers. The *Reader's Guide to Periodical Literature* is an excellent guide for the more commercial magazines. The *Directory of Associations* lists over 35,000 professional, trade, cultural, educational, governmental, religious, recreational, and other associations. Last but not least, *Writer's Market* is published yearly as a trade book. It's loaded with advice for the aspiring writer on specific formats. Your local library reference room will have most or all of these

Major publishers are looking for best-sellers.

Writing Books

Just about everybody has a secret dream to become an author. Writing a book is a chance at immortality. It's also a chance to solidify your reputation as an authority. Through book promotions, you'll appear on talk shows, be quoted in the press, be called for speeches and lectures, and enhance your career prospects overall. "She must be successful. She was on Oprah last week!" You also may make good money as an author.

Not everybody has the time or inclination to write a book, however. It's a major project, something that you won't want to take on casually. If you've been flirting with the idea, here's what you need to get started.

If you've never written for publication, you might want to start writing articles for magazines and newsletters before you tackle a book assignment. This experience will help you hone your style. The task of organizing an entire book can be daunting. The secret is to break down your project into small components. Pick a theme. List ten secondary topics. These are your chapters. Each chapter could be the focus of a magazine article. Research your topic at the library, but write from your immediate experience wherever possible. Conduct personal interviews with experts or people who may serve as examples.

Don't give yourself the excuse, "I don't have any time." Set aside at least one hour a day while the house is quiet, either late at night or before breakfast, to work on your project. Steer clear of distractions, television, and telephone.

Decide early on whether you want to approach a major book publisher or self-publish. The advantages of book publishers include: wide distribution potential; a cash advance of up to $5,000 or more for a new author; others handle production; and it's their risk, not yours. Disadvantages include: your book will go out of print within one year if not a big seller; most authors never see royalties beyond the initial advance; and you lose some editorial control. Publishing houses usually own the property, too. You'll have to negotiate to share profits from magazine excerpts, newspaper serialization, book club rights, or film deals. You'll probably want to bring in an agent and a lawyer at this point.

It's not easy to interest a major publisher in your work. Send a query letter or proposal before you start to write. Most publishers will want to see a table of contents and at least one sample chapter before they act seriously on your proposal. Most proposals are rejected. Even if a publisher pays you an advance, the book may not be published. Once a book is published, it may not be widely distributed if it doesn't show immediate profit potential.

There are, however, notable success stories. Physicist Fritjof Capra tried unsuccessfully to interest every major New York publisher in *The Tao of Physics* when it was new. Finally he found an obscure British publisher to handle the work. This book became an international best-seller which inspired a vast wave of popular writing by astrophysicists and philosophers. Capra's book did great things for the British publisher who took a chance. It also helped to make Capra a prominent voice in the international scientific community and, ultimately, in the Green movement. Capra told us that now he has several New York publishers bidding for upcoming work.

If you are a new writer, seriously consider the self-publishing alternative. Self-publishing may not sound as prestigious as selling to a major publisher. Many people think that self-publishers couldn't get their books published by a major publisher. Though this is often the case, it reflects more on the economic limitations of large scale publishing than on the quality of self-published books. For those who think that self-publishing carries a stigma, you can patiently explain, "We've decided to form our own publishing company."

With self-publishing you take responsibility for writing and production. You decide the title, what your book should look like, how many pages, how large, and what's on the cover. The advantages of self-publishing include: there's no risk of being rejected; you write exactly the book you want; production takes months, not years; and you can profit even with small print runs. The disadvantages of self-publishing include: you need editorial assistance and self-discipline; you're responsible for pro-

Self-publishing is an attractive option if you have a highly targeted niche market.

duction; and you're now responsible for sales and distribution.

Don't confuse self-publishing with "vanity press." Vanity publishers generally claim that in addition to producing your book they will furnish promotion and distribution services. Vanity press books, however, rarely return even a fraction of the author's investment. If you want to make money in self-publishing, learn everything you can about marketing and distribution. Consider yourself in book sales until the last copy is sold, remaindered at a discount, given away, or burned.

We know several self-publishing success stories. With an initial investment of $5,000, one fellow we know broke even from book sales and related speaking engagements in the first nine months. It's all gravy now. Another fellow, David Harp, supported himself through graduate school teaching music and self-publishing. His *Blues Harmonica for The Musical Idiot* became a popular classic and led to several other titles. David went on to become a psychologist and write the successful self-help book, *The Three Minute Meditator.* David has written and self-published over seven titles and sold over 100,000 books through self-publishing.

We also know self-publishing failures. One fellow took a second mortgage on his house and invested over $33,000 in self-publishing. As a known author, he believed that he had a secure market for his product. He hired professionals to typeset his book, arrange for printing, and produce direct mail marketing flyers. His first print run was 5,000, which included 1,000 hardback editions for library sales. After two years he was still nowhere near breaking even.

Our friend could have produced the same book for less than $5,000. He could have made back his money if he had followed a low risk marketing strategy. Even though he had written his book on a Macintosh computer, he had paid to have the text completely reset by professional typesetters. He could have saved a few thousand dollars by giving his disks to a service bureau to produce the original pages. He could have saved several thousand dollars more by reducing his initial print run. A commercial book publisher such as Whitehall in Wheeling, Illinois, will work with initial print runs as low as 1,000. Unit costs decrease with larger press runs, but startup costs for your initial investment increase.

Consider partnership with an independent small press publisher or distributor.

The cover price of your book should be five to eight times your production costs. This may sound expensive, but note that you'll probably be selling part of your run to distributors for as much as a 60% discount off the retail price. If you are writing a book for the popular market, keep your list price under $20.00. Also, avoid round numbers. Numbers such as $14.95 sell better than $15.00.

There's much to know about the field of self-publishing, and plenty of first-rate resources to show you the way. Read the books by self-publishers on self-publishing. Tom and Marilyn Ross's *The Complete Guide to Self-Publishing* is a comprehensive introduction to self-publishing, possibly the best general reference book written on the topic. Dan Poynter's *The Self-Publishing Manual* is outstanding for its market savvy and detailed resource listings.

Gordon Burgett's *Self-Publishing to Tightly Targeted Markets* is a masterpiece of strategic marketing advice. Burgett urges you to focus on marketing and distribution even before you start to write. This is a key to writing for specialty markets. Know in advance what your readers want and the size of your readership. Write exactly the book they want to read. Focus your promotion to reach this targeted audience. Find what's most appropriate to promote your book: speeches, seminars, conferences, schools, bookstores, direct mail, at or through a business.

If you still feel queasy about self-publishing but you want some of its advantages, consider co-op publishing. A growing number of existing small press publishers will enter co-op ventures with you. In these cases the author puts up part or all of the production costs in exchange for sharing profits with the publishing house. There are also a growing number of independent distributors who will market your book to libraries and bookstores in return for a share of the profits.

If you are even moderately successful with a self-published book, consider offering your property to a major publisher. Your previous success will give you added bargaining strength—better percentages and a bigger advance. A larger publisher means better distribution, more sales, and wider dissemination of your ideas.

If you go with a major publisher, include a clause to retain full title to your book when the publisher has ceased to promote it actively. Your contract may also include the right to purchase unsold or remaindered copies at a deep discount. From the start, you may want the right to purchase a quantity of books at or below wholesale prices. This is particularly advantageous if you have means of distributing books directly to an established audience. For example, if you are a pastor of a large congregation, you might want to obtain 500 or more books and sell them through the church library.

For more leads, including how to find a publisher, an association of self-publishers, and where to get your book printed, see "Books and References" in the back of this book.

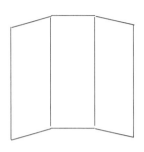

Suzanne Strisower, Certified Hypnotherapist, hands out this brochure at speaking engagements to promote her private sessions and workshops. The original is printed with copper ink on beige stock, 8 1/2" x 11".

THE INNER JOURNEY™
SUZANNE STRISOWER
171 MAYHEW WAY, SUITE 203
PLEASANT HILL, CALIFORNIA 94523
(510) OR (415) 945-6339

THE INNER JOURNEY™

Hypnotherapy
with
SUZANNE STRISOWER, C.H.T.

Suzanne Strisower, C.H.T., has helped clients of all ages achieve goals in their personal and professional lives for the past 10 years. She is a counselor and certified hypnotherapist with a private practice in the San Francisco Bay Area. Her East Bay location offers convenience and she is available at flexible hours.

Suzanne has been on radio talk shows and done workshops and presentations nationally. Suzanne is available to speak before your group or club on therapeutic hypnosis, including these topics:

- *How Hypnosis Works–Live!*
- *Unlocking Your Unconscious*
- *Using Hypnosis To Release Tension, Stress, Anxiety, And Fear*

For more information and a free telephone consultation, to make appointments, or to obtain a current schedule of workshops, please call Suzanne at (510) or (415) 945-6339.

About Hypnosis and Being a Hypnotherapist

Hypnosis is a learning experience and an exploration of an individual's psyche and subconscious mind. It is a quest and gentle pursuit of some inner truths or understandings of events that lead to resolution of problems and to feeling at peace. I am honored to participate with clients in their processes. I feel like a "stage hand" who just facilitates the changing landscapes and events for the clients, however they direct and edit the events in their own lives. The conscious mind is always able to watch and filter anything the subconscious mind presents that it doesn't want to share or deal with at a given time.

Suzanne Strisower offers hypnotherapy in a way which is interactive, relaxing, and empowering. A typical private session lasts 90 minutes. "It is like watching your own movie unfolding in your mind's eye, experiencing emotions and sensations of your body and recreating them to attain your goals of healing and productivity." It is you who decides what to change, and at what pace.

Benefits of The Inner Journey™

Optimal Health:
- Relax and release stress
- Lessen chronic pain
- Release trauma
- Heal memories of abuse
- Create positive patterns for relationships
- Weight loss and smoking cessation

Peak Performance:
- Access creativity
- Increase motivation
- Build confidence
- Eliminate negative patterns
- Experience mastery

Personal Growth:
- Discover your own inner world
- Understand unexplained connections with people or circumstances
- Visualize your future
- Look at things in great detail
- Gain wisdom and understanding to deal with your professional and personal relationships
- Finding your life's work, direction, and purpose

What Suzanne's Clients Say

"I feel a tremendous sense of peace and relief. I have a love for my parents and loved ones that I haven't experienced in a long time."
—T.S.
Nurse

"Suzanne has a wonderful voice which naturally puts you in a relaxed state."
—M.C.
Elementary School Principal

"I can't believe how vividly I could go back and experience past memories that I had totally forgotten about and how they could be changed."
—J.R.
Computer Engineer

"...helped me get right to the heart of my [weight] problem. I just dropped 10 pounds in the following week."
—K.R.
Financial Title Owner

"...gave me lots of new information and understanding about my current situation."
—B.A.
Deputy District Attorney

"...I'll incorporate her materials into my talks!"
—R.P.
Radio Show Personality

The Inner Journey™• Workshops and Private Sessions • Please Phone for a Free Consultation
SUZANNE STRISOWER ———————————————— **(510) or (415) 945-6339**

8

Direct Marketing

DIRECT MARKETING HAS BEEN CALLED the main alternative to advertising in the major media. We believe that for most independent professionals it should be the first alternative. The whole point of direct marketing is to generate direct responses. Direct marketing includes direct mail, personal sales, telemarketing, print, and other non-advertising approaches. Direct marketing also reinforces personal marketing efforts. Have brochures, newsletters, and books available following a speech. Pass out handouts at clubs, expos, conferences, book signings, parties, and networking events. Give brochures, pens, novelty items, and holiday gifts to established clients when they visit you.

This chapter covers our favorite direct marketing strategies. These are the ones we also think will work best for you.

"Selling Lite"

Many professionals cringe at the prospect of selling their services. We've all struggled to end an unwelcome sales call. We've suffered the bombastic salesperson who has overstayed his welcome. Some salespeople even adopt a prospect's breathing rhythm, speech patterns, and body language to ingratiate themselves.

141

Nevertheless, every professional in business needs to develop a presentation that wins clients. There has to be a more professional approach, and there is. Non-manipulative selling has become the sales philosophy of many Fortune 500 companies, including IBM, American Express, Xerox, and AT&T. In their book, *Non-Manipulative Selling*, Tony Alessandra, Phil Wexler, and Rick Barrera develop these low-key strategies.

They encourage you to target likely prospects rather than performing "razzle dazzle" sales. They believe in maintaining a professional demeanor rather than making small talk. Ask questions and gather facts rather than "studying" your prospects. Make a proposal, not a canned "pitch." Confirm a purchase that is clearly in the client's interest rather than "closing a sale." Reassure the client about his decision rather than "reselling."

By whatever name you call it, consider using non-manipulative sales. This is not the same as the "soft sell." It's really a fundamental change in attitude toward the prospective client. The secret, if there is one, is to emphasize the process rather than the "close." Ask yourself, "Am I being regarded positively by the client?"

Our own version of non-manipulative selling is "Selling Lite." We call it "lite" as in lighthearted, and as a backhanded compliment to all those other "lite" products. Here are eleven steps to "Selling Lite:"

Sell your service by being helpful, not by forcing a sale.

1.) Identify yourself
2.) Identify your prospect
3.) Establish rapport
4.) Discover prospect's needs
5.) Stress the benefits
6.) Encourage feedback
7.) Overcome objections
8.) Propose a sale
9.) Close
10.) Verify
11.) Reassure

1.) Identify yourself. Clearly identify yourself and your institutional affiliation right from the beginning. Your first few sentences are critical in creating a favorable impression.

2.) Identify your prospect. Make sure that the person you're speaking with has the interest and the authority to evaluate what you're offering.

3.) Establish rapport by commenting on something you already know about your client, shared interests, or a mutual business contact. Request permission to continue.

4.) Discover prospect's needs. Use open ended questions to carry the conversation forward: How would you use our service? What are your most pressing needs?

5.) Stress the benefits of your service in order to create interest: save time; save money; improve profits; be healthier; gain awareness; etc.

6.) Encourage feedback. Your prospect will appreciate a pause at this point. Listening to feedback at this point will reveal the prospect's reservations and apprehensions. You'll minimize sales resistance.

7.) Overcome objections with reasoned arguments rather than evasions or broad denials. Realize that objections usually indicate genuine interest on the client's part. Overcome objections before you propose a sale whenever possible. This way you minimize rejection.

8.) Propose a sale. Use closed questions that require "yes" or "no" answers when you are ready to test the client's commitment. Your sales message should reiterate the benefits of your service.

9.) Close. Use multiple options to avoid an absolute "no." Have fallbacks. Obtain either a commitment to purchase, a commitment for a future purchase, a personal appointment, a consideration of purchase, or put the prospect on your mailing list.

10.) Verify. Wrap up the call by reviewing your agreement and verifying the terms. Review any notes you've taken to insure accuracy. Leave the client feeling comfortable whether you have completed a sale or not.

11.) Reassure. If a prospect decides to purchase, reassure him that the decision is wise. If a prospect decides against purchasing, leave yourself a reservoir of goodwill to call again.

"Closing" usually is the most troublesome aspect of sales. Here are some popular strategies. Some of these strategies sound more manipulative than others. Just for fun, guess which strategy we like the best:

Assumptive closes
Direct closes
Fallbacks
Incremental closes
One more yes

'Closing' is the most difficult aspect of selling.

Assumptive closes work from the presumption that the sale has been made, whether or not the client has voiced a commitment. One assumptive close is the forced choice: "Do you want the regular edition or the gold leaf special edition?" The sale is presumed; only the choice of certain options is at issue. Another assumptive close uses open-ended questions such as: "Which color do you want?" A third assumptive close is the order-blank close. When reasonably confident of a sale, the telemarketer starts to write up an order. He notes the buyer's name, address, and finally closes with: "And how would you like to pay for that?" or "And how about a second one for a friend?" An obvious drawback to assumptive closes is that they will backfire if the salesman seems too aggressive.

Direct closes. It is a direct close to ask the client if he is ready to purchase or not to purchase. "Can I sell you our set of encyclopedias?" This approach is useful when you're up against an absolute time limit. However, it's not particularly effective in persuading unsure buyers.

Fallbacks. When there is difficulty coming to a close, look to fallbacks. Ask why the client is reluctant. "Do you want a different color?" "Do you need structured payments?" "May I call you back later with more information?" "Do you know somebody else who might be interested?" "Did I do something wrong?" If this last question does not regain your client's trust, it may at least give you some feedback on your sales approach.

Incremental close. Let the client make the decision to close. Lead but don't push the client toward a close by suggesting incremental commitments. Use questions such as: "Do you need more information?" "Would you like me to send you a printed rate sheet?" "Would you like to be on our regular mailing list?" "Do you need additional assistance?" "Do you need more time or are you ready to act now?"

One more yes is a specialized assumptive strategy. Elicit a series of "yes" replies to easy questions. "Does homework get tedious? Do you like to save time? Would you like to double your reading speed?" Build a rhythm with a series of such questions. The final question closes your transaction. "Now, would you like to order our speed-reading instruction book?" In general it is always better to ask "yes" questions. Avoid questions that are likely to elicit a negative reaction.

The incremental close is at the heart of our own "selling lite" strategy. It is definitely low-key and possibly less efficient than assumptive closes. However, it's especially suited to people who think of themselves as professionals rather than as sales representatives. This approach also minimizes "call reluctance," the dread that some people feel at the thought of having to make "sales" calls.

We use the incremental close in our own publishing business. We focus on process rather than the goal of a sale. We don't hire commissioned salespeople, so there's no financial pressure to make a quota. The goal of our cold calling is to get prospects on our mailing list and let our brochures sell the service. When prospects call back, they're looking for assistance, not a hard sell. The incremental close fosters long term relationships with established clients, and it has served us well for over seventeen years.

> **Listen to what your prospects are really saying.**

The approach that works best for you depends on the nature of your business and your personal style. When we train new staffers we often give them a short script to follow. Working from notes can help you stick to your call agenda and stay in control. Experienced callers improvise more freely. One fellow we know becomes friends with his regular clients. He asks about the kids, the dog, how business is going. After a while he finally closes with, "Well, it's about time again to renew your order. Can I put you down for the usual?" Experiment and develop your own approach.

Successful callers have an agenda and stick to it.

Telemarketing Tips

Telephone manners should be obvious, but they're not. How many times has a brusk receptionist kept you waiting interminably? Make sure that you and your staff use good phone communication. Here's our one-minute mini-course (drum roll, please):

TELEPHONE MANNERS—TOP TEN TIPS:
1.) Answer and return calls promptly.
2.) Speak slowly and clearly.
3.) Be courteous and wear a "telephone smile."
4.) Avoid interrupting your caller.
5.) If you have to interrupt, say "Excuse me, but...."
6.) Pause and listen—avoid monologues.
7.) Summarize and take notes for follow-up.
8.) Set a time limit for each call.
9.) When leaving a message, spell out your name and address.
10.) When leaving a message, repeat your telephone number.

Nothing is worse than missing calls. Generally, a good answering service is better than an answering machine or voice-mail retrieval. A certain number of casual callers tend to hang up on recorded messages. However, a friendly recording is better than an unreliable answering service. Some callers actually prefer an recordings because they can leave a more detailed message than with a human secretary.

A good answering machine with basic functions costs less than $100. A sophisticated machine that accepts incoming calls of any length and has a remote call retrieval is not much more expensive. Voice mail services run around $10 a month and up. Keep your outgoing message short and upbeat. A 10 or 15 second message is fine. Resist the temptation to turn this message into an extended commercial for your service. Make a personal appeal to the caller to please leave a message so that you can call them back personally.

We've found that when we leave an emotionless outgoing message on our business phone up to 40% of our callers do not leave a message. When we "punch up" our message and personally encourage a reply, we lose only about 10%. Our message goes something like this:

We are away from the office working on production of the Spring catalog. But your call is important, so please wait and leave a message....

A good answering machine is better than a poor receptionist.

Don't get too cute with your messages or you will also lose serious replies. Save the in-jokes, exotic music, James Cagney and Rod Serling impressions for your personal machine. Don't put them on your business phone.

A good answering service runs $10 per month and up. Expect to pay a premium for twenty-four hour operators, call forwarding, and other special features. If you hire a service, get one that not only performs competently but also is sensitive to your professional image. Some services are unreliable. They lose or garble messages. A more subtle problem is the rude or uncaring operator. One of our prospective leads was a therapy referral service. Before we could explain the purpose of our call, we encountered a curt message taker who left us on hold interminably. We can only imagine what impression this person may have made on a prospective client. Before choosing an answering service, call patrons of the service and ask them if they are satisfied.

For many professionals, the telephone is their most cost-effective marketing option. Telephone leads may come from general sources such as the telephone book or newspapers. You also may develop leads from culled lists such as former clients, their friends, and referrals. You may target by neighborhood as well. For example, tree trimming is valuable to suburban residents but unnecessary for uptown apartment dwellers. Obtain a reverse directory from the library or your local telephone company. A reverse directory cross references telephone numbers by address rather than alphabetically by name. This way you obtain telephone numbers by knowing the street address.

Whether your leads are cold (random), warm (inquiries from flyers, ads) or hot (current or recent clients), be prepared for rejection. Depending on your objectives, it may take 100 calls to net one committed sale. For instance, let's say that you're cold calling. It may take 100 leads to net 50 completed calls. The other 50 will be answering machines, no answers, busy signals, or "He's not available right now." Out of 50 completed calls, you might set up 20 office presentations. Out of 20 presentations, you might net one to three actual sales or contracts. Expect to hear "no" more often than "yes," but don't be deterred. One psychotherapist complained to us that business was down. Inquiries were coming in, but they were not resulting in clients. Apparently the therapist's own anxieties about the general economy were scaring off prospects. "When I seem needy, people don't schedule appointments." It's important to project confidence when you solicit new business.

Project competence, too. Win prospects over by offering them something valuable in the initial call: A good suggestion, a business tip, a piece of advice, an assurance of help, or perhaps simply a "telephone smile." Limit what you give away free, however. Close by scheduling a personal appointment or other appropriate commitment from your prospect.

Stationery, Cards, and Brochures

Letterhead stationery and envelopes are essential, even if you have no other printing needs. Small scale businesses use their letterhead stationery, rather than specific business forms, for letters of introduction, billing, and all general business correspondence.

We've seen some striking full color stationery, but one or two colors usually does the job. Off-white or beige paper connotes an elegant, "upwardly mobile" flavor. The softer contrast of colored paper often is preferable to the starkness of black and white. Paper with a high rag content feels more like cloth and looks richer. If your budget permits, ask the printer about embossed (raised) lettering for an added touch of elegance.

You may want to include business cards with introduction mailers or hand them out personally. Reinforce your professional image by coordinating your stationery and business cards. Use the same logo art, typefaces, texture and color of paper. Business cards need to be of thicker stock than stationery, but can have the same feel, color, and style.

A brochure works like an expanded business card. Almost every professional could benefit from having a brochure.

Whenever possible, keep business correspondence to one page. A simple block format, with each new paragraph flush left, is simple and elegant. The more formal approach is to single space each paragraph, with a double space between paragraphs. Alternately, you may want to double space the entire letter. It's less formal. Here's a hot tip: More people will read a personal "P.S." than any other part of the letter. So, put your most compelling argument or best benefit here.

After obtaining stationery and business cards, many independent professionals find it useful to make up a brochure describing their services. The most effective brochures combine elements of display advertising, directory listings, and personal solicitations. The front of the brochure should target your audience. Make it attractive with eye-catching graphics or photography. Inside, devote a couple hundred words or more defining the specific benefits and features of your service. It may be appropriate here to include fee schedules, available hours, locations, and refund considerations. Establish credibility and trust with the use of photographs, biographical statements which include formal training and experience, and client testimonials.

Don't just let your brochures gather dust around the office—use them! Prepare copies of your brochure to hand out at speaking engagements

#1 Since 1974

SERVICES & CLASSES IN BUSINESS · THE ARTS · WELL BEING

O·P·E·N
EXCHANGE ™

POB 7880, BERKELEY, CA 94707   (510) 526-7190
FAX: 540-1057, BOX 51   527-4273

2/28/92

To All New Staffers:

Please use this popular block letter format in all correspondence to be sent from our office.

Use a simple flush left format with no tabs at the beginning of a paragraph. Single space between lines. This enables you to fit a lot of copy on a page. Double-space between paragraphs. This helps to separate ideas and direct the reader's attention.

After you have composed a rough draft, center the body of the text on the page. If the letter is longer than one page, remember to use a blank sheet, not a second letterhead, on subsequent pages.

Make your final salutation friendly and professional.

Warm Regards,

Janet Geis

Janet Geis
Publisher

P.S.— Handwritten notes are always attention-getters! Put your most important message here!

This block letter format is excellent for business correspondence. Put your strongest message in your handwritten postscript.

and other public events. Ask your current clients to take copies to friends. Mail them to prospective clients. Distribute extra copies throughout the community where you might target prospective clients. For example, if you are a veterinarian, distribute your brochures at pet stores. If you offer hiking parties, distribute at sports equipment stores. Be inventive, but move brochures.

Flyers, Posters, and Handbills

On a very small scale, you can achieve wondrous results with just a few dollars worth of flyers. You'll find announcements of every description on telephone poles, bulletin boards, kiosks, car windshields, in laundromats and store windows in any town large enough to have a copy store. Vista, a state-supported community college in Berkeley, California, encourages teachers to print and distribute their own flyers, even though the Vista class catalog is mailed and widely distributed in stores.

Handbills—essentially flyers distributed by hand—are immediate and personal. They can be taken home, written on, and shared with friends. The standard sizes are least expensive: typing sheet size (8 1/2" x 11") or legal size (8 1/2" x 14"). For extra economy, print your message twice on each sheet, then cut the sheets in half with the store's paper cutter. Print hundreds of copies inexpensively in black ink on white or a light pastel. With bigger budgets, consider posters printed on thicker, larger stock with multi-colored inks.

Design a flyer or poster to be readable from a long distance. Make the title large and bold, at least a quarter to one half the size of the entire page. Put your telephone number or address in one or more obvious locations on the page. Use one or two art clips or photographs in a way that directs attention to the written copy. Keep your design simple and clean. Your message should stand out at a quick glance. Avoid typefaces which are hard to read.

At the bottom of your poster, consider cutting tear-off tags with your printed telephone number. This keeps respondents from having to fish for pen and paper to copy your number. Tear-off tags' main drawback is that they cheapen the overall look of the flyer. They're okay for private piano lessons. However, they're probably too tacky for an uptown performance concert. An upscale alternative is to affix multiple "Take One" reply forms to each flyer. Of course, this adds greatly to your production expenses.

Distribute your flyers in retail stores and community centers, or mail them to prospective clients. Target your clientele as much as possible. For example, if you offer computer repair, leave your flyers at the local Radio Shack rather than the nearby Laundromat. Stretch your budget with

Using flyers and brochures is a low-cost way to kick-off a new venture.

Bodywork therapist Richard Adelman credits flyers with greatly expanding his practice. He mails flyers to rented lists, posters around town, and distributes them in stores. The original is an 11" x 17" tabloid.

cooperative ventures. For example, a psychotherapist and a bodyworker might complement each other's work. They could fit two announcements side by side on one flyer. Consider co-op mailings, too. You can mail two or three flyers stapled together with one first-class stamp, so long as the total weight is under one ounce. Share the work of distributing flyers. If you hire a student to post notices or distribute flyers in stores, you can cut your costs in half by having him leave two different flyers at the same time.

Newsletters

A newsletter is not just a scaled-down version of the daily paper. It's a direct conversation between editor and reader. A newsletter editor becomes known for his personal opinions and feelings. Newsletter readers want specialized information, and in a hurry, too. Whether stylishly produced or quick and dirty right off your typewriter, newsletters convey immediacy and impact.

Newsletters can serve several purposes. Company newsletters boost employee morale. Customer newsletters are good public relations, the ultimate "lite-sell" for new products and services. Readers take the contents of a newsletter more seriously than an advertising circular. Independent professionals stay in touch with clients, recruit new business, and reinforce their expert image with newsletters.

Newsletters are less likely to be seen as 'junk mail' than ad circulars.

Just about anyone can publish a newsletter. One dentist publishes hygiene hints in his newsletter. A small business accountant keeps his clients abreast of filing deadlines and interpretations of tax law. A skeptics group publishes inaccurate psychic predictions and disseminates them to the mass media. A medical doctor summarizes new research and translates it into plain English in his newsletter. A Realtor advises neighborhood prospects of prices and market trends. A Wall Street investor offers "insider" information and gets top dollar for subscriptions.

Use the newsletter as a natural extension of your current practice. You may want to start by sending it free to current clients. Sell newsletter subscriptions by advertising in special interest publications and using targeted mailings. What starts as a free newsletter can become a viable money maker of its own!

Your newsletter may contain several elements:

Masthead
News
Gossip
Advertisements

Masthead. Include an information box with the name and address of your organization, names of the editor and staff, the frequency of publication, and subscription costs, if any.

News. An eye-catching headline with news or statistics important to your readers is a great place to start. For example, highlight trends, changes in government regulations, issues in health and safety, or some news item already familiar to your readers because of mass media coverage. Build your story with a slant relevant to your readers.

Gossip. Warm, immediate, and personal, gossip reinforces the bond between you and your readers. Talk about people, their promotions, retirements, births, birthdays, anniversaries, vacations, intrigues, and jokes.

Advertisements. Classifieds, display ads, and personals may be appropriate and useful. Advertising may be exclusively in-house or from outside organizations. Your readers probably will appreciate ads for services and products relating closely to the theme of your newsletter.

Newsletters are a sophisticated way to announce services and events.

Don't worry about maintaining a regular publishing schedule. Publish a new edition when you have extra time and motivation. If you are already publishing a regular schedule of events or classes, consider upgrading it to newsletter status. You'll find that the combination of news and editorial will make your mailings more valued, less like "junk mail," and more like a complimentary magazine subscription.

The style and size of newsletters vary widely. The simplest ones are typed on letterhead stationery and quick printed at the nearest copy machine. For extra room use legal size paper (8 1/2" x 14"). Another standard for printers is exactly double letter size (11" x 17"). This page, folded, printed on both sides, is the equivalent of four letter pages. If your budget allows, upgrade paper stock, add extra pages, and consider binding. If your newsletter grows bigger than you can handle on your typewriter or home computer, you might want to hire a designer or a production assistant to help with the details.

Here are some design tips: Divide your newsletter page into one, two, or three columns. Break up your text into big rectangles of various lengths and widths that fit into the columns. Most people read the front page, so put your most striking copy there. Put your most important ideas in headlines or titles. Most people read from the top to the bottom of the page, so put key ideas "above the fold." Use subheads to break copy into manageable chunks. Many people skim subheads, so put strong ideas there, too.

Some thoughts about type: Conventional typewriters are quick, cheap, and homey in appearance, but they limit your typestyle options. Professionalize your publication with desktop publishing or typesetting if your budget permits.

DENISE JAYNE FASHIONS AND COLOR (815) 555-9018

1116 ASHFORD STREET, MIAMI BEACH, FLA 30469

S P R I N G · F A S H I O N · N E W S L E T T E R

Spring Fashions Show New Colors

Are you ready for the new fashion colors this season? The trend will be on beiges and grays, with burgundy accents. But the best colors for you always are the colors that suit your complexion and your personal tastes. Explore with me the colors that will work best for you in my upcoming series of classes and personal consultations.

Celebrate My New Offices! Come to My Open House
On Friday, April 25, 4-7p.m.

We've moved to spacious new quarters downtown. Here's a chance to see and touch the new Spring fashions. There will be coffee and light refreshments. Door prizes, too!

Sneak Peek Fashion Show, March 20.

I've invited several of my friends in the fashion industry to model some of the new fashions that will be available this Summer. Here is a special opportunity to get a sneak peek at the daring new bathing suits that you'll be seeing on the beach this summer. We'll be accepting orders at this time, too.

Attend My New Color Coordination Workshop
Saturday, May 10, 10a.m.-4p.m.

A color analysis can improve your image. Here's how to use color in all facets of your life: home wardrobe, workplace, and romantic relationships. First we'll explore how color can affect your physical, emotional, and mental well-being. Then you'll learn how to use color effectively to make the professional and personal statement you want. Class includes a follow-up personal consultation. Only $85 for the day.

And remember to bring a friend!

Denise Jayne

Denise Jayne
Denise Jayne Fashions and Color

DJ: mr

Simple newsletters require only your letterhead stationery and a typewriter or home computer.

We designed a newsletter for a graduate environmental management program with excellent results. The newsletter is distributed to personnel officers in major corporations, public service agencies, former program graduates, and prospective new students. It keeps professionals informed of environmental management issues and also serves as a recruiting device. The newsletter typically features an interview with the program's director, a directory of the program's thesis library, and an advertisement for the program itself. The advertisement includes enrollment information, academic requirements, and testimonials from former students. Next to word of mouth and selected mass media advertising, this newsletter became a major source of new students for the program. The newsletter also lends prestige to the university which sponsors it.

Catalogs

The catalog business has grown increasingly sophisticated in the last ten years. Because of competition, the pressure is on to produce elaborate, full color catalogs. You have to select merchandise carefully. You have to analyze mailing lists in great detail. Some catalogs are an extension of store merchandising, such as the famous Sears catalog. Others are home-based operations where a person stocks his garage with mail-order specialty goods. The popular themes for specialty catalogs reflect social trends. Clothes, toys, books, audio and video cassettes, music, natural living products, and high-tech products are among the favorites. Catalogs targeting children, seniors, outdoors types, and just about every hobby and specialty interest also are popular.

Successful small-scale catalogs target a well defined niche market.

You can make money with a small catalog business or a really big one, but there is little room in between. "The economics of the catalog business are such that money can be made if sales are under $1 million because the business can be operated out of a garage.... Once over that, earnings of over $4 million are needed to show a profit" (*Bay Area Business Journal*, December 1985, page 26). So, plan to stay small, or try to go really big. Develop a little home-based desktop publishing operation or raise enough capital for a major publishing enterprise.

If you want to run a profitable catalog business, you'll almost certainly have to accept Visa and MasterCard. When we registered for adult classes in 1989, over 75% of our business was on plastic. Unfortunately, becoming a merchant vendor is no longer simply a matter of requesting it from a bank. One Bank of America officer told us that it is policy not to accept any merchant who has not been in business for at least two years. Apparently some banks are afraid to assume the financial risk. If you're starting a catalog, however, you can't afford to wait two years to accept credit cards.

If you have a working relationship with a banker, you probably can get around such restrictions. A catalog publisher we know who lives in a small town was given merchant status based on her reputation in the community. If you can't work through a bank, there's another alternative. Some private companies lease or sell electronic telephone credit card machines. They also provide merchant status as part of their service, and often at less than bank rates. Get leads from any private merchants in your area who sell sophisticated telephone equipment.

Successful catalog companies analyze their mailing lists in great detail. The marketers at L. L. Bean have depended on direct mail as their main source of business for about 70 years. They build mailing lists from responses to newspaper advertising. The company also rents and exchanges mailing lists, including competitors' lists. They analyze their lists down to the zip code. "The company knows how many catalogs it has to mail to a customer who has responded to an ad before he or she actually buys something from the catalog" (*Consumer Trends to Watch,* a publication of *American Demographics* magazine).

Direct Mail

The use of direct mail has grown at double digits during the 1980's, from $6.7 billion to $22.1 billion annually (*Newsweek,* May 27, 1991). Although proposed postal increases threaten to slow the growth of direct mail, it remains one of your most powerful marketing tools.

Direct mail rates of response tend to be higher than comparable newspaper advertising.

If you can hand it out, you can also mail it: announcements, catalogs, newsletters, coupons, surveys, sample gifts, product deliveries, and contests. If you are prospecting for clients outside the local area, direct mail is even cheaper than telephone. It's the same postage to reach Hawaii, Maine, or your next door neighbor.

Where do you get a mailing list? Here are the best sources:

Advertisements
Referrals
Rented lists
Trade lists
Your own client base

Advertisements. Include a line such as, "Free brochure mailed on request," in all your ads and announcements. Some prospective clients would rather receive a mailer than contact you directly. These are hot leads—names you'll want to keep.

Referrals. Ask satisfied clients, friends, and associates to give you the names and addresses of others who would be interested in your service.

Rented lists. Businesses and membership organizations frequently rent their lists. Publications often rent their subscription lists, too. If you market sporting goods, consider renting the mailing list of a local sporting magazine. A reasonable price to pay is $50 to $100 for one thousand names, for use on a one time basis. Mailing list companies (see your telephone directory under "mailing lists") rent lists by occupation, zip code, income, and lifestyle preferences. Prices start at about $15 per thousand names for lists marked "resident" or "occupant." Lists which sort by occupation or specific interest run somewhat higher.

Trade lists. Your own list is a business asset which you can sell or trade. Look for opportunities to expand your list in creative ways. For example, a cooking school and a gourmet food store might swap client's names on a one for one basis.

Your own client base. Collect the name, address, and telephone number of every paying client and everyone who inquires. Try to use your list at least once a year, more likely quarterly, bimonthly, or monthly. Consider discounts for established clients or "two for one" specials to any client that brings in a friend. Maintain your client list if you don't use it for direct mailings. You'll certainly want it for other forms of direct marketing such as telemarketing or business visits.

> *A direct mail campaign is only as good as your mailing list.*

The effectiveness of a mailing list depends on several factors:

Hot or cold?
Current or stale?
Clean or dirty?

Hot or cold? The list may be cold or hot. A cold list is a list of names chosen at random. For example, a random mailing to every tenth "occupant" in your city would be a "cold" mailing. The response to a cold mailing typically is less than one percent. Thus it takes, on the average, more than one hundred pieces to generate one active respondent from a cold list. Your own clients probably constitute a hot list. The people who know you and have responded favorably to your service in the past are most likely to respond to your solicitations again. From our experience, any response over 10% is "hot."

Current or stale? An old list tends to be a dirty list. When renting a list, inquire as to how often it is updated. Ask if it is sorted for duplicates, too. Keep records of your response so that you can determine if a particular list is cost-effective and worth renting again.

Clean or dirty? A list also may be clean or dirty. If a list is reasonably free of misspellings, errors, duplications, and out-of-date addresses it is "clean." Some errors are easy to catch. We once purchased a commercial mailing list that was so dirty that we returned it unused. A casual visual inspection revealed pages with three or more addresses for the same person and several different misspellings for the same name. We estimated that the list was 20% in error just by random checking.

You can't always tell just by looking at a list. For example, if a list is sorted by zip code, the same person may be listed twice at two different addresses. You have to resort the list by name to catch this duplication. You also have to date entries so that you know which address is current. Another kind of duplication occurs when people are listed at home and at work under their business name. Some of these errors are hard to clean. Considering that about 20% of all Americans move every year, a list grows old quickly. You must work to maintain it.

There's no easy way to maintain a mailing list. If you use the same list regularly you'll want to develop a system for cleaning names. The post office will provide address corrections for an additional charge. If you code an address entry, you can track how many mailings you make to any address and when it generates a paying response. Keep all returned mail and contact the addressee by phone to update the address. Purge your list of duplications at the same address. Date each entry and remove unresponsive names after a certain date. Analyze your response rates by zip code and area. Beef up mailings to the best geographical areas; cut back unresponsive areas. Track different mailing lists you use and know which work best for you.

What kind of mailing list will work best for you? It's cheaper to maintain a list "in house," but it's less wear and tear to contract with a mailing list maintenance company. When we first started publishing, money was tight. We had under 1,000 names, so we maintained our own list. Now we rent lists and also contract with companies to update two lists of our own. We use "resident" lists for neighborhood saturation. We rent the lists of other organizations whose memberships are similar to our readership. We also maintain a list of past and prospective advertisers that we target with special solicitations and announcements. We update the prospective advertiser list almost every time we do a mailing, but we leave prospects on the list for over five years. (We're overdue for a cleaning!) We still get 5% to 7% response from this list, so we're happy.

Your own client base is your best source of names.

How long should you keep a name on your list? It depends. Musician Jim Grantham told us that he hasn't deleted names from his list in many years. "My feeling is that I'm networking. I keep my musician friends on the list even though I know they don't take my classes. And I figure that former students refer others." Bruce Tessler, director of the San Francisco

School of Art, says that he mails a quarterly catalog to prospective students. He deletes a name after nine months if the person hasn't enrolled. This cuts mailing costs, but it's probably too soon. Keep your names on the list for at least a year or two, and see what happens.

Is it better to stuff your flyers in envelopes to hide their contents? Maybe. Envelopes do protect your letter. They add a touch of class. They also make it easier to disguise a sales solicitation. Would recipients want to throw away your mailer if they could see through the envelope? Maybe, but it's been our experience that envelopes aren't worth the extra expense. We want to shout our message, not hide it in an envelope. What you see is what you get, direct and honest. We've mailed flyers to targeted clients both in envelopes and free standing *with equal results*. In this vein, consider mailing post cards. Post cards save you postage, too.

The rate that you pay for postage depends upon the number of pieces mailed, their classification, and their weight. Since postal regulations change frequently, contact the post office directly for current information. Ask about provisions for mailing first class, first class pre-sort, bulk rate, non-profit rates, second class, third class, or fourth class.

If you are mailing more than 200 pieces, you may qualify for bulk rate discounts. If you are willing to do a bit of work—sorting and rubber banding your list by zip code—you qualify for substantial discounts off the first class rate. Computer generated lists excel here. "Pre-sort" first class saves you several cents per piece. If you have a newspaper or catalog that qualifies for second or third class classification, you may mail for less than half the current first class rate. If your organization is non-profit, you may mail for about one-fourth the first class rate. Larger mailings and heavier pieces are figured at a "per pound" rate which can save you money. There are greater savings for ten digit zip codes, also.

Will direct mail make you money? Here are two statistical guidelines:

Rate of response (ROR)
Return on investment (ROI)

Rate of response. People in the direct mail industry expect about a 3% response rate, but this is a rough average. If you're mailing to an "occupant" list, figure on around a 1% return. If you're using a rented business list, guess at about 2%. If you're using a list of people who have made active inquiries, estimate around 5%. For your own established client list, figure maybe 10%. Based on your rate of response, calculate the return on your investment.

Return on investment. Add up all your direct mail expenses—list maintenance, publishing, preparing, labeling, postage. Based on your

Use a professional mailing service to help you manage larger lists.

estimated rate of response, what will be the return on your investment?

Here's an example. Let's pretend that you want to market a $100 seminar. For the sake of simplicity, let's ignore all other expenses involved in producing the seminar—room rental, handouts, etc. Let's assume that you want to spend $1,000 on mailing. It costs you $1,000 to mail 1000 pieces. You'll need at least 10 enrollments at $100 each to get back your initial $1,000. Let's say that your mailing list is good for a 3% response. That means that 1000 pieces will generate 30 students. Thirty students at $100 each will yield $3,000. Starting with $1,000 and ending with $3,000, your return on investment is three to one, or 300%.

Remember, this is only an example. Your numbers will vary. For example, if you charge students $300, not $100, you only need ten students, not thirty, to triple your money. In other words, a 1% rate of response yields a 300% return on investment. But is your seminar hopelessly overpriced at $300? You may have to test market at different prices. Experiment and play with the numbers. (You also might want to test different ad media. For instance, would newspaper advertising generate a better return on investment than direct mail?)

Test market before you commit to a major direct mail campaign.

Test market before you commit major resources to a direct mail campaign. Ignoring this advice can be very costly. One Realtor spent $35,000 printing and mailing 25,000 pieces, with virtually no response. If he had started with a test mailing of just 1,000 pieces, he would have found out that his mailing didn't work. Then he would have had money left to try something else.

Direct mail marketing can be highly refined. With a computer technique called merge-purge, you can mix lists from several sources without sending out duplicate pieces to the same name or address. This can save you a lot of money. Ask about merge-purge capabilities before you rent or trade a list.

Another sophisticated technique is the split run. The purpose of the split run is to test the effectiveness of two different mailing pieces. Let's say that you're marketing a fitness training program and you don't know exactly who will respond. The title of one flyer might read, "Fitness Over 50!" The title of the second flyer might read, "Fitness At Every Age." Divide your mailing list into halves, then code and track responses. The title that produces the best rate of response is the one to keep for future mailings.

If direct mail marketing is going to be a major part of your business, consult with a direct mail marketer to help design and prepare your materials. For lists over one thousand names we also recommend that you hire a mailing list company to label, sort, and deliver your pieces to the post office. Private mailing services can help you determine which class of mail will be the most cost-effective. They know postal procedures and can get through the bureaucracy with minimal delay. A competent preparer will be able to give you a quotation in advance of your mailing. This includes a breakdown of per-piece costs for mailing, affixing address labels, and, if applicable, a modest delivery charge to the post office.

Direct Distribution

If you can mail it, you also can distribute it on the street, in offices and other public places. Place posters on walls, poles, kiosks, and in store windows where managers are sympathetic. Hand out coupons, handbills, and leaflets on any public street. Distribute newspapers, catalogs, and brochures at supermarkets, liquor stores, restaurants, retail stores, professional offices, libraries, churches, and community centers. These are the locations that typically reach young, active people with discretionary income. Many of the chain stores make it a policy to refuse to carry locally distributed materials. You'll rarely see flyers in a MacDonalds or a Baskin Robbins. If you leave materials without permission, they'll probably be thrown out before the end of the day. For best results, we suggest you concentrate on locally owned and operated establishments.

If your service is specialized, your choice of outlets may be different. For example, if you organize ski trips, leave your materials at local sporting goods stores before you attempt to leaflet every Laundromat. (Incidentally, flyers are trashed in most Laundromats, so don't leave more than 5 copies.) Don't waste your flyers or spread yourself too thin.

For the most effective street distribution build your own route list. Go to the busy main streets. Look for stores that have flyers in their windows or provide space for free literature on the floor or counter. First, ask the manager for permission. Leave no more than 25 copies initially. Increase that number only once you are certain your material is reaching the public and not the trash can. It's a rare outlet that will move more than 100 before they get tossed out. The competition among free periodicals for precious store space is getting fierce. Replenish and uncover your stacks as often as you can afford it, perhaps as much as once each week.

Get permission to leave materials in stores and community centers.

Consider purchasing racks for your periodical if budget permits. Local bookstores, restaurants, liquor stores, and boutiques may permit you to place wood or wire racks on counters or near the doors. Supermarkets and carry-outs often require you to pay for space in their stores. In downtown areas or where store space is at a premium, consider purchasing free standing news racks. Racks tend to get lost or damaged frequently and need constant maintenance, so plan your budget accordingly.

In many cities you can hire a distribution service to put out posters and periodicals. Some companies will rent you street racks so that you don't have to purchase or maintain your own. However, it's cheaper to keep distribution in-house. A classified ad in any local newspaper will attract reliable people with their own transportation to distribute your literature and update your route lists. We've tried employee cars, but we prefer hiring independent contractors who provide their own transportation, insurance, and supplies. Costs are less and the cars seem to last longer.

With street distribution you're playing percentages. Generally it takes about 100 flyers, brochures, or catalogs to generate one paying respondent. Still, street distribution provides excellent exposure, even if people don't respond immediately to your solicitations. When stores provide you with display space, they implicitly give you endorsement and legitimacy.

Fairs and Expos

Fairs and expositions are great places to test new market lines and to network with others in your field. The best expos to attend are well promoted, "don't miss" events with wide community acceptance.

Whole Life Expo is a world's fair of health and well being which is held in several cities every year. Co-founder Alan Goldman says that a well-designed booth is both "interactive and engaging." A booth you can walk into is most effective. A large placard or banner attracts attention. People will enter a booth to watch a video tape, try out a machine, or get a sample foot massage. Give them brochures and handouts. Have products for sale as well. And it can help to have a gimmick. Free food, a clown, a mime, a sandwich board, funny hats—all can attract people to your booth. During hot summer fairs, give away free iced tea and offer a shady place to sit.

A booth at a fair or expo may cost several hundred dollars or more. If you cannot afford one yourself, consider sharing space with one or more other groups or individuals with business interests similar to yours. This not only saves money, it also gives you additional support staffing the booth. A three day expo might require at least thirty hours, not even counting set up and preparation labor. For all your efforts, fairs may increase name recognition, although not necessarily direct sales.

Will you make money with a fair booth? Probably so—if you're selling refreshments. Otherwise, don't bank on an expo to generate direct sales. Go for general exposure and try to build your list of prospects for later follow-up. One therapist told us that he got six months worth of client leads from just one weekend at a health fair. Just keep your expectations within reason. Alan Goldman explains: "Don't look at the Expo as everything you do. It is only one component of your marketing. Also do networking, leads, and ads." That's good advice, and we second it.

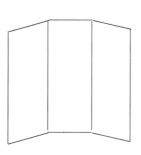

Jamal Mogannam, J.D., mailed this brochure to a targeted list of about 2,000 local professionals and businesspeople in the Arab-American community. This both established Mogannam in his community and brought in new business. The original is 81/2" x 11" on a standard paper stock.

Judith A. Bloomberg

The Law Office of Jamal F. Mogannam is pleased to announce:

JUDITH A. BLOOMBERG has become Special Counsel with the firm and will continue to specialize in the field of Immigration and Naturalization including:

Relative Visa Petitions
Permanent Residence
Work Authorization
Business/Investor Visas
Deportation Defense
Political Asylum
Naturalization
Appeals

JUDITH A. BLOOMBERG has been an attorney in San Francisco for 9 years, specializing in immigration law. She is a graduate of San Francisco State University with a Master's Degree in Speech Communication. In 1981, she received the degree of Doctor of Jurisprudence from Golden Gate University in San Francisco.

"Committed to serving our community."

The Law Office of
JAMAL F. MOGANNAM
550 Kearny Street, Suite 505
San Francisco, California 94108

THE LAW
OFFICE OF
JAMAL F. MOGANNAM

550 Kearny Street, Suite 505
San Francisco, CA 94108
(415) 392-2677
FAX: (415) 392-6101

Jamal F. Mogannam

JAMAL F. MOGANNAM was born and raised in northern California, and graduated from the University of California at Berkeley in 1979 with a Bachelor's Degree in Rhetoric. His studies at Berkeley included Real Estate Law, Economics, and spoken and written Arabic. In 1985, Jamal received the degree of Juris Doctor from San Francisco Law School. In 1987, Jamal became a member of the California Bar.

Jamal has worked in residential and commercial real estate with Mogannam Realty and Grubb & Ellis Brokerage Services. In 1985, Jamal joined the Law Offices of Jerome Marks, first as a law clerk, then as a contract attorney. In January, 1988, Jamal joined the Law Offices of Lilienthal, Fowler, and Rudderow as an associate attorney, with an emphasis on business law, real estate law, and landlord-tenant disputes. In July, 1989, Jamal founded his current private practice, tailored to serve the needs of the Arab-American community in the Bay Area.

Jamal has been active in the Arab-American community as a member of the board of directors of the Ramallah Club of San Francisco and has participated in local politics to promote the interests of our Arab community. Jamal is currently a member of the San Francisco Relocation Appeals Board, having been appointed in 1988 by Mayor Art Agnos.

The Law Office of Jamal F. Mogannam offers a wide range of services, including:

Immigration and Naturalization
•
Landlord/Tenant Actions
•
Business Escrows
•
Living Trusts
•
Business Litigation
•
Bodily Injury
•
Partnerships/Corporations
•
Contracts/Leases

Please call us for a free initial consultation.
(415) 392-2677

When You Are Buying or Selling a Business...

The Law Office of Jamal F. Mogannam can provide you with complete escrow and transaction services.

BUSINESS ESCROWS
Flat fee regardless of the amount of the purchase price*

$600.00 with Alcoholic Beverage License
$500.00 without Alcoholic Beverage License

Fee Includes, with no extra charges:

*Escrow Instructions
Notices of Bulk Transfer
Liquor License Applications
Demand Notes
Installment Notes
Security Agreements
Financing Statements
Inventory Certificate
Bill of Sale*

You will always receive personal attention and prompt responses to your inquiries regarding the status of the escrow. All escrow funds are deposited into an interest bearing escrow account to prevent loss of interest on Buyer's money. Discounted rates are available for drafting of Purchase Agreements, Leases, and Partnership Agreements requested with escrow services.

Escrow costs not included.

9

Publicity In the Mass Media

ANDY WARHOL SAID that in the future everyone will be famous for fifteen minutes. When your time comes, have a statement to make, a book to plug, a product to sell, or a seminar to promote. We say, make the most of your fifteen minutes!

Anyone can get publicity. Just do something kooky or dangerous—climb a skyscraper or threaten the President—you'll get your 15 minutes on tonight's evening news.

Not everyone gets *good* publicity, the kind that helps build your business. This chapter is about getting *good* publicity.

The difference between advertising and publicity is that with publicity the media, not you, controls the message. Another difference is that advertising costs you money, but publicity is free. Well, not exactly free. In contacting the media, you pay for postage, phone calls, stationery, printing, and travel expenses. It takes time to get results, too. As they say, time is money, and money is money.

Good publicity doesn't come without effort. Is it worth your effort to go for it? Maybe. Reports are mixed. As with all other kinds of promotion, we urge you to experiment a little and see what clicks. Publicity is no free lunch, but it might just add a little spice.

The Impacts of Publicity

Publicity can reinforce other marketing efforts. Publicity can mean legitimacy, a form of testimonial from the media. Publicity is something others say about you, while advertising is something you say about yourself.

Publicity means wider name recognition. An individual can greatly benefit his career or cause by becoming known to the media as a knowledgeable expert. The familiar guests that you see on *Nightline* or *McNeil/Lehrer* are listed in what one writer coined the "golden Rolodex." Several of our friends and acquaintances appear regularly on local radio and television talk shows. We call that the "silver Rolodex." If your service is local, this is all the celebrity status you may ever want or need.

Publicity carries no guarantees. Enjoy it when you get it!

Publicity may or may not make your business grow. Its impacts may be subtle or direct. Publicity may add to your name recognition. You may appear more legitimate in the community if you have been featured prominently on television or in a newspaper story. And maybe, just maybe, publicity will bring you new clients.

The effects of publicity can be slow and cumulative or direct and immediate. Our storefront school had been in operation for many years, yet our next door neighbor never seemed to notice. Then one night he happened to catch our 30 second public service announcement sandwiched somewhere between the evening news and Johnny Carson. Afterwards our neighbor greeted us with newfound astonishment and awe. We had become larger than life; we were his "brush with greatness."

Still, you never know for sure if publicity will generate many paying clients. The public service announcements for our adult school on television and radio have had no immediate impact other than a few requests for catalogs. The publicity may have added incrementally to our credibility and community standing, but it didn't pay the phone bill. A client of ours, the owner of a well known dance school, has appeared "on every television channel in the San Francisco Bay Area." He finds that television publicity brings in "a small residue of business, not suddenly 200 students."

This isn't unusual. One fellow who has received national attention for "peak performance" trainings assessed the impact of a feature story in the *Sunday San Francisco Chronicle*. He said that he heard from many nice people, but that it was probably a net loss considering the time he had expended. What really helped his career was an article in the *Wall Street Journal*. Corporations then contacted him to do seminars. It also led to an appearance on *The Tonight Show*. Local coverage was helpful in obtaining national coverage, which, in his case, was extremely beneficial.

What will your experience be? Since you can't count on publicity with any regularity, don't try to build your business with it. A publicity director at one of the nation's biggest news radio stations told us that even when they give generous coverage, they never know if the public will respond.

Approaching the Media

The mass media consists of general circulation newspapers, radio, and television. Here are three areas that get publicity in the mass media:

1.) Promotional—grand openings, galas, publicity stunts
2.) News—demonstrations, protests, news conferences, features
3.) Commentary—expert analysis, critique, interview

Package your message in simple terms for easy consumption.

It's easier to get coverage in newspapers than on radio or television because there are many more newspapers. It's also easier to get local coverage than national coverage. A low risk strategy is to start by approaching your local neighborhood newspaper. If you're more ambitious, plan an event with a colorful visual component that will play on television.

To interest the media in what you do, package your message in simple, easily understood terms. A catch phrase for this is "high concept." A high concept is an idea that you can express in a phrase. You know a high concept when you hear it: "Whole Earth Catalog." "Eternal Child Syndrome." "Women Who Love Too Much." "Couch Potato." "Weight-Watcher."

Some professionals find dealing with the media personally distressing. We sympathize. If you have a sophisticated message, you don't want it turned into a cliche. The media, however, thrives on journalistic shorthand. We asked noted biologist and population control advocate Paul Ehrlich, what he thought about being labeled a "doom and gloomer" by the media. He answered without blinking, "If you can't stand the heat, you get out of the kitchen."

Labels do facilitate communication. At least they give people an approximation of what to expect. Embrace labels. Use them as a starting point for dialog, rather than an albatross.

To the media, the worst sin is to be boring.

The media is looking for stories that are informative, entertaining, or of human interest. The media wants to generate goodwill with publicity. People in the media want to make the world better, too. However, they have to entertain while doing it. The worst sin is to be boring.

Wherever you seek publicity, be sure to take a non-commercial approach. If your material looks like advertising, they expect you to pay for coverage. You can, however, plug a book, announce a workshop, or promote a service with creative publicity.

Sometimes it's useful to link up with a non-profit organization for publicity. If you are a member of a church or club that has non-profit status, you may be able to obtain sponsorship for a special project or program. Classes, film series, conferences, parties, and other publicity events are more likely to get media coverage when submitted on letterhead stationery from a non-profit organization. If your service is for-profit, consider sponsoring a charitable or educational event. Corporate charity runs, toy collection drives, and such generate goodwill with the public. Local media even may want to co-sponsor such events.

As magazine publishers, we have two important prerequisites for publicity. First, the material cannot look like advertising. Second, it should be interesting to readers, whether or not they know anything about the subject. If the article is about astronomy, you shouldn't have to be an astrophysicist to understand and enjoy reading it. The ideal story is about "real people" and also touches on universal themes.

Developing Your Slant

Tailor what you say to the needs of the media. To approach a local radio station, for example, ask yourself, "How will my announcement inform, interest, or entertain their audience?" You can promote any service in many different ways. Develop a slant based on the effect you would like to achieve. Your slant probably will fit into one of these general categories:

Community service
Unique or offbeat
Human interest
News

Here's how these different slants might work. Let's say you are publicizing an accounting firm. A community service approach would be to offer a free seminar about taxes. An offbeat approach would be to demonstrate accounting in a swimming pool with waterproof pens and paper, perhaps with a tag line about "Keeping Afloat" financially. A human interest approach could be to tell the story of the chief executive officer's "humble beginnings." And a newsworthy angle might be to throw a big bash celebrating a corporate landmark, the 10th anniversary, for example. It only takes a little imagination to develop a slant to promote your service. Business startups and anniversaries, in fact, are two of the best times to go after publicity.

Sometimes a writer or editor will choose the slant in advance. We were interviewed once by a writer who, unknown to us, was doing a hatchet piece on the failure of alternative education. Almost everything we said was taken out of our original context and used by the writer to make her own point. We were never directly misquoted, but our original ideas were badly distorted. We learned from this that there's no guarantee that you will like what somebody else writes or says about you.

Up to a point, controversy actually can be good for business. "I'd kill for a bad book review in the *New York Times*," said one successful author. Bad press often is better than no press. "Just make sure that you spell my name right." However, the full weight of public opinion against you can be devastating.

You're more likely to receive good press coverage if you are honest, direct, and positive in your comments. Your goal is to get your story told in much the same way that you would tell it yourself, in your own words. Avoid cynicism, personal attacks, and negative asides, even if they are deserved. They make you sound weak or spiteful, and they do not generate sympathy for your cause. They may be libelous, too.

Finally—and this may offend some of our friends in journalism—but you should avoid "off the record" comments. Don't volunteer anecdotes that could become headlines in the *National Inquirer*. Assume that everything you say to a reporter or interviewer is always "on the record."

> *Assume what you say to reporters is always 'on the record.'*

Newspapers and Magazines

The print media includes general circulation daily newspapers, weeklies, monthlies, quarterlies, shopping and entertainment guides, school papers, trade journals, ethnic and neighborhood papers, circulars, and freebies or "throwaways" of every size and description.

Before you submit publicity material, obtain a profile of the publication's readership. Virtually every commercial publication that carries advertising also compiles demographic information about its readership. Ask the advertising department to send you a readership survey. Read the articles and advertisements to get a feel for the audience they are reaching. You'll want to write your own submittals in a way attractive to each publication's readership.

Here are the most common ways to get publicity from newspapers and magazines:

Columnists
Community calendars
Guest editorials
Letters to the editor
News and feature stories
Press releases

Columnists each have their own individual style. Columnists have their special beats: the city, fashion, food, entertainment, sports, science, business, and more. Unlike reporters, columnists have wider latitude as to what sees print. Columnists, after all, are hired for their personality appeal as well as their writing flair.

Some smaller community papers give publicity features to paid advertisers.

Tweak the columnist's fancy. *San Francisco Chronicle's* Herb Caen, for example, has a weakness for wacky puns. He loved it when the "Colon Hygiene Institute" changed its name to the "Inner Beauty Institute." The owners of "U C Flowers," a flower stand near the University of California (U.C.) Medical Center, got coverage simply by sending him their business card. An insurance agent made the top of the column when he celebrated his 40th birthday by handing the Golden Gate Bridge toll taker $41, a dollar for his own fare and the balance for the next 40 cars. "A bit toll house kookie, but nice...," added Herb. Nice publicity, too!

Community calendars are a regular feature in many periodicals. Some editorial policies favor "non-profit" organizations or free events over paid services. Modify your materials accordingly. We've found that announcements for "open houses" and "free informational meetings" usually are published with more frequency than more commercial statements. Mail your announcements on letterhead stationery, and be sure to include the name and telephone number of a contact person. If you regularly publicize events, develop an address list of each local newspaper that has a calendar section. On each address label include, "ATTN: Calendar Editor."

Guest Editorials are an indirect source of publicity. Some papers feature guest editorials, your opportunity to sound off on a particular theme or issue. For example, if your firm installs solar panels, you might want to encourage an editorial supportive of solar tax credits. Remember to include your organizational affiliation with your name, address, and telephone.

Letters to the editor are an often overlooked source of exposure, and much easier to get published than you might think. Letters are a favorite feature among readers. Many papers do not even receive as many letters as they would like to publish. Almost half of the letters that we've written to local community papers have been published.

When writing your letter, stay within your area of expertise. Be direct and concise. Write to voice your opinion on a particular topic or to "set the record straight" about something that saw print. Close the letter with your name, organizational affiliation, and the city where your organization is located. This, of course, enables readers to contact *you,* even if your full address and telephone number are not published with your letter.

News and feature stories are the mainstays of most newspapers and magazines. Stories may be focused around hard news events, human interest, entertainment, or public service messages. Smaller community papers often give free publicity to paid advertisers. Ask the advertising department at a particular paper about their policy. It may be worthwhile to pay for an ad to have a feature written about your service. Most editors assign reporters to cover these assignments, but some accept articles from freelancers "on spec." If you want to write, ask an editor about their policy and submittal format.

The larger publications are divided into departments. There's a different editor for the city beat, style, food, entertainment, education, business, and the like. The managing editor may assign story ideas or, more commonly, delegate this responsibility to each feature editor. Call the paper and you may be directed to one or more appropriate departments. Talk directly with an editor if possible, because they are the ones who decide what will get printed. If you need to confirm a reporter's credentials, ask to speak with his editor.

Take a reporter to lunch!

If you're in contact with a staff reporter, consider inviting him to lunch or for drinks. Underpaid reporters appreciate the treat, and you may hear some insider's gossip. It also won't hurt your chance of being featured sometime in the future.

Press releases are published by many newspapers when they have extra space to fill, as "filler." It's less expensive for a paper to use your press release than to hire a reporter to do a story. The editors of smaller, local papers generally are most receptive to granting you publicity. They tend to be close to their community and more approachable.

Limit the length of your press release to four typed pages. If you can summarize your material in one or two pages, do it. We have used the

SAMPLE CALENDAR ANNOUNCEMENTS AND NEWS RELEASES:

The New Therapy Center

666 Freudian Drive, Vienna, Ohio 43606 • (419) 555-5692

CALENDAR LISTING
FOR IMMEDIATE RELEASE
Expires 3/1/92
CONTACT: Audrey Lane at (419) 555-5692

FRIDAY, MARCH 1, 1992

HOW TO CHOOSE A PSYCHOTHERAPIST:
Attend a free lecture 7-9 P.M. at the New Therapy Center
Conference room, 9500 Freudian Drive. Call Audrey Lane
at 555-5692 for details.

(28 words)

TOP—Here is a sample calendar announcement which might be sent to local newspapers which feature calendars. Some papers publish calendar listings free; others charge. Ask your local paper for details and set up your copy in their preferred format.

The New Therapy Center

666 Freudian Drive, Vienna, Ohio 43606 • (419) 555-5692

PUBLIC SERVICE ANNOUNCEMENT
NEWS RELEASE
Expires 3/1/92
CONTACT: Audrey Lane at (419) 555-5692

THE NEW THERAPY CENTER IS SPONSORING A
SPECIAL ONE-TIME LECTURE ON THE TOPIC,
"HOW TO CHOOSE A PSYCHOTHERAPIST."

THE LECTURE TAKES PLACE FRIDAY, MARCH 1,
1992, AT THE NEW THERAPY CENTER CONFER-
ENCE ROOM, 9500 FREUDIAN DRIVE. PLEASE CALL
AUDREY LANE AT 555-5692 FOR MORE INFORMA-
TION

(46 WORDS)
(15 SECONDS)

CENTER—Here is a sample news release to be sent to newspapers, radio, and television stations which give free publicity to community groups. Take a non-commercial approach for best response. Radio and television stations prefer the "ALL CAPITAL LETTERS" format, which is easier for announcers to read on air.

The New Therapy Center

666 Freudian Drive, Vienna, Ohio 43606 • (419) 555-5692

PUBLIC SERVICE ANNOUNCEMENT
NEWS RELEASE
Expires 3/1/92
CONTACT: Audrey Lane at (419) 555-5692

FINDING THE RIGHT THERAPIST

The New Therapy Center is sponsoring a special one-time
lecture on the topic, "How To Choose A Psychotherapist."
The lecture takes place Friday, March 1, 1992, at the New
Therapy Center Conference room, 9500 Freudian Drive.
Please call Audrey Lane at 555-5692 for more
information.
A major dilemma facing prospective therapy clients is
finding a therapist that meets their particular needs. The
New Therapy Center has formed a special referral hotline
to address this pressing need.
The New Therapy Center was founded in 1974 by
Sigmund Lane, a noted therapist and writer on humanistic
therapies....
(198 words)

Audrey Lane
Publicity Coordinator
AL: bb

BOTTOM—Here is a sample news release which might be sent to local newspapers which run longer publicity features. Ask your local paper for details and what is their preferred word length. Be sure to cover the basics, "Who, What, When, Where, Why," in the first couple of sentences.

following "shot gun" strategy very effectively, and you can too: Mail a one page, typed press release to all local newspapers. Have another set of labels ready for all the newspapers you contact regularly. Include the name of a contact person on each address label, or simply print: "Press Release." If you have the time or staff resources, make a personal follow-up call after one week. Call to confirm that your material was received. If not, mail it out again and be sure to address it personally to the appropriate editor or decision maker. If the editor tells you that he does not intend to publish your release, ask how you might rewrite it to improve your chances. Chances are that you'll get useful feedback. However, even if you get a flat "No!," call back in six months. There may well be a new editor who will look more favorably on your submittal.

Keep a scrapbook or file of all the publicity you receive.

Keep a scrapbook of all the publicity you receive, especially major features and articles. Quite apart from the sentimental value, the track record that you build makes subsequent coverage easier to obtain. If you get coverage in one paper, send a clipping to the editors of other papers to arouse their interest. Periodically, develop a fresh "slant" or theme in order to get the attention of a paper that has already given you coverage.

Radio and Television

There are plenty of opportunities to obtain media coverage. Entertainment, news, and talk shows have a voracious appetite for witty and outgoing experts on every subject. These shows look for stories that are topical, controversial, and filled with human interest.

Community calendars
Feature stories
Free speech messages
Independent productions
News conferences
News releases
Public service announcements
Talk shows

Community calendars. Many stations read public service announcements once or more each day on a feature like "Community Calendar," or "Billboard of Events." In this case, follow the same instructions as for public service announcements, but address them, "ATTN: Community Calendar."

Feature stories. The local news people do both straight news and feature stories. Contact the stations and ask for the appropriate feature or assignment editor. Visual stories especially appeal to television. During the 70's, our ecology classes never were "sexy" enough to make the evening news. However, juggling in the park made the local news. How to get a date at the all-night grocery brought out a field crew with cameras. Now, even ecologists have learned how to package their message in entertaining ways. Earth Day 1990 was an international media event.

Free speech messages are an important but often overlooked source of publicity. Most broadcasters provide regular air time to individuals and representatives of organizations who wish to speak out on social and political issues. A representative of a top rated radio station admitted to having trouble finding people to make rebuttals to station editorials. If you wish to air your opinion, contact the public service director. Speakers that appear relaxed and self-assured come across the best. Practice reading your speech until it becomes second nature. For television, avoid sparkling jewelry or intricate clothing patterns which distract the viewer. Ask if they can put the text of your speech on a TelePrompTer so that you can appear to be looking directly into the camera all of the time.

Talk shows are always looking for interesting new speakers.

Independent productions include public service announcements, documentaries, talk, and interview shows. Broadcast television stations regularly accept public service announcements made on 35 mm slides (adding an announcer's voice over), video tape, and film. Production costs vary. A single slide used as backdrop may cost only a few dollars. An elaborate professional film with actors and voice-overs will run many thousands. Some stations will help you produce your own television show.

Some television stations make video equipment available to community groups without charge. Contact your local cable and public service channels, where community access opportunities still abound. Many cable companies provide a channel to show these programs, too. Cable's audience for community programming still is quite small, but the production experience is worthwhile, even without wide exposure.

Some commercial radio stations will air your own pre-recorded audio cassettes of public service announcements. One station even recorded our announcement while we read it to them over the telephone. Some local public radio stations let you do your own programming. Berkeley, California's KPFA helped to pioneer public access radio over 25 years ago. Community groups can produce and host their own programs with the assistance of station facilities and technical staff. Ask! Ask! Ask! Make inquiries at your own local television and radio stations to see what is possible.

News conferences. A news conference is a direct invitation for news people to meet you face to face. If you have an announcement or event which you believe is newsworthy, call the media and invite them to attend.

If you aren't sure that your event warrants a news conference, ask the opinion of one or more news directors or editors. Incidentally, news conferences used to be called "press" conferences, but this implied favoritism toward the print media.

Call or write the news departments of broadcast and print media at least two weeks in advance if possible. Provide refreshments for the press. Make a brief prepared statement. Then be ready for questions from reporters.

News releases. News can be "hard" or "soft." Hard news—wars, airplane crashes, kidnappings, and such—happen with little thought to how the media will react. Soft news—anniversaries, open houses, celebrations, charity drives—are events staged for their impact in the media. And they are a mainstay of news programming. The purpose of a news release is to issue a statement or reaction to an event which in turn becomes news. Hard or soft, seize the stage. As news person Scoop Niskar says, "If you don't like the news, go out and make some of your own."

News releases are similar to public service announcements, but longer in length. It's generally okay to run three or four pages. Mail them to news directors or assignment editors. For best results, phone in advance, inquire about specific formats, and establish a personal contact in the news department. Then make a follow-up call to find out if they got your release.

Public service announcements generally are given to community groups whose activities are charitable or educational in nature. You may not have to be incorporated "non profit," but your activity needs to appear non-commercial. Radio and television stations often provide announcers to read public service announcements at regular intervals in their programming schedule. Television stations frequently provide their own visuals if you provide written copy. Some television stations encourage you to provide your own slides.

Submit public service announcements on letterhead stationery. Indicate if your organization is non-profit and tax-exempt, a plus in appearing non-commercial and worthy of publicity. Double-space type. Include the name of a contact person. Indicate the date your announcement is effective and the date it expires. For example: "Effective now through October 1991." Your mailings will be more effective if you address them to the name of the public service director. However, since the people holding this position seem to change almost monthly, you may want to prepare address labels in advance simply with, "ATTN: Public Service Director."

Most stations accept more than one announcement length as standard. Standard lengths are 30, 20, 15, and 10 seconds. Station require-

> *Hold a news conference if your comments affect public policy.*

ments vary, so inquire first. It's a smart idea to prepare several announcements of varying length. Mail the longest ones in first. Call the public service director after your mailing and inquire as to the status of your announcement. They won't promise to use your announcement. However, if you keep calling, you won't be forgotten. If you don't make the schedule with your 30 second announcement, mail in the 20. Then the 15. Finally, send in the 10 second announcement. If they use the shortest one first, they'll never consider the longest ones. Repeated mailings, as always, improve your chances of coverage.

Talk shows always are looking for the new and unusual. Consult your local newspaper or *TV Guide* and check out the morning news, the A.M. shows, noon news, evening news, the locally and nationally produced talk shows. If you're new to publicity, start with radio, where the opportunities are greater. In many cities, radio talk shows abound at every hour of the day and night. Contact the show's producer rather than its host. If you are the proposed guest, have somebody telephone on your behalf. This could be a friend or coworker. It appears more professional to be represented by a "publicist." Send a query letter or a copy of your press kit. If they want you, they may schedule an advance interview with the producer.

Incidentally, you don't have to be a scheduled guest to participate in many talk shows. Radio and television call-in programs present a great opportunity for you to talk with the host and air your opinions in a public forum. One night we were listening to a local radio talk show whose guest had not shown up, apparently stuck in traffic. The program's topic was non-credit classes, one of our particular specialties. Not to miss an opportunity, Bart called the show to offer his expertise. The grateful host interviewed Bart and kept him on the air for half an hour!

The Press Kit

Press kits help to obtain media interviews.

You may want to prepare a press kit for your initial contact with the media. A press kit contains material about your program, the person or people behind it, and your specific availability for interviews or other coverage. Send copies of your press kit to newspaper and magazine editors, radio and television show producers, and public service directors. In the San Francisco Bay Area, for example, you might need about 100 copies of your press kit. Not uncommonly, an initial mailing results in talk show interviews, feature articles, and public service announcements.

The components of a well prepared contain the following items:

News release or cover letter
Background sheet
A list of questions

Newspaper/magazine clippings
Photographs

The news release is a one to four page story about you or your program. Keep it short and sweet. Bear in mind that media people are besieged constantly with reams of publicity material and cannot be expected to dig out sublime meanings. Include journalism's five "w's"— who, what, where, when, and why— in the first sentence or two. For example:

> *John Doe Marceau, famous East Coast mime, is here in Oregon this August to promote his new book, Don't Ask Me!*

> *The Dallas Adult School is celebrating its tenth anniversary this October with a series of parties and special events. Famous alumni available for interview include....*

In addition to or in place of the news release, you may include a cover letter stating the nature of your request for publicity. If you have the staff time, address the letter personally to the contact person at each station.

Background information includes additional corroborating data not provided in the press release or cover letter. This adds credibility and legitimacy to your request. The background sheet is a kind of publicity resume. Include your organization's legal status and a summary of your track record in the community. Individuals include academic degrees, credentials, and dates of previous media appearances. One or two typed pages is usually sufficient.

Prepare *a list of questions* that you'd like to be asked and that you're prepared to answer. Submit this list to producers in advance. One sentence questions and one or two sentence answers make for good dialog. Producers of entertainment shows may want to revise or rehearse your "script." They want to know that you're prepared, and they want you to look good! The news media, however, won't limit their questions to what is on your list.

Newspaper/magazine clippings from former interviews and feature articles add legitimacy to your request. It also can save time for the new interviewer or reporter. Earlier stories often are quoted in new introductions, building favorably on your growing reputation.

Photographs of individuals, groups, landscapes of office settings can give your press kit a professional touch. Television producers prefer to "see" what you look like in advance. Some magazines and newspapers use photographs you provide rather than going to the expense of doing their own, especially if yours are good.

Assemble the contents of your press kit in an attractive folder or

It's common for the media to quote directly from your own news materials.

ELEMENTS OF A SAMPLE PRESS KIT:

Assemble these materials in an attractive binder or loose in a pocketed folder.

COVER LETTER OR NEWS RELEASE: A cover letter is a good introduction to a city editor or producer if you are seeking an interview. A news release is good if you are highlighting an important event or wish to make a public announcement.

The New Therapy Center
666 Freudian Drive, Vienna, Ohio 43606 • (419) 555-5692

4/14/92
ATTN: Harry Smithe
The Georgia Graham Show
1119 Plaza Tower
New York, New York 90021

Dear Mr. Smythe:

This is a follow-up to our phone conversation of 4/1/92.

I believe that you will find Sigmund Lane to be an exciting and humorous interview guest for Georgia Graham. Dr. Lane's credentials as a therapist, coupled with his insight and wisdom, make him a superb choice.

Please call me at your earliest possible convenience to book an interview.

Sincerely,

Audrey Lane
Publicity Coordinator
AL: bb

The New Therapy Center
666 Freudian Drive, Vienna, Ohio 43606 • (419) 555-5692

PUBLIC SERVICE ANNOUNCEMENT
NEWS RELEASE
Expires 3/1/92
CONTACT: Audrey Lane at (419) 555-5692

FINDING THE RIGHT THERAPIST

The New Therapy Center is sponsoring a special one-time lecture on the topic, "How To Choose A Psychotherapist." The lecture takes place Friday, March 1, 1992, at the New Therapy Center Conference room, 9500 Freudian Drive. Please call Audrey Lane at 555-5692 for more information.
A major dilemma facing prospective therapy clients is finding a therapist that meets their particular needs. The New Therapy Center has formed a special referral hotline to address this pressing need.
The New Therapy Center was founded in 1974 by Sigmund Lane, a noted therapist and writer on humanistic therapies, ya ta ta da ipso lorem ya ta ta da datta ipid so in facto ya ta da dat.
(198 words)

Audrey Lane
Publicity Coordinator
AL: bb

The New Therapy Center
666 Freudian Drive, Vienna, Ohio 43606 • (419) 555-5692

RESUME: Dr. Sigmund Lane

Education:
Masters Degree in psychology, University of Vienna, 1971
Masters in Public Health, University of Colorado, 1974
Ph.D., University of New York, 1976

Work Experiences:
Personnel Director, New York Stress Bureau, 1977-1984
Staff Director, Chicago Health University, 1985-1989
Founder and Director, New Therapy Center 1989-present

Authored: *The Id and the Ecstasy*, Harper, 1979
Executive Stress, Dutton 1989
Beyond Therapy, Harper, 1992

Media Appearances:
2/13/87: Oprah, topic of "Job Burnout"
3/29/88: Phil, discussing stress
4/14/88: KCBS Radio with Tom Tomlinson, topic stress
9/19/90: NBC Morning Show, topic recent book

BACKGROUND MEDIA RESUME: If focusing on an organization, tell about its corporate track record. If focusing on an individual, highlight accomplishments, books authored, past media appearances, previous interviews.... Keep it short and sweet; 2 pages is probably sufficient.

QUESTIONS AND ANSWERS, give producers an idea of how and what you're prepared to talk about. They also make excellent crib notes for overworked researchers and interviewers! Remember, however, an interviewer is under no obligation to stick to your prepared questions, just as you're free to improvise on your answers.

The New Therapy Center
666 Freudian Drive, Vienna, Ohio 43606 • (419) 555-5692

SUGGESTED INTERVIEW QUESTIONS AND ANSWERS:

Q: When did you first realize that you were a born therapist?

A: *To lken lkein linell sdeine.*

Q: How did you start the New Therapy Center?

A: *Hd fasdfas lkj; fal skdf;a sldf j;alsdj f;alskj.*

Q: How are the problems of corporate executives different from other people?

A: *As you go, so it dfkjn lksdfq woe rn d flka qwe now.*

Q: In your new book, *Beyond Stress*, you say that, "To cure stress, you need to get beyond wero mn wene." If this is so, then why?

A: *When you dqein dsfk fjhe dksi kjs oeir nn.*

PHOTOGRAPHS: A 5" x 7" black and white glossy reproduces well in newspapers. It also shows that you're professional and presentable, especially important for TV interviews. (We've received color slides unsolicited, but that's probably overkill.) Consider including photos of your service and staff. The more visuals, the better.

Each press kit can cost a few dollars to assemble and mail. Unsolicited kits may not be read. For best results, phone ahead before you mail. Then phone again to follow-up.

THE WELL STREET JOURNAL

From February 29, 1991

Corporate Execs Curb Stress At New Therapy Center

Sigmund Lane Director

A major dilemma facing corporate executives is finding a therapist that meets their particular needs. The New Therapy Center has formed a special group to help chief executive officers cope with the stresses particular to their profession. Noted authority Sigmund Lane says that corporate executives should spend more time with house pets and children, rather than focusing exclusively on trying to make money. These radical views greatly upset many of the executives we polled, but delighted their children and Rover. The executives themselves found that they actually liked their families once they were reintroduced. Many of them did not realize that spending 100 hours a week working was unusual or unhealthy. The New Therapy Center was founded in 1974 by Sigmund Lane, a noted therapist and writer on humanistic therapies....

PRESS CLIPPINGS: Copy and include press clippings, notices, reviews, and other favorable media notice you've received personally or for your service. The more you have, the more you are likely to get (until you become hopelessly overexposed.) If you have authored a book or tape, you'll also want to include it with your press kit.

binder. We have received press kits bound and embossed with gold leaf lettering. This is impressive, but not really necessary. Almost any binder from your local stationery store is good enough.

A press kit can really help you to obtain interviews in print and on talk shows. Mail each press kit in a manila envelope to each media contact. Telephone ahead to get the name of each public service director, editor, or show producer if you have the staff time. Call back about one week after your mailing to make sure that your material was received. Ask if you need to follow up with any additional information. If you are turned down, inquire why. Most media contacts will offer to "keep your material on file" if they do not intend to use it immediately. Mail them updated press releases every time you initiate a new publicity campaign. You don't need to send out the complete press kit again for about a year.

The Interview

Give interviewers a list of prepared questions.

Your quest for publicity inevitably will lead to a personal interview. The interview is a critical test of your skills as a communicator and expert. Here are some popular interview formats:

Live television/radio call in
News conference
News show
Newspaper feature article
Television/radio interview show

Typically, the media will decide in advance how to slant your story. A magazine editor might want to focus on how trendy your service is becoming. A lifestyle reporter might want to do a personality piece about the founder. A news reporter might look for controversy. Almost any slant will work if allows you to get your story out.

Prior to the interview, review your goals. You may be promoting a book or a workshop. You may want to appear as an expert on a particular topic. You may be the spokesperson for a company under media scrutiny. Ask yourself: What message do I want to underscore during this interview? For talk shows, prepare a list of questions with succinct one or two sentence answers and give it to the producer in advance of the interview. Knowing what you're prepared to talk about makes for a more lively exchange.

Emphasize dialog, not monolog. Long speeches tend play poorly on talk shows. A big mistake of the nervous novice is to talk too fast or too much. Give your interviewer space to respond and react. He wants to sound brilliant for asking the right questions. If you push too hard, you'll

PUBLICITY LOG:

Copy this form and adapt it to your own needs. Develop media contacts and nurture them with follow-up calls. This will help you keep a running tally:

Media Source (radio, TV, or publication name, address, phone—) (Get local leads from your yellow pages.)	Contact person (publicity director, reporter, or producer—)	Press kit or release mailed (date—)	Press kit or release received (date—)	News release, calendar announcement, article, or interview to be on date— If not, why not? When to try again—

lose audience sympathy, not to mention your interviewer's.

The media relishes experts. During the interview add ideas and anecdotes that reinforce your expert or authority image. Discuss your track record, how your work has changed people's lives for the better. Except in the case of live programming, your interview may be edited. Sometimes an innocent remark is excerpted out of context. Minimize problems by sticking to one or two main ideas. Add only those comments that reinforce your message. If you have to be critical, offer it as "constructive criticism."

During an in-depth interview, be prepared to deal with tougher questions. Serious journalists will not limit themselves to the questions you provide in advance. If you get surprised by a question, it's better to say, "I can't comment *yet...*" than to say something you'll regret. Acknowledge problems that are part of the public record. Don't lie. Avoid petty attacks or cynical asides, even "off the record." Take the high road—the impression you make is *never* off the record.

If your enterprise is new and experimental, you may be pegged as kooky or offbeat. During one interview, we had to field these loaded questions: "What was the strangest class you have ever offered?" "What *really* happens in those massage classes anyway?" To defuse the rhetoric, return to your main theme. "Our classes focus on therapeutic, non-sexual bodywork offered by licensed practitioners. And bodywork is only one of thirty categories offered by our school. Let me tell you about the others." Redirect the interview onto issues that reinforce your goals.

Avoid cynicism and black humor, especially with print reporters. Innocent jokes can read deadly serious in print, even where the reporter preserves the original context.

Project a personal image consistent with your interview goals. Avoid appearing unkempt, unprepared, discourteous, or ill at ease. Dress appropriately for your profession. This is critical if you expect to be photographed. A performer dresses differently from an expert. If in doubt, dress as though you were going to a job interview. On camera, avoid large pieces of jewelry which may flash bright light. Also avoid small print patterns, which sometimes create wavy motion lines. If your body is different from the fashionable "norm," you may want to play down the distinction by dressing conservatively. Don't distract the audience from the point you wish to make.

If your first "fifteen minutes" of fame are entertaining, you'll be invited back for more. Members of the media are always looking for an interesting story. Whether you are the story's author, hero, villain, victim, or fool is largely up to you.

10

Advertising In The Mass Media

EACH OF US IS BOMBARDED with over 1,500 advertising messages every day. Most are forgotten by the next morning. Getting your message heard over the thunder of other voices is tricky business.

Decide where to advertise by reviewing the nature of your service, your budget, and the advertising medium. Your primary advertising options are newspapers, magazines, radio, and television. Mass marketed products do well in the national media, general circulation magazines, and large local newspapers. Specialized products and services do better in the local print media and specialty magazines. The mass media simply is too expensive for many small scale operations. Advertise successfully by tracking your responses and spending your ad dollars selectively.

181

The Benefits of Advertising

Advertising influences customers in many ways. Advertising may help to:

Change brand loyalties
Create a new demand
Educate and inform
Reach the undecided
Reinforce existing decisions.

Advertising can heighten consumer consciousness. Advertising enlarges markets and also may reduce unit costs. Even professional services can benefit from advertising. The Federal Trade Commission found that "lawyer advertising, once banned as unethical, promotes competition and leads to lower attorney's fees for uncontested divorces, wills and other ordinary legal services" (*San Francisco Chronicle*, December 7, 1984, p. 13).

Some services benefit more from advertising than others.

Will advertising build your business? Our answer is a qualified yes, but opinions are divided. In *Marketing Without Advertising*, business experts Michael Phillips and Salli Rasberry argue that advertising usually isn't cost effective for small businesses and community based services. Their recommendation is to focus almost exclusively on personal and direct marketing strategies. In a similar vein, media critic Robert L. Heilbroner maintains, "The merchandising of a product—designing and packaging and distributing and servicing it—probably far outweighs the effects of the propaganda that will ultimately be launched on its behalf." Other marketing efforts, it seems, are far more important to your success than advertising.

Then why advertise? In a crowded marketplace, it's risky not to advertise. Heilbroner explains, "Advertising is a kind of trench warfare in which few victories are won, but many defeats are staved off. If all sellers of automobiles canceled their TV ads, it is doubtful that auto sales as a whole would fall. On the other hand, if any single seller [quit advertising], his territory might well be lost [to] his competitors" (*Harpers,* January 1985, p. 73). The safe strategy, then, is to advertise as much as your competition.

Some businesses are more "market driven" than others. Advertising can increase market share in a highly competitive market. Mass marketed consumer products rely more on advertising than professional services, which benefit most from personal marketing. Luxury items also benefit more from advertising than basic services. You may need new shoes, but nobody "needs" $150 designer running shoes. When marketing a novel kind of service, advertising is useful to educate and to create new market demand. Startup businesses benefit from advertising, if only to announce to the community, "We're here."

The direct benefits of advertising are not always easy to calculate. One marketing director for a metropolitan extension school exclaimed about the effectiveness of a radio campaign. She had spent over $20,000 on a series of very slick commercials, complete with a theme song written by the author of a MacDonald's hamburger jingle. She justified the cost because it represented a reasonable percentage of her total revenues, which had been growing. However, she really didn't know if her ads were the reason for the school's success.

The director at another university offered an alternative approach. One of his good friends was the manager of a local radio station. The manager arranged for him to be a regular guest on a popular talk show. This way he became recognized as a local authority while generating priceless free publicity for his school.

One way to find out if your advertising works is to stop advertising and see what happens. The owner of a well known Bay Area dance school went cold turkey for an entire year just to find out. "I stopped advertising in newspapers and pulled my phone directory advertising. I even tried to stop word of mouth. If people asked me what I did for a living, I told them I was a janitor."

What happened? Even though this school was well-established, the number of students dropped considerably. The owner determined that about 50% of new students came from the Yellow Pages (the bigger display ads pulled better for him), 25% from newspaper advertising, and 18% from his location itself. The balance came from publicity and word of mouth. There is a cumulative or synergistic factor, too. Students say, "Gee, you seem to be everywhere! I saw your ads and your television appearance."

No advertising is expensive if it produces results.

Wherever you advertise, demand results. Most small businesses can't afford to spend money on the vague promise of "name recognition" or "market saturation" at some unspecified time in the future. Repeat ads that pay for themselves. Rewrite ads that generate inquiries. Give your ads a chance to work, but drop them and try something else if they're not paying off. No advertising is expensive if it's making you money.

Advertise more when you are starting out or expanding your business. Reach out to as many new people as possible. If your business is more established, spend your ad budget more conservatively and concentrate on "getting more bang for the buck." Expect one dollar of advertising to generate at least three dollars in client revenues if your business is mature.

Why People Distrust Advertising

Does advertising promote wasteful consumption? Does the consumer lifestyle harm our psyches and threaten the physical environment? In many respects, yes. Advertising is a tool that, like many other tools, has been subject to abuse. We're no apologists for the industry, and we won't excuse the excesses. However, let's set aside the bigger philosophical issues for now. Let's explore why people resist and deplore so much of the advertising they see and hear.

People distrust advertising because they suspect that they are being manipulated. Advertisers hire marketers to create artificial distinctions between almost identical products. Marketers credit the relative successes of Coke versus Pepsi or Hertz versus Avis more to the ingenuity of advertising campaigns than the relative merits of the products.

Consumers resent overt manipulation by advertisers.

Since the purpose of advertising is obviously self-serving, it's natural to be skeptical of advertising claims. One friend put it more directly: "Advertising is lying." One day we are supposed to buy Coca-Cola because it has four percent less sugar than Pepsi. The next day we are presented New Coke, with its cleaner, *sweeter* taste. Hertz is better because it is number one. Avis is better because it is number two and they "try harder." In the cross fire of claims and counterclaims, the perceptive consumer only wants to run for cover. No wonder so many people tune out advertising. And no wonder some professionals eschew advertising as undignified and unethical.

SUBLIMINAL ADVERTISING SELLS?

Ads are not meant for conscious consumption. They are intended as subliminal pills for the subconscious in order to exercise an hypnotic spell, especially on sociologists.

—Marshall McLuhan
Understanding Media

Vance Packard's *The Hidden Persuaders* is the classic introduction to the psychology of marketing. It's a treasure trove of post-Freudian analysis applied to mass media advertising. The book discusses our yearnings and fantasies, for instance why men relate to car headlights like women's breasts. Who has a wilder imagination—the public, ad agencies, or sociologists?

In the more recent book *Doublespeak,* William Lutz details how advertisers use linguistic tricks to confuse us. For example, consider the rule for "parity products." Since all toothpastes are essentially the same, no brand is better than any other. Therefore, it's legal to advertise every brand as "best." However, if one brand claims to be "better" than another, legally they are obliged to prove it. "In the world of advertising, 'better' means 'best,' but 'best' means only 'equal to.'" Then there are the "weasel" phrases. These are dangling modifiers that may be technically true but intentionally misleading. "You get more when you shop at our store." More of what? People feel misled, then insulted, once they decode the empty content of a weasel phrase.

Perhaps the most entertaining (and arguably most paranoid) media critic is Wilson Bryan Key. In the books *Media Sexploitation* and *Subliminal Seduction,* Wilson finds secret sexual cues to be pervasive in all mass media advertising. The controversy surrounding subliminal messages goes to the heart of why people distrust advertising. Let's explore why.

Subliminal messages allegedly work by arousing the consumer, and then transferring this arousal to the product for sale. The idea is to keep subliminal impressions just below the conscious level so that consumers are stimulated to purchase without quite knowing why.

In the 1950's a well-publicized experiment utilized subliminal cuts in movies. Messages such as "I'm thirsty" or "I'm hungry" flashed on screen for just a fraction of a second, too quickly to register consciously. Apparently this sold lots of extra soda pop and candy. Subsequently, the Federal Communications Commission and Bureau of Alcohol, Tobacco and Firearms banned subliminal cuts in movies, broadcasts, and ads. It turns out, however, that the original experiment may have been a hoax. There is still no conclusive scientific evidence that subliminal messages influence outward behavior. Still, people are no less suspicious of advertisers.

Does subliminal advertising work?

The overt use of sex in advertising is obvious. Key, however, insists that advertisers routinely insert subliminal intimations of sex, death, and love in print and on television. Key's books are collections of hundreds of television and magazine ads. He highlights secret airbrushed images of sex organs, skulls (the death wish), goblins (fear), and animals (companionship/fidelity). Children dressed as adults become subliminal sex objects, according to Key. He finds the word "cancer" (the death wish again) airbrushed in a cigarette ad on a pair of skis. Key contends that words that sound like "sex" or contain similar sounding vowels and consonants have a measurable physiological impact, too.

Key testified for the prosecution at the 1990 trial of the heavy-metal rock group Judas Priest. Key contended that the misspelled word "suicide" and drawings of sex organs and demonic faces are hidden in their album cover. The prosecution argued that these messages contributed to the suicide shootings of two teenagers. The defense countered that subliminal advertising isn't effective and that, even if it is, the band didn't use it. The judge ruled for the defense, commenting that even if hidden words were on the Judas Priest album, they were not put there with the intention to do harm. The debate continues.

Don't dismiss Key entirely until you look at the pictures reprinted in his books. Also, consider why so many product models are identified by EX, SE, ES, EZ, 666, 7000, or similar combinations. We found the following listed under "Sexy Cars" in an ad appearing in the *San Francisco Chronicle*, Sunday, August 11, 1985. Say them aloud:

> Alpha Romeo GTV-6
> Chrysler GTS
> Isuzu Impulse
> Mazda RX-7S
> Nissan 300 ZX

Apple computer lovers enjoy the voluptuous Macintosh SE, SE-30, and fX. PC "business users discover SX appeal" with the 386SX (*Computer Currents,* July 30, 1991, cover). What could feel better on your tummy than Tums-EX? Consumer reporter David Horowitz demonstrated the word "sex" spelled out unmistakably on specially designed cans of Pepsi Cola *(The Tonight Show,* 7/27/90). Is anything sacred? As a client of ours noted, "Even the word *expert* sounds like sex."

Is all this pure coincidence, an insider's occasional joke, or common industry practice? Personally, we doubt that subliminal techniques really increase sales. However, we suspect that many advertisers are using these techniques, just in case.

Quality Advertising

Quality and integrity sell without gimmicks.

So much for the Dionysian approach; we prefer the Apollonian. In other words, bring your message into the daylight, up front for everyone to see. The job of advertising is to convey a benefit to an audience. Being clever is no substitute for being informative. There's no direct correlation between entertainment value and sales results.

Use sex only if you're selling a sexy product. Then be direct about it. It's okay to look sexy if you're selling sports cars or romantic vacation cruises. However, it's not particularly useful if you're marketing business classes. Exaggerated sexual innuendoes even may insult your target audience.

Use humor, but not as a substitute for describing your product. If people remember the joke but forget the product, the ad was a failure. If your audience is sophisticated, you even can play to their skepticism. The television ad campaign for Isuzu cars featuring sleazy salesman "Joe

Isuzu" was hilarious and effective. When Joe says that the Isuzu only costs one dollar, the words "He's lying" flash on screen. The advertiser was, in effect, inferring that car salesmen and ad copy writers can't be trusted. How refreshing!

The first duty of advertising is to sell. The artistic and ethical challenge is to create effective ads that do not compromise the integrity of the advertiser or the dignity of the audience. The best advertising informs, entertains, and enlightens, as well as sells. Advertising needn't be crass or unprofessional. The secret is to create advertising with the same honesty and dedication to excellence with which you practice your profession.

Try a non-manipulative approach. Stress quality and conscience. Start with the presumption that your audience is media savvy and can anticipate any attempt to manipulate. This is especially true of baby boomers, the first television generation. Stress the unique benefits of your product or service—and do it in an upbeat, entertaining way. Here are a few advertising approaches that you can apply with honesty and directness:

Celebrity endorsements
Comparative ads
Money back guarantee
Real people testimonials
The active corporate executive
The educational approach

Celebrity endorsements. Some ad experts encourage celebrity endorsements. Others say that they are too expensive for the results achieved. Celebrity pitchmen command more initial attention than non-celebrities, but their persuasive powers may be limited. Does it really matter that Michael Jackson likes Pepsi or that Elton John drinks Coke? Celebrity testimonials are more credible if the celebrity is an expert on the topic of the advertisement. Personally, we're willing to believe that Jane Fonda knows more about exercise than Ed McMahon does about Alpo dog food.

Comparative ads. Compare your service to competitors and explain why yours is better. Refer to your competition by name if they are better known than you are. Burger King mentions MacDonalds in its ads. Pepsi compares itself to Coke. Avis attacks Hertz. If you're number one in your market, however, avoid naming a smaller competitor and thereby giving him free advertising. If there are many providers in a market, consider non-specific comparatives such as these: "Nobody beats our price." "We're faster." "You've tried other weight loss programs. Try ours last."

Money back guarantee. Stand behind your product or service with a guarantee of performance, and put it in your advertising. This lowers

Your guarantee probably will increase sales.

consumer resistance and makes new people more likely to try your service. Make the guarantee as comprehensive as you can, given the realities of your service. Naturally, a psychologist can't guarantee "complete happiness or your money back." Nobody expects a travel agent to offer a complete refund if the weather turns bad during your Hawaiian vacation. Offer what you can within reason. Assure your prospective clients that you are doing everything to satisfy them.

Real people testimonials. The "real people" in national ads usually are professional actors and models. However, you can use real "real people" in your ads to reinforce your message. "What people have to say about our service..." or "Satisfied customers include..." are reliable ad approaches. The presumption is that this is what others have said about your service, not what you have chosen to say about yourself. Testimonials are good "word of mouth."

The active corporate executive. For big companies or small, the direct appeal of the corporate executive lends credibility and sincerity to the pitch. Here is a person who is willing to put his own reputation on the line to endorse a service. Remington's Victor Kyam liked the shaver so much he "bought the company." Chrysler's Lee Iacocca became its number one car salesman and saved it from bankruptcy. And here's a personal favorite: Tim Hansen, of Hansen's sodas, dressed for safari à la Indiana Jones, flying his biplane to Sri Lanka, searching for the most sublime herb for his soft drink. Your own image on a brochure or ad can be just as reassuring to your clients.

The educational approach. To market professional services, take a no-nonsense, informational approach. Specialty services usually need more explanation than mass marketed services. You know what to expect from the typical refrigerator, but there is, for example, no "typical" computer software program. If your service is relatively new or untried, you have to spend more of your marketing budget simply to explain what you offer. Educational ads can be direct and effective in such cases. Many print ads read so much like articles or editorial features that the editors often feel obliged to issue the disclaimer, "Paid advertisement," in small print below the copy.

A core of your prospective customers remains highly resistant to all advertising inducements. They don't impress easily and they don't buy to impress others. They may respond to reasoned arguments, but they decide to purchase, ultimately, for their own reasons. They tend to do more comparative shopping. They look beyond the appeals of advertising and assess the motives of the advertiser. If your values seem to resonate with theirs, they are much more responsive.

'Real people' endorsements lend credibility.

Newspapers and Magazines

The print media has changed dramatically over the past 30 years. The decline of the "Lou Grant" style independent daily metropolitan newspaper marks the end of an era of print journalism. However, the profusion of specialty publications of every description has created exciting new possibilities for niche marketing.

Print advertising is ahead of television, radio, and direct mail in total sales (*Newsweek*, May 27, 1991). We believe that there is a good reason why. In marketing specialty products and services, there are many advantages to choosing print. Long, complicated messages translate better into print. You can read them at your own pace and in any order. Broadcast messages, by contrast, run at a set pace and in a set order. Print is tactile and portable. Print has "reference" or "tear-out" value. You can save it and reread it at your leisure. By contrast, very few of us go to the trouble of recording and reviewing broadcast commercials. Print requires your active participation and concentration. Readers are more attentive than viewers or listeners. Readers recall printed ads twice as well as viewers.

Readers are more motivated to act than viewers or listeners.

Choose the publications appropriate to your readership. There are local entertainment guides and shoppers which pinpoint specific districts within every major city. There are specialty directories highlighting the unique talents of holistic health practitioners, business consultants, specialty schools, and professional services of every description. There are trade publications for every profession and business, from doctors to jewelers, grocery buyers to funeral directors. And there are magazines targeting every interest, age, income, hobby, and personal philosophy. National magazines such as *Time* and *TV Guide* publish regional editions so that local advertisers can afford to take advantage of regional coverage. Also inquire about separate zip code runs or break-outs. Advertising in specialty directories and magazines often lends prestige to your promotional efforts. For instance, if you advertise in a Sierra Club publication, it says to the membership, "I care about the environment, too."

Consider print advertising in one of these four ways:

1.) Classified advertising
2.) Advertising inserts
3.) Directory listings
4.) Display advertising

1.) Classified advertising emphasizes text and contains little or no graphics. Classifieds often are located toward the back of a publication. Frequently the classified section is divided into subject categories, making it a kind of directory. If your budget is small, start with the classifieds. Usually classified advertising is less expensive than other print advertising. Ads are sold by line, by word, or by character, depending on the policy of the paper. Individuals and small scale businesses often find classified advertising more effective dollar-for-dollar than other forms of advertising. Start by trying the local district papers; they are cheaper than the area-wide dailies. Write your ad using complete sentences and adopt a conversational tone. Avoid abbreviations unless they seem to be standard format in the publication. Some papers sell classified listings with the option of logos, larger type, and borders to help your ad stand out.

2.) *Advertising inserts* in larger newspapers and periodicals can be plain or sophisticated. They range from single page flyers to the Sears catalog supplements that accompany your Sunday newspaper. The distinct format of an insert can reflect the individual character and graphic design of the advertiser, making it stand out as special. Inserts may be less expensive than purchasing the same amount of space as advertising. Often you can place an insert into all or part of the publication's total print run. This way you can target the prime neighborhoods in your community. Usually inserts are published separately and inserted by hand into the larger publication. Ask the advertising department of your local newspapers if they carry inserts

3.) *Directory listings* are available from the telephone company as well as a myriad of catalogs and publications which target special interest

Classified ads are cheaper and often more effictive than display advertising.

DISPLAY VERSUS CLASSIFIED ADS:

Display advertising often works best for retail storefronts and "brand name" products with trademark identification.

Classified advertising often works best for specialty services, independent professionals, and teachers.

Classified ads look less commercial than display ads. Classified ads often produce a more immediate response. People read the classified pages when they are ready to act.

When offering a service to the general public, try classified ads before you try display advertising. It's cheaper. It's easier. It's less commercial. It's more immediate.

groups. Formats vary widely. The Yellow Pages and their district competitors, including the Asian, Hispanic, and Women's Yellow Pages, use a combination of telephone listings and display advertising. Since display ads in the phone book are expensive and you are committed for one year, do not contract for a big ad at first. Give your enterprise a year or two to get on a firm footing, and test market your designs in other media. Some catalogs use paragraph formatting; others print business cards at a standard rate. The logo listing format, a combination of masthead art and an accompanying statement of philosophy, has become very popular in new age publications. Longer directory listings often work best for professional services that need longer more detailed descriptions. Directories represent the best and the worst of the publishing world. Ask for a current copy of the catalog; find out how and where it is distributed. Beware of "vanity" publications, with little distribution except to paid advertisers (all sellers, no buyers).

4.) Display advertising emphasizes the graphic element. Display advertising normally is sold in blocks of space, by the page, fraction of a page,

THE YELLOW PAGES:

Telephone directory advertising gets mixed reviews. It can be extremely effective. However, it's very expensive. You have to commit to one year at a time. So, if your ad doesn't draw, it can be a costly mistake.

Some professionals tell us that the Yellow Pages is their main source of new clients. Some tell us that their ad draws, but not enough to justify the high expense. One person told us that her ad cost thousands of dollars and didn't get her one client.

A medium sized display ad in the Yellow Pages can cost you as much as your office rent. So, unless you can afford the expense, we recommend that you keep your telephone directory ads small the first year. This is especially true if you are an independent professional in private practice. The first year, it's probably enough to list just your business number.

Enlarge your ad once you know that it's pulling, and once your practice is more established.

The Yellow Pages may be too expensive for a smaller startup business.

THE ELEMENTS OF A DISPLAY AD:

On this page we've designed a display ad using five basic elements: headline, title, graphic, description, and call for action.

On the opposite page we've manipulated the basic elements to create four alternate ad designs. Notice that each ad contains all five basic elements. You can vary size, layout, and exact text, depending on what you want to emphasize.

Remember, most people read ads from top to bottom and from left to right. Use art or photos to stop the eye or focus attention on some element of your copy.

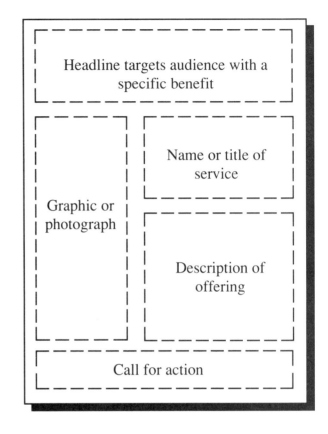

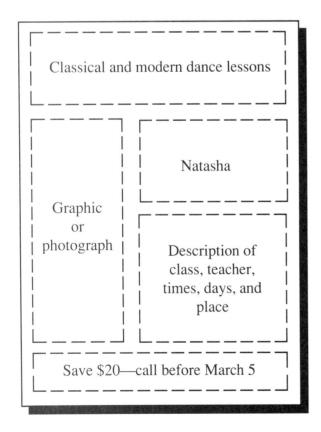

or by the "column-inch." For instance, one column-inch refers to an ad one inch tall and one column wide. Since column sizes and prices vary with each publication, ask for a rate card prior to submitting copy. See that your ads are designed so that they can be reduced or enlarged 75% to 150% and still be readable. This may save you from having to redo your ad when you want to place it in a different sized publication.

There are several elements to the visual design of a display ad. These include:

> Color
> Contrast
> Drama
> Placement
> Size

Color heightens all other aspects. Use "spot color" to draw a person's eye to a certain portion of your ad. One color can make an ad 25% more effective. The single most often used and most eye-catching color is red. The full color effect uses four inks—magenta, yellow, blue and black on white paper—an impressive effect that easily can triple the cost of an ad. Full color may be worth the expense if you're going for a look of prestige.

Contrast is created by juxtaposing white with black, images with copy, headlines with text, open space with detail. The biggest mistake that novices make is to try to cram too much copy into a display ad, allowing no open space. Reverse headlines, white letters on black background, stand out more than black on white. This technique, however, looks heavy-handed if overused.

Drama is created in many ways. Headlines command attention. Borders and boxes organize your ideas. Smaller graphics and spot color move the eye from point to point. Faces, words, and type styles convey emotion and personality. Include photographs to increase reader recall.

Placement on the page can make an ad more effective. Advertising experts prefer the top of the page to the bottom; the outside columns over the inside; the right page over the left, the front of the publication over the back. Ads also tend to work better next to reading matter, not stacked under another ad. Preferred placements include the inside front cover, the inside back cover, the two-page centerfold, and next to a publication's table of contents. Directory listings benefit from early placement, also. In an alphabetical class directory one enterprising instructor listed "Aardvarks and Economic Theory." In the telephone book note the number of "AAAAA" plumbers and such. Some publications charge extra for preferred placement. Others will accommodate if you request. The back

Design display ads with open space to draw the eye.

DISPLAY AD SIZE AND PLACEMENTS:

The 2/3 page ad effectively dominates its page. The tall 1/4 page ad can be very commanding for its size.

Ad designs vary greatly, but in general: Larger is better than smaller. Taller is better than wider. Publications charge extra to guarantee exact placement, but it may be worth it: The right side is better than the left side of facing pages. Higher on the page is better than lower. The front of a publication is better than the back (the back cover and inside back cover are exceptions.) The inside front cover or near the editorial masthead are prime.

The designs displayed to the left each command a whole page for the price of just half of a page.

cover and inside front cover may cost at least 50% more than the inside page rate.

Size. The larger the *size* of an ad, the more likely it is to stand out. A larger ad costs more than a smaller one, but the proportional discount usually makes a larger ad a relative bargain. Bigger is better, but repetition is best. Purchase an ad that you can afford to repeat a minimum of three times in any one publication.

Effective advertising designs include:

3/4 or 2/3 page design which "commands" the entire page
1/2 page top (above fold)
tall outer column
1/8 page, outer column
Checkerboard

Radio and Television

Overall, the broadcast media reaches a wider audience than print and has a more immediate impact. However, the attention span of the viewer or listener is shorter than the reader's. Broadcast messages are forgotten more quickly. That's why it is important to keep messages simple and to repeat them often. Continuity is important, too. All ads in a campaign should have a similar look and style.

Advertising on radio is growing in popularity for smaller scale enterprises. Radio, like print, reaches highly targeted audiences, which means that there is little waste coverage. The radio audience largely is self-selecting. People tune in to their favorite station when they're in the mood

Stress how your service is unique.

TV COMMERCIALS REMEMBERED...

"The single most important feature of an effective commercial is a clear statement of how the product advertised differs from its competition. Humor, jingles, information about the convenience of the product and details about its benefits also increase an ad's effectiveness, according to a study conducted at the University of Southern California School of Business."

—*TV Guide*
May 9–15, 1987

for rock, classical, news, investment advice, gardening tips, or sports. Ethnic groups are highly segmented, too.

Radio is more portable than television, a great way to reach the commute crowd. Local advertising is much less expensive to produce and air than television. Many radio stations will produce a commercial for you and include it in your price. A daytime spot on a top station in a major metropolitan area can cost several hundred dollars or more a minute. At night the price can drop to $15 a minute. Typically the station will expect you to purchase a package of one minute spots over the period of a week. Radio can be less expensive than print, but it is not nearly as good for communicating complex messages.

Radio can be cheaper than print, but requires more repetition.

Here are some tips for making the best use of radio:

1.) Identify your product and stress a benefit from your very first sentence. Remember, attention spans are short.

2.) Emphasize one compelling idea or theme.

3.) Stretch the listener's imagination. You can put your listener on a mountaintop, in a submarine, or on Mars. You can be a talking lion, a Roman gladiator, or a precocious two-year old.

4.) Use compelling music to reinforce your message.

5.) Capitalize on events, time, weather, holidays, and seasons.

6.) Don't hesitate to include a call for action. Ask the listener to write, telephone, visit your store.

7.) Reinforce your advertising with repetition.

Television's two greatest assets are its compelling images and its universality. Television's visual impact is undeniable. Since television reaches more consumers than any other single medium, this is the place for widest exposure. TV's universality is at once a drawback, too. If you are "narrowcasting" to a niche market, you waste much coverage broadcasting on television. You are paying, in effect, to reach viewers outside your target demographics: those who have no interest in your service. Local cable television is more targeted and less expensive, but audiences are small. Weigh all factors when you consider where to advertise.

Television is expensive to produce. A simple half-minute videotape commercial produced in a studio can run several hundred dollars. If you need to hire actors, rent props, or do on location shooting, costs can skyrocket into the thousands. Nationally aired commercials typically cost hundreds of thousands of dollars just to produce, as much or more than the network shows they sponsor. Airing the spot just once on prime time can cost many tens of thousands more.

The cost of local television advertising puts it beyond the means of most small service businesses. Even if you can afford it, TV advertising is still a gamble. We know one fellow who spent many thousands of dollars marketing expensive guitar lessons on a major San Francisco television station. Over the course of a year he saturated the late night viewing audience with his message. He certainly caught the attention of other local musicians. Still, he lost a lot of money. Admittedly, our experience with television is in a diverse urban marketplace. People in smaller communities, places with only one or two local stations, can saturate their market less expensively, making TV ads more cost effective.

Negotiate for discounts and extra free spots with advertising reps.

Television and radio advertising usually is sold by the minute, the half minute, or the quarter minute. Ten second mini-spots are available in some markets. Stations like to sell packages, with an ad being repeated at regular times over a week, a month, or longer. Rates are usually most expensive during the holiday season and cheapest in January. Night slots can be one tenth or less the cost of day slots. Negotiate for lower rates, possibly even for a certain number of free spots, as part of your package.

WHO'S WATCHING?

"It isn't easy to tell who's listening to radio and watching TV. Unlike magazines and newspapers, there are no purchase records for broadcasts—no cancelled checks or subscription lists.

"...Today's viewers are often loners with split-second attention spans who page through dozens of channels by remote control, switch off halfway through a program, or use the medium as background noise while their attention is focused elsewhere.

"Measuring such an unruly audience is a job that never can be perfected."

—Brad Edmondson
"Who's Watching the Show?"
American Demographics, January 1986

If your organization is non-profit, a station may agree to air your public service announcements as part of the deal.

Many stations sell blocks of time (half hours or more) to advertisers to produce their own shows. These programs often have the format of talk or news shows, but they are really thinly-disguised commercials. Real estate seminars, health and beauty aids, and hair restorers are prominent late night TV fare in the San Francisco Bay Area. This kind of program, sometimes called an "infomercial," represents a million dollar investment. On a smaller scale, San Francisco radio station KEST sells weekly half hour time slots for only a few hundred dollars per month. Financial advisers, network marketers, religious leaders, and psychics each have developed their own niche markets on this station. We know one enterprising individual who bought a time slot, produces her own talk show, and then interviews other experts for a fee. She thus promotes her own business and made a profit selling radio time, too.

Target niche markets by producing your own local shows.

Negotiating with Sales Representatives

The majority of advertising sales representatives are honorable people who will not misrepresent their product to close a sale. However, since most sales reps work on a commission basis, they clearly are interested parties. Remember that you, too, are an interested party. So demand performance. Let your rep know from the beginning that you will renew your ads only if they make you money.

Here's how to find out more about a particular publication, radio, or TV station. Obtain demographic data on publications from *Ayers Directory of Publications.* For broadcast media, also consult *Standard Rate And Data.* These references usually are available at your local library. Also, call the advertising department of any publication or station and request demographic data. Look for audiences that are similar to your own in age, income, occupation, geographic region, and lifestyle.

Does the publication or station already carry ads for services similar to your own? For print media, request back issues from your sales rep, or go to the library stacks. See which advertisers stayed with the publication and study how their ads may have changed. Ads that work tend to be repeated. Call advertisers and ask them about their response. Don't be shy; it's your money.

Ask your rep for a rate card and study it carefully. The rate card usually notes sizes and prices, including discounts for repeat commitments. Negotiate price before you commit. Some commissioned sales reps can discount off their commissions and pass the savings on to you. Other reps are not allowed to discount the price from their rate cards, but can offer you free publicity or production assistance to close a sale. You'll never know if the price is flexible unless you ask. Also, get free advice from the sales rep on how to design your ad. Sales reps make their living by knowing what sells. If your first ads don't work as well as expected, ask the rep for more ideas. Graphics designers and media producers may know their art, but not necessarily what *sells.*

Generally sales reps want you to commit to the largest ad for the longest time. Ad reps will promise you a cheaper insertion rate if you agree to run your ad over a long period of time. If the ad works, this makes good sense. But if you are still in the "trial and error" stage of marketing, avoid signing a binding contract. We've seen advertisers obligated by contract to ads that didn't work and drained their marketing budget.

If you commit to a lengthy contract, try to include an escape clause which will enable you to get out early by paying a somewhat higher unit rate. Also, find out if there are extra costs if you need to make editorial or copy changes. For example, you may change your address, pricing, or simply need a copy revision to make the ad more effective.

Test market before you commit to a lengthy contract.

Compare the costs of advertising by referring to a statistic called CPM, or cost per thousand. Cost per thousand what? It might be homes, individuals, or pet cats. So ask your ad rep exactly what his CPM is measuring. You may also find it useful to compute how much it costs to reach an individual listener, viewer, or reader. To do this, find out how many people your ad will reach. A $500 ad may be less expensive than a $200 ad. Here's how: If the $500 ad is seen by 1,000 people, your cost per individual is 50 cents. If the $200 ad is seen by only 200 people here your cost per individual is $1.00, twice as expensive.

When advertising in print, know the difference between circulation and readership. *Circulation* refers to the actual number of copies sold over the counter and by mail to subscribers. *Readership* is an industry calculation which includes primary subscribers and pass-along readership. Right or wrong, most publications assume that there are three readers for every copy printed. A publication with a circulation of 100,000 copies may estimate a total readership of 300,000.

A publisher or broadcaster may ask you to revise your ad copy. They even have the right to reject your advertising. The Supreme Court guarantees free speech and free press, but not for commercial purposes. Broadcasters may determine which commercial messages are appropriate and which are not. Freedom of the press means freedom for publishers. In effect, if *The New York Times* won't take your ad, you're free to publish your own newspaper. (On the company copier, right?)

Different media enforce differing standards. Congress banned television cigarette advertising many years ago, but *TV Guide,* the nation's largest circulation magazine, carries cigarette ads. Local standards vary, too. Some publications do not permit ads for bodywork, psychic arts, "get rich quick" schemes, or "X-rated" movies. Others ban ads for liquor and junk food. Ads also may be rejected for substandard production quality, the dubious reputation of the advertiser, or on the vague grounds of bad taste. Rightly or wrongly, if a publisher or broadcaster won't accept your particular ad, it's generally not worth your effort to make a federal case about it. Simply find another place to advertise. There are plenty of alternatives.

Advertising Agencies

An advertising agency can run a campaign for you, handle your market research, produce and design your ads, and place them in the proper media. Ad agencies usually charge top dollar, but you can expect really polished work. Ad agencies tend to know commercial mass markets very well, but some are not as skilled in serving specialty markets. Make sure that whomever you hire has a "feel" for what you want to accomplish with your advertising.

Hire an ad agency, or consider forming your own!

If you do most of your advertising in print, you may not need an outside ad agency at all. Many publications offer their own copy writing and advertising design services. If your budget is modest and your design uncomplicated, save time and money and let the publication do the job. Publications often will design ads for little or no extra charge just to get your business.

If you advertise regularly and exclusively with the print media, consider forming your own advertising agency. Many publications give outside ad agencies a 15% discount off their retail rates. What constitutes an outside agency is open to interpretation. Sometimes all you have to do is say, "We're an ad agency. We'd like your agency discount." Some media reps expect to see special stationery and business cards with a different business name to qualify as a bona fide ad agency. If you qualify, your 15% discount will save $150 on your first $1,000 worth of advertising.

Being an ad agency is like being an executive producer or a prime contractor. You may do some of the work yourself, but you're free to contract out if it suits your needs. Most independent professionals we know prefer to write their own ad copy, then contract out for typesetting and design.

If you're planning to advertise on radio or television, we recommend that you contract with a full-service ad agency. Many local radio and television stations can produce spots for you "in house." An ad agency, however, can plan an overall strategy that may involve several stations.

Effective advertising often reflects personal values and philosophy.

ADVERTISING IN THE LIGHT:

Jane and James Baraz have run a display ad for Multi-Pure Water Filters for several years with excellent results. (See opposite page.) Successful advertising, however, is more than producing technically competent ads. We asked Jane and James to share their philosophy:

Q: How do you earn your living?

James: Mostly through network marketing two products, Light Force Spirulina (a vegetable protein supplement) and Multi-Pure Water Filters.

Q: Why are you two more successful than most people at network marketing?

James: We're networkers. I love to hook up people with other people. We've been doing it for several years, have been very fortunate, and at this point we have many people in our downline.

Q: You are also one of the main Vipassana meditation teachers on the West Coast for the organization Insight Mediation West.

James: I spend a majority of my time in meditation, leading classes and retreats, and doing Dharma (meditation-related) activities. These produce no direct income, although participants are generous in giving donations. But it is Light Force and Multi-Pure that produce most of our income and allows me to have a flexible schedule for teaching, too.

Q: Are most of your Light Force customers also meditators?

Jane: Not necessarily. But the same people who practice meditation are also into health. A lot of meditators are vegetarians, and Spirulina is a good source of protein for them.

Q: How do you blend your business and meditation activities?

James: For years I kept it as separate as possible. But Right Livelihood is an important aspect of meditation that hasn't been fully addressed. One of the places I run this ad is *Inquiring Mind*, a magazine specifically targeted to the Vipassana community. Now, when I conduct classes and retreats, I might mention it casually when we hold sharing circles at the end. Then, if people want to, they can ask me for more information.

Jane: James likes to say, "The Dharma is my best product."

You'll appreciate the input on production, sets, and hiring announcers and actors, too.

Here are some tips on selecting an advertising agency:

1.) Get referrals from other businesses, your local Chamber of Commerce, or the telephone book. Plan to interview several agencies.

2.) Compile a list of your goals in advance. Talk frankly with each agency about your needs.

3.) Ask about an agency's philosophy of business and track record. Discuss current and previous clients and the campaigns they ran. An agency's size is not as important as how they'll fit with your needs.

4.) Look for stability and continuity in the management team.

A personal appeal lends credibility to this drinking water ad.

Request a financial report from the agency if you expect to become a major account.

5.) Rank the finalists based on how well you believe each will support your goals. Seriously talk money with the top contenders. Then make your final decision.

Lastly, here are some tips for getting the best results from an advertising agency:

1.) Set your objectives in advance. Make sure that your goals are understood.

2.) Cultivate honesty in your relationships. Avoid becoming combative or advarsarial. You're now working with a team.

3.) Deal directly with the creative people, not through a layer of administrators or secretaries. Encourage them to take chances, to break the mold.

4.) Be frank in your criticisms, but always give your reasons if you don't like something.

5.) Try to be consistent in your appraisals and reactions.

6.) Don't nit-pick. Expect the agency to be responsible for details.

7.) Trust the process; then hold the agency accountable for results.

A handy little volume that can help you to work with advertising agencies is *How to Advertise* by Kenneth Roman and Jane Maas. Other resources are noted at the back of this book.

11

Writing To Persuade

FROM TIME TO TIME we hear this complaint: "My ads aren't pulling, even though I wrote good copy." The fact is, being a good writer isn't enough. It's also important to be a *persuasive* writer.

Whether it's ads, brochures, flyers, or radio spots, all your copy should serve your marketing goals. In this chapter we offer guidelines, including specific words and phrases, to help you to write more persuasively.

Ten Guidelines for Persuasive Writing

Good writing is good communication. Persuasive writing also has a job to do. It must convince as well as communicate. Because your message must compete with so many others, you can't afford to waste words. You can't afford subtlety. You have to make your point directly and with impact. Persuasive writing is easy to read, and often fun to read, too. A sales pitch is okay—so long as it is an *entertaining* sales pitch. However, you have to be credible. If your audience isn't openly skeptical of product claims, they certainly are more media savvy than ever before.

Here are our ten stylistic guidelines for persuasive writing:

1.) Know your purpose.
2.) Address your audience.
3.) State one priority message.
4.) Highlight unique benefits.
5.) Make every word count.
6.) Organize for impact.
7.) Use plain English.
8.) Don't use jargon.
9.) Be concrete.
10.) Use action words.

1.) Know your purpose. Decide what you want to accomplish before you start to write. Your copy can teach, motivate, explain, recruit, analyze, inspire, justify, solicit, report, or more. For marketing purposes, you probably want your copy to generate active inquiries if not actual sales.

2.) Address your audience. Use familiar language and a common frame of reference. Speak directly to the acknowledged aspirations, fears, hopes, and desires of your target market. Use personal pronouns, "you" and "I," much the same as if you were talking directly to an individual client in person or over the phone.

3.) State one priority theme. Don't send your audience in many directions at once. We know a lawyer who is a part-time bodywork therapist. When he tried to advertise both occupations together, he got no response. It's hard to market double themes of any kind. For example, it's not credible to be "the highest quality" and "the least expensive" at the same time. If you want to be safe, pick one priority theme per announcement.

4.) Highlight unique benefits. What special benefits do you offer your clients? It might be experience, location, personal service, speed, price, quality—or whatever you choose. Benefits are engaging, but facts are boring. Consider this case: One of our clients was marketing a portable electric heater. His brochure contained schematic diagrams of how to open the heater and change the filter. Prospective buyers didn't care, because a filter is supposed to be easy to replace. But look at the benefits our client forgot to mention: This heater is small enough to fit on a bookshelf. It alone can heat a large bedroom or living room. It's also baby-safe, cool to touch, saves energy, cleans the air, and is a cooling summer fan! Aren't specific benefits more engaging than filter diagrams? Entice your reader with benefits.

5.) Make every word count. Don't cram too much into a limited space. Avoid footnotes and other "fine print" that make copy less readable.

Commercial writing has a job to do: Motivate prospects to respond!

Where you don't have room for details, infer your point. For example, don't list 20 benefits where five or six will do. Include a phrase such as "And more…" to state the unstated. If you're announcing a class schedule in limited space, don't cram in every date. Use a phrase such as, "Call for information and a complete calendar of events." Make your copy representational, not necessarily all inclusive.

6.) Organize for impact. Never stray from your theme. Most people read ads from top to bottom. They read text blocks from left to right. Ideas should build logically. Sentences should flow, one to the next. Put your most important ideas in the headlines and subheads. Intersperse headlines and body copy to direct your audience from point to point. Use **boldface,** *italics,* and CAPITAL LETTERS to command attention and create interest. But use sparingly, like fine spice—too much looks gimmicky.

7.) Use plain English. Use simple declarative sentences and contractions. Short sentences are easier to read. Words with fewer syllables are easier, too. Test your copy by reading it aloud. Will it come across as academic, stilted, or rambling? We tell therapists, "Don't write here for your peers, your college professor, or for Dr. Freud. Write for your clients." *Time* magazine, for example, is written at about a tenth grade level of vocabulary. If you have to choose between sophistication and clarity, always choose clarity. Someone once said, "Write to express, not to impress."

8.) Don't use jargon. Avoid bureaucratese, corporatese, academese, doublespeak, and other confusing derivations of basic English. Use special language only to target a specific audience. For example, only computer hackers will appreciate, "Access time of 5 ms and one free gigabit of memory!" Avoid abbreviations, even in a classified ad, unless everybody else in the category is using it. Be professional, but let people know you're a human being, too.

9.) Be concrete. Make your point with specific examples. "I lowered my health care costs 21%. How much will you lower yours?" Write about people, places, and feelings. Use examples familiar to your target audience. Detailed philosophical justifications can reduce readability. Relax and assume that your audience will select itself. Use idioms which attract your target group. For example, "Responsible Investing" automatically says that you are sensitive to pro-environment and civil rights themes. Idioms, unlike jargon, convey some meaning, even to general audiences.

10.) Use action words. Use active verbs and expressive adjectives. Write in the present tense. Use direct questions and direct answers. Create lush, memorable images. Avoid cliches—surprise your reader with something fresh. Stress positives. Turn weak negatives into strong positives. For example, turn "Don't forget…" into "Remember…." You're on thin ice

Write in the same style that you speak.

using bad taste, sick humor, or cynicism, any of which might upset or repulse people. Be upbeat! Let your enthusiasm shine through!

Persuasive Appeals

Persuasive writing works with both intellectual and emotional appeals, often on many levels simultaneously. These may include:

Emotional appeals
Inner directed appeals
Intellectual persuasion
Outer directed appeals
"Whole brain" approaches

Emotional appeals are many and varied. You can make a bad situation good. You can range from negative to positive emotions, from fear to confidence, hate to love, poverty to wealth, loneliness to belonging, curiosity to satisfaction. You can conjure up images of greedy misers, cuddly puppies, caring husbands, lusty Amazons, smart women executives—or whatever you choose to identify with your service.

Inner-directed appeals focus on personal values, authenticity, and the quest for selfhood. Inner directed appeals work especially well for therapy, art, and new age activities, but almost any service can be marketed this way. Here are two unlikely slogans with inner directed overtones: "MasterCard—master the possibilities!" "Be all that you can be, join the Army!" The inner-directed audience is a minority of the total market, but it is an affluent minority. Inner directeds are resistant to traditional advertising but responsive to targeted approaches.

Intellectual persuasion is advertising for the thinking person. Make your point directly and appeal to logic. Use an immediate, "high concept" headline that states your case. Examples: "Seven reasons why we serve you better—" "Our clients say that we're the best. Here's why you will, too." Back up your claim with facts, statistics, and testimonials.

Outer-directed appeals create desire or envy in the mind of the prospect. Driving a Cadillac equals success. Wearing a certain designer label proves that you're hip. Outer directed appeals to fad or fashion can be very effective for a majority of buyers. Conventional advertising tends to emphasize style over substance, appearance over reality. In fact, many people buy health related products to improve their personal appearance, not to improve their health.

"Whole brain" approaches. Wherever you can, take an integrated approach to advertising. Appeal to the head and the heart, to intuition and

Advertising should highlight the service, not call attention to itself.

to reason. Express values and promise results. The "whole brain" approach puts the focus where it belongs, on showing clients the many ways that they will benefit from your service. Avoid the "no brain" approach, advertising that calls attention to itself but fails to make your service memorable to prospective clients.

Moving Clients to Respond

Judge your persuasive writing by the response it elicits. If you don't get response, it wasn't very persuasive. Don't be impressed by beautiful prose that doesn't get the job done. The job of persuasive writing is to turn a passive, perhaps skeptical observer into an active inquiry, if not an actual sale. To accomplish this, structure your material to include these four elements:

Persuasive writing should invite active response.

1.) Arouse interest
2.) Identify a need
3.) Specify a solution
4.) Call for action

1.) Arouse interest. Use a powerful idea or emotion to arouse interest—curiosity, love, elation, wisdom, health, wealth, friendship, sentiment. The offer of "something for nothing" also is a common arousal. "Free" is probably the single most attention-getting word you can use. "Sale," "discount," and "$" work well, too. Consider using a more subtle approach to market professional services. One mutual fund ad asks the question: "It is 11 p.m. Do you know where your money is?" This is a clever parody of a public service announcement that asked, "Do you know where your children are?" Experiment with your own copy by switching the order in which you present ideas. You may organize for logical or dramatic effects. Intentionally withhold bits of information to create ambiguity and suspense. For example, don't include your price and prospects will have to call for more details.

2.) Identify a need. Pain, loneliness, frustration, fear, anger, grief, and sadness are universal emotions. And who doesn't want to be prettier, healthier, stronger, wiser, wealthier, happier, and more popular? Target your audience, identifying a specific need. "Have you ever missed a cultural event because you didn't want to go alone?" "Reduce the isolation, confusion and lack of motivation of being self-employed." "Looking for a place to have a good time, get some exercise, and maybe meet someone new?" "Coffee, chocolate, sweets, alcohol, nail-biting, rich foods, over-spending, cigarettes—learn how you can control such habits."

3.) Specify a solution. Explain how your service fulfills a particular need faster, better, longer, cheaper, more effectively than anyone else. "We are unique because we use in-depth confidential matchmaking as well as high tech video profiles to help arrange the best possible matches for our clients." "I like to function as an old style general practitioner. I believe that health care should be especially caring, very personal, and offer the consumer freedom of choice." "We offer a personalized travel service that caters to the busy professional whose needs are not met by the conventional travel agency. In most cases you can complete your travel arrangements from your home or office." The more specialized the service, the more you need to explain it.

4.) Call for action. Your presentation is not complete without calling for some kind of client response. The response may be an immediate commitment to purchase or a low risk inducement to inquire further. "We're here to insure that making your business move doesn't interrupt your work. To learn how we can help you get to your new destination, give us a call." "To receive this astounding catalog, send $2 to the following address." One direct approach is to print a response coupon. Leave space for the prospective client's name, address, telephone number, and include boxes to check if they wish to receive more information, catalogs, etc. Consider using time deadlines to motivate response: "Please respond

> *All persuasive writing should include an explicit call for action.*

PERSUADE WITH POWER, PLEASURE, OR RAPPORT:

BUSINESSPEOPLE, use power words. Power words express a "can do" attitude. Use words with impact: now, strong, important, sensational, commitment. Avoid weak words: might, possibly, perhaps, could.

FOR RECREATION AND FUN, use pleasant words. Pleasant words have lots of "V's" and "L's": lullaby, love, learn, like, velvet, voluptuous, and very. Unpleasant words sound harsh and guttural. Avoid using too many "S's" in one sentence.

THERAPISTS, use rapport words. Rapport words establish a bond between you and the client. Use words that demonstrate empathy and concern: trust, feeling, safe, express, you. Avoid sounding clinical or overly negative—you'll reinforce fears.

within 15 days for an extra discount." "Good only through August 31." Or simply request a call or visit: "Please telephone for additional assistance." "Drop by for an initial interview. There's no obligation." Don't leave out your call for action, thinking that you're being sophisticated or subtle. Don't assume that your readers know what you want them to do. Be specific, direct, and lead them to one or more options for response.

These four elements—arousal, need, solution, and call for action—are part of all persuasive writing. Sometimes the elements are combined in a single phrase. "Have Work You Love" both arouses interest and identifies a perceived need, fulfilling work. A title such as "Cartooning for Fun and Maybe Profit" implies a need and expresses a solution. A phrase that targets a very specific audience practically does it all, such as "Born Again Singles" or "Spiritual Gunhandling for Gentle People." And a television phrase that sticks with us after decades actively combines arousal, need, solution and action: "Bad Breath? Try Cloretts!" Loud, yes. But elegant in its simplicity!

The best persuasive writing is simple and direct.

Promoting Specialized Services

Specialty services, by definition, are not for everybody. The challenge is to make your copy accurate while appealing to the right people.

Your writing may function like a sieve or a funnel. It may attract general inquiries or specific purchases, more responses versus the right responses,

---

HIGHLIGHT NON-CASH PAYMENT OPTIONS:

Take a competitive advantage and boldly highlight all payment options other than cash. This may be especially important if you are offering a higher priced service or promising convenience as one of your benefits. Here is a list of popular payment options:

American Express
Billing
Deferred interest billing
Insurance accepted
MasterCard
No payments for 30 days
Visa

*Teaser ads
arouse
curiosity and
coax a broad
response.*

quantity versus quality. Sometimes it's better to say less in print. You end up fielding more inappropriate inquiries but may get more live prospects. Shorter ads, "teasers," often focus on arousing interest and coaxing response. "Need extra income? Call 555-9876." It also may be better to say less when you expect clients to make a large financial or personal commitment. Explain it in person, not in your initial advertising. Consider this strategy: Attract lots of general inquiries with an initial announcement. After personal contact, evaluate which prospects are serious and which are not. Send a more detailed brochure only to the serious leads.

If your announcements are more specific, client inquiries will be more targeted. One music teacher insists on publishing a lengthy directory listing which attracts a very special kind of student. "Listening and feeling will allow your music to come through you freely, and listening and feeling will happen by bringing technique, improvisation, theory, composition, rhythm studies, singing, and body awareness exercises into a comprehensive music experience...." Michael would rather work intimately with five inner directed students than with a barrel full of people who want to play "like Chet Atkins."

Sophisticated advertising approaches such as catalog listings often focus on just two elements: need and solution. Identify need before solution. It is usually more effective to start with the word "you" rather than the word "I." The point is to show empathy and understanding for the reader's situation. Our popular formula for directory listings is two paragraphs. The first paragraph, the largest, is a "you" statement. "Are you having trouble coping with illness or pain? You may feel tense, overwhelmed, or demoralized. This often creates a vicious cycle by interfering with your body's ability to heal the physical ailment...." After the "you" paragraph comes a first person statement of relevant credentials and experience. "I provide specialized counseling for just such situations. I am a licensed psychotherapist with many years experience in stress management, pain control, anxiety reduction, and grief counseling."

You may not stay conscious of the mechanics while you write. However, always keep your audience in mind. Who are they? What attracts them to your service? Poll current clients periodically to find out what is drawing them to your service. Some minor point you may have buried in small print such as "relief from the pain of sports injuries" may be your biggest selling point. If so, make it bold and prominent!

Titles are especially important. Your title or headline is the most read part of your announcement. Most readers will skim the title, but only about 10 to 20% get past the title to the body copy. So make sure that your title says something that will motivate prospective clients to read further. (We don't encourage using arcane or nonsense words.) If your title or business name doesn't specifically target your audience, add a subtitle or second line, e.g., "Heliotrope: The Open University." A longer title can be effective, but make sure that it emphasizes a benefit. Avoid jargon words in your title. Avoid vague or overused phrases, too. For example, everybody is interested in "growth," and everybody does things in a "holistic" way. These titles are effective because they say a lot about their service:

Angry? Depressed? Confused? Counseling & Hypnotherapy
Damn Good Resume Service
Designing for Shared Living: Workshops and Consultations
Immigration Attorney with Humanistic Values
Sculpting with Clay For Higher Creativity
Support Group for Women Who Love Too Much
The Computer Tutor

Once you've chosen a business name, avoid changing it. Changing your title is a waste of valuable name recognition. If you're outgrowing a title, try fleshing it out with a more descriptive subtitle. If you must change an established name, use both old and new names in all publicity and advertising for at least one year to familiarize clients with the change. In 1980 we changed our magazine's name from "Open Education Exchange" to "Open Exchange," but in 1991 people still wrote checks to the old name.

The popular wisdom is that display advertising works better than classified advertising. For storefront businesses and mass marketed prod-

AVOIDING THE HARD SELL:

One bodywork therapist thought about closing her directory listing with, "Try me—I'm the best!" We suggested a more reserved and conversational approach. For instance, talking directly with a prospective client, you might say, "Call me and let's discuss how we can work together," or words to that effect. We pointed out that "I'm the best" might come across as too boastful and shrill.

"Why not? It worked for Muhammad Ali, didn't it?"

"Yes," we replied, "but you wouldn't go to him for a back rub, would you?"

The value of a service is doubted if a professional tries too hard to "sell" it. For this reason, a whisper is often heard above a shout.

Write with dignity appropriate to your service.

ucts this is true. Specialty services, however, benefit from longer announcements, one hundred to five hundred words in length. For these services, classified ads or directory listings are more cost-effective. An accountant in private practice—let's call him John Jones—wanted to promote his service by using his business card as a display ad. The card simply read: John Jones, Accountant/Manager, Financial Management/ Tax Service. His address and telephone were included, too. It was a nice enough card, but it didn't give any particular reason to use John's service.

John needed to convey a sense of what he actually could do for his

Stress a tangible benefit in your headline or title.

HEADLINES MAKE YOUR FIRST IMPRESSION:

Most people read headlines. Less than 20% read the body copy. Advertising guru David Ogilvy says, "When you have written your headline, you have spent eighty cents out of your dollar" *(Confessions of an Advertising Man).*

Some experts say that the best headlines evoke curiosity. Others say that the best headlines explain as much as possible. Maybe they're both right.

A headline or title needs to identify what is being offered. It also needs to encourage your audience to want more. A good headline targets your audience and evokes curiosity at the same time. See how the following do both:

7 Warning Signs of Depression

Are You Paying Too Much for Auto Repair?

Soothing Touches: Sports Injury Pain Relief

The Bottom Line: Low-cost Bookkeeping for Small Business

Where to Find Single Men

Sometimes you may want to use the name of your service as your headline. Most of the time, you'll probably name the service at the bottom of your ad, along with the address and phone number.

clients. Why should a person choose John's service rather than the firm down the street? John does something called "financial management," but for whom? It might be for big corporations, salaried professionals, people in private practice, or people who have declared bankruptcy. We don't know if John knows or cares anything about stock investments, real estate, corporate restructuring, estate planning, or non-profit corporations. John may want to say that he's a generalist. Still, pitching to everybody is appealing to nobody. And John probably is less of a generalist than he thinks. If John's clients are major corporations, he's probably not out to solicit business from hardware store managers or school teachers. But if John works daily with the problems of wage earners and people in small business, his announcement should reflect this expertise.

John's revised announcement might read something like this:

> *Your finances are complicated, and you need someone you can trust. It's time to begin organizing your records in preparation for the April 15 tax deadline.*
>
> *If you're self-employed or an independent contractor, you probably have questions about what expenses are deductible. You also need to know how to keep income and expense records, how to make quarterly estimated tax payments, and how the tax laws now affect you.*
>
> *If you're a wage earner, you especially need to protect your investments and keep up with new developments in real estate and financial planning. Working with me will put money back in your pocket.*
>
> *I specialize in helping people like you to develop strategies to lower your taxes and plan for the future. I have lived and worked in the community for over 8 years. My clients include....*

The best listings read as if you were speaking directly to a prospective client.

Secret Magic Words

Often a simple word or phrase can arouse interest, express concern, and command attention. Marketers always are looking for persuasive and attention-getting words. Almost every expert's short list includes "free," "new," "now," "you," "money," "health," and "sex." Our list here emphasizes words which best describe specialty services. Use your common sense to choose what's appropriate. "It's fun" may describe ballroom dance but not cosmetic surgery:

Act now!
Announcing
Attractive

More magic words...

Authentic
Bargain
Beginners especially welcome
Bonus!
Call for a free brochure
Call for more information
Call today!
Certified
Classic
Discover
Distinctive
Easy
Eight ways to
Excellent
Exclusive
Expert
Facts
Famous
Fast!
Find out more by calling
First
Free
Free initial consultation
Fun
Genuine
Gift
Guarantee
Handouts and book list included
Health
Helpful
How to
Individual attention
Insurance accepted
Last chance
Limited offer
Love
Magic
Make money!
Make new friends!
Meet new people
Mistakes you should avoid
Money

Money back guarantee
Networking and social time
New
No obligation
Now
Outstanding
Pay later!
Personalized service
Popular
Powerful
Price is going up
Professional
Proven
Quality
Quick
Rare
Recommended by
Refreshments provided
Reliable
Respond within 15 days for this bonus_____.
Results
Safety
Save
Secret
Service
Seven tips
Sex
Small classes for personalized attention
Special
Successful
There is no obligation whatsoever
Tips
Twenty reasons why
Unique
Valuable
Value
We care about you
We're here to help
Wealth
Write today!
You
You can become more_____.

More magic words...

Now that you've gotten a prospect's attention, what are you going to do with it?

Use "magic" words like spice. A little goes a long way. Too many in the wrong combination and you'll ruin the stew. According to a Yale University study, the 12 most persuasive words are: Save, Discover, Safety, Health, You, Guarantee, Love, Easy, Money, Proven, Results, and New. We tried to put them all together in this one dynamite solicitation: "You will Discover 7 Easy New ways to Save $, Improve Health, and find Love with Safety—Proven Results Guaranteed!" See, it's easy to go overboard.

The real secret to imbuing words with magic is to use them in their proper context. "You" and "new" in a headline may not increase reader response. Uniqueness and newness are qualities perceived by the reader, not simply foisted on him by a copy writer. If your service really isn't "new," don't use the word! Too many readers will resent being misdirected if your headline is inappropriate. Take care not to get so wrapped up in technique that you forget you're communicating with a living, breathing person. Offer him an idea, but don't bully him with it. Respect the intelligence of your reader. Allow him to draw his own conclusions. Chances are, he will anyway!

Overcoming Writer's Block

For some of us, writing never comes easy. Even experienced writers can get stuck when writing promotional copy. For those of you who experience writer's block, here are a few tips.

Good writing starts with a good idea.

First, eliminate distractions. If you don't have a quiet space of your own, go to a nearby library. Writing can be pure joy, but it takes concentration. The more you write, the more natural writing becomes. With practice, you eventually get beyond technique and find a writing "voice" that is distinctly yours.

Some people are paralyzed by fear. Overcome fear by realizing that the words you write are no more than personal notes until you choose to share them. No draft is necessarily final. You can always rewrite. In fact, a good way to get started is to write down everything that comes to mind, without filtering. Fantasize, daydream, free associate—and take notes. Ideas and themes culled this way may be diamonds in the rough. Mine for ideas before you polish your prose.

If you can't write at all, talk into a tape recorder. If you find talking to a machine awkward, talk to a friend and leave the tape machine on "record." Have your friend prepare a list of questions and "interview" you. Transcribe your conversation and make it your rough draft, ready for editing and polishing.

If you're a relentless perfectionist, you may tend to overwrite. We've seen people drain all the life out of original drafts due to endless rewriting. Don't agonize endlessly trying to write 'perfect copy,' because nobody can. Relax! For the moment, forget that you're trying to promote something. Get out your favorite personal stationery. Write a letter to your favorite aunt or your best friend. Tell her all about the exciting new enterprise that occupies your time. Go into as much detail as you possibly can. This letter can become your rough draft.

Dialog is also an excellent way to break through creative blocks. Often when we hear a first draft we react, "Is this what you were trying to say...?" "No, what I *really meant* was...." While the person is saying what he really meant, we write it down word for word. When we read it back, we get credited with being brilliant rewrite editors! The point is to get outside your own head and touch base with a live person. For most of us, saying what we mean is easier than writing it. This is truly finding your "voice."

Some people just can't seem to get started. There may be only one sure cure for this. Commit a block of time to writing and don't get out of your chair for any excuse. For ongoing projects, set aside a regular time each day. If sentences are not flowing easily, write phrases or words. Write without regard to style or organization. If you write yourself dry, spend your scheduled time editing a previous day's work. Sooner or later, you'll find your voice and the words will flow.

Get your ideas down on paper or into a tape recorder. Edit afterwards.

The panic of a deadline may get you to write. This method of last resort releases adrenaline and stimulates creativity. There certainly are more pleasant ways to write, but few more effective.

If all else fails, there are plenty of skilled professional writers who can draw out your ideas and make them sound brilliant, crisp, and enticing.

Copyrights and Trademarks

A copyright is a legal statement of ownership of a literary document, photograph, or drawing. Copyright material with the symbol "©," the date the owner's name, and the phrase "All rights reserved." This format is good in the United States and most countries internationally. You can embellish, too. (See our copyright notice at the front of this book.)

Put your copyright notice on all original materials, including class handouts, newsletters, and brochures. This notifies the public that you intend to register your copyright for full legal protection. This initial step costs you nothing. It also lends an air of importance to your document.

To register your copyright with the federal government, request forms at your local library or directly from the Copyright Office of the Library of Congress, Washington, D.C. 20559, (202) 479-0700. Filing costs at least $10 per notice. Copyright owners have the rights to reproduce, distribute, perform, display, or adapt original material. Copyrights owned by individuals last 50 years after death, and then are owned by the estate. Copyrights owned by corporations last 75 years after first publication. Before 1978 different laws applied. Anything published before 1922 is in the public domain. Anything not copyrighted is in the public domain.

If you want to use artwork, photographs, or writing under somebody else's copyright, call or write for permission. Offer to credit the original source. If your venture is non-profit or not highly commercial, many owners will grant one-time publishing permission at no cost. If you use somebody else's copyrighted material without permission, you could be guilty of violating copyright laws and liable for civil prosecution.

Registering a copyright or trademark insures legal proof of ownership.

You may publish brief excerpts of original material under "fair use provisions" of the copyright law without securing permission. This includes quoting passages for purposes of teaching, commentary, reviews, and news. Make it a habit to credit your source to protect yourself against liabilities of all kinds. "According to today's *National Requirer,* 'Aliens have landed on the White House lawn.'" Notice, *we* didn't say that aliens landed. We were quoting an outside source.

Should you register your copyright with the federal government? Yes, if you want legal recognition of ownership. Does a copyright offer protection against plagiarism? Yes and no. You probably would win a copyright infringement suit if somebody copies your work without permission. However, a copyright is little protection against someone taking your ideas and making their own version. A client of ours was concerned about being interviewed as a source of "background" information by another author. Would our client receive credit for his original contribution? We cautioned our client that his claim would be hard to prove. It would be up to the author to give credit where he saw fit. The rule is this: Your published words are protected against theft, but your ideas are not. In short, if you want to protect your work, you need more than a copyright. You also need to become famous for what you think and do.

Now about trademarks: Names, titles, logos, and symbols usually are not protected by copyright laws. If you have a unique motto or art emblem that distinguishes you from potential rivals, you may qualify it for a trademark. When applying for a trademark, put the designation "TM" to the side of the art. Service businesses sometimes are designated with "SM." Putting "TM" or "SM" with your art costs nothing, so we always recommend doing it. This protects your work temporarily and is a statement of your intent to file for registration. After your trademark registration is approved, "TM" or "SM" is changed to the symbol "®." Registering a trademark costs at least $200. For forms and details contact the Patent and Trademark Office, Washington, D.C., 20231, (703) 557-3158.

EDITING FOR IMPACT:

	Instead of...	Consider...
Wordy to concise:	Many of the clients say that our service is outstanding and that it has met their needs in a variety of ways that improve their lives...	Our clients cheer: "I've never been treated better!"—Jane Sayer, Nurse "You're the best!"—Jim Ng, Stockbroker
Vague to concrete:	The treatment is effective for many common complaints and health problems...	Hypnotherapy is especially effective for treating phobias, compulsive eating, and stopping smoking...
Dry to engaging:	The accounting process combines quarterly revenues with end of the year analyses in order to maximize the amount of your return...	John takes the time to explain accounting in language you can understand. You'll know where your money is going and feel in control...
3rd person to 2nd person:	A person entering into our program will be invited to participate...	You are cordially invited to participate...
Academic to conversational:	These paradigms are primary to our understanding of the world around us...	Here is a whole new way to look at the world...
Negative to positive:	If you don't attend, you'll be missing out on something really special...	You'll experience something really special...
Past tense to present:	I have taught ballet throughout the United States and Europe...	I teach ballet throughout the United States and Europe...
Shrill to reassuring:	Incredible! Fantastic! You won't believe how great our service is until you try it!...	Give us a try. We stand behind our service with this guarantee...
Jargon to plain English:	Our neuromuscular reconditioning program improves your PDQT ratio...	You'll feel rested and relaxed after a soothing therapeutic neck rub...
Dull to motivating:	Our staff has years of experience conducting wilderness expeditions...	Our staff of talented, enthusiastic wilderness guides shares their love and respect for the outdoors...
Generic to unique:	I am a computer consultant who can solve just about any of your technical problems...	With 6 years experience as computer consultant to Hewlett Packard, I am uniquely qualified to...

PROMOTION CHECKLIST:

Use this checklist to make your promotional materials more effective:

1.) ADVANCE PLANNING

☐ *Are you targeting active prospects?*
Make sure that your message will reach people who need and want your service. Expect to go through a period of trial-and-error testing. Minimize your investment until you know what's working for you.

☐ *Is there sufficient lead time?*
Give yourself enough time to prepare and produce your materials thoughtfully. Plan events and special promotions with enough lead time to meet media deadlines. Notify prospective clients and participants three weeks or more in advance so they can fit it into their schedules. This is especially important for seasonal activities—Christmas retreats, semester startups, tax service deadlines, etc.

☐ *Is the price right?*
Break into new markets by pricing your service slightly lower than the prevailing competition and emphasizing the bargain, or by pricing your service slightly higher and stressing quality. Price your service too high, however, and people will not pay it. Price your service too low and people won't value it. If you accept payment in forms other than cash—insurance, billing, credit cards, etc.—highlight them prominently.

☐ *Are the times and dates convenient?*
Many services and events enroll better "after hours." Career people—those who can best afford higher priced services—usually have more free time during lunches, evenings, and weekends. Also, they have more disposable cash for impulse spending at the beginning of the month right after payday.

☐ *Is the location suitable?*
Choose a central location, a safe neighborhood, clean streets, and bright lighting. The best environment is warm, friendly, spacious, comfortable, quiet, and clean.

PROMOTION CHECKLIST, Continued...

2.) ANNOUNCEMENT CONTENT

☐ *Is your content accurate?*

Double-check telephone numbers, addresses, days, dates, times, and prices very carefully. Make sure no information is garbled or omitted by mistake. Make sure that your copy covers all the necessary points.

☐ *Do you arouse interest?*

Use titles, photos, and graphics to draw people into the text. Use titles to describe your service and to target your audience. Put your most important benefit in the biggest, boldest headline.

☐ *Do you address needs and aspirations?*

Speak to issues that are important to your prospects. Stress why clients would want to use your service. Hypnotherapy, for example, might be offered to stop smoking, to lose weight, for psychological counseling, past life regressions, or for entertainment. Use what's appropriate for your audience and for you, too.

☐ *Do you offer a unique solution?*

Tell how your service is special. How are you bigger, better, faster, cheaper, more personalized, more convenient, newer, more established, or more committed than other similar services?

☐ *Do you include testimonials?*

Publishing testimonials from happy clients may be the most convincing element you can add to any announcement. Use three to six testimonials, keep each one short (one to four sentences, maximum), and include the client's full name, profession or institutional affiliation, and photo if available.

☐ *Is there a call for action?*

Spell out the response you want. That may be an immediate purchase, inquiry, partial payment, or office visit. Consider including a time-value inducement, for instance, "Prices increase after November 3." "$25 in advance; $35 at the door." Overcome resistance with "free introduction" or some other low risk inducement.

PROMOTION CHECKLIST, Continued...

3.) ANNOUNCEMENT STYLE

☐ *Is it readable?*

Effective copy reads like spoken English. Long sentences with complex dependent clauses lose readers. Abbreviations, specialized words, and technical phrases make your reader work too hard to get your point. Read your copy out loud to check it.

☐ *Are you to the point?*

Use the fewest possible words to make your point.

☐ *Are you concrete?*

Make your case with specific examples and testimonials. Elaborate philosophical justifications are not persuasive. A phrase or idiom that identifies your world view is sufficient. Your market is self-selecting, and respondents tend to be sympathetic to your point of view.

☐ *Does your copy sound shrill?*

It should tantalize and invite without appearing to be hype. Exaggerated claims can be hip or humorous. "Announcing the biggest event since the invention of fire!" But if overdone, humor can backfire. People don't take you seriously.

☐ *Are you guilty of false modesty?*

Don't be subtle. Spell out why your service is special. Say it with pride and authority.

☐ *Are you personable?*

Some copy reads as if it came from a computer. You can be technically accurate yet dry and unappealing. Let your humanity shine through the copy. Make it clear that you really care about your clients.

☐ *Are you inspiring?*

A sense of purpose and vision makes an enterprise more attractive. Express this by projecting integrity, honor, and pride.

PROMOTION CHECKLIST, Continued...

☐ *Are you being overly negative?*

Focus on marketing the solution, not overstating the problem. In general, avoid sounding depressing, cynical, or angry. Also, don't waste too much copy attacking your "competition." This may work if you're David fighting the giant Goliath. Still, it's better to focus on your own strengths rather than someone else's weaknesses.

☐ *Are you persuasive?*

Read your copy to other people to check it. Reading it should convince them of the value of your service. If not, why not?

4.) FOLLOW-THROUGH

☐ *Can prospective clients reach you?*

Make sure that the telephone is being answered at designated hours. At least make sure that an answering service or machine is doing the job.

☐ *Do you return calls?*

Return messages within the week, daily if possible. Notify prospects if you will be away and unable to respond promptly. Before a scheduled appointment or small scale event, call back to confirm and remind early registrants.

☐ *Are you friendly and enthusiastic?*

Personal contact motivates prospects. Be available. Be warm. Be encouraging. Give prospective clients every possible reason for using your service.

☐ *Are you doing your paperwork?*

Obtain names, addresses, and telephone numbers for future contacts such as direct mail or telemarketing. Collect other demographic data to build a client profile and better target your market.

☐ *Are you getting feedback?*

Ask respondents how they found out about your service and what attracted them to it. Use this to revise promotional copy. Track your responses to evaluate the effectiveness of your promotion campaign.

Sue Roberts is a successful psychotherapist in private practice who commutes between two offices in the San Francisco Bay Area. We asked Sue to tell us how she developed her business:

Q: How did you get started in private practice?

Sue: When I worked at the Center for Special Problems, part of the San Francisco mental health system, clients kept asking to see me privately after I quit working there. Shortly afterwards, I branched out on my own.

Q: How did you get more clients?

Sue: I dance for recreation, and somebody from my dance group sent her husband. I promoted therapy for women by distributing flyers. I also advertised in two Bay Area professional directories, *Common Ground* and *Open Exchange.*

Q: What campaigns worked particularly well for you?

Sue: I wrote an article about the "Eternal Child Syndrome" that appeared in *Open Exchange.* I made copies of the published article and gave it out as a flyer and a mailer. It really helped to establish me in the community. I even met someone at a party who had the article put under his windshield by a knowing friend. Writing a couple of articles helped me achieve a critical mass of being known. Writing gives you a status and credibility. That led to teaching classes at community centers, singles groups, and elsewhere.

Q: What happened next?

Sue: For a while, "Eternal Child" and "Peter Pan" issues were very big, but this died down. The next wave of interest was "women who love too much," drug and alcohol recovery, and co-dependency issues. This fit in with my family background and professional expertise. I helped found a professional organization of therapists specializing in ACA (adult children of alcoholics) therapy. Since then I've done a lot of work with substance abusers and children of alcoholics. An article published in *Recovering* magazine also helped establish my credentials in this area. Of course, after 20 years as a therapist, I've already earned my stripes.

Q: What advice can you offer to newcomers?

Sue: Perseverance is important. Keep running your ads and get out into the community.

12

Graphics With Impact

Hᴇʀᴇ ᴀʀᴇ ᴇssᴇɴᴛɪᴀʟ ᴛɪᴘs for designing and producing attractive stationery, flyers, brochures, newsletters, and display advertising. Think of published materials as an extension of your personal wardrobe. In a way, it's as if you were choosing a tie to match a suit, or shoes to go with a dress. Coordinate all of your printed designs to reinforce your theme. Look stylish, look tailored, and make your own personal statement. Whether you produce your own material or hire design assistance, make it a point to be involved in the process. That way you'll obtain the best results for the least expense.

Ten Guidelines for Graphic Design

Use design to underscore your prose. The age of media has made us more visually oriented than ever before. Pictures convey an immediacy and impact beyond what words describe. Typestyle, color, texture, size, and paper stock also can reinforce your intended message. Even if you want to look "non-commercial," it takes planning to achieve the design you want. If you ignore the elements of design, it may appear that you just don't care.

Even if you don't think of yourself as artistic, learn enough about design to achieve the effect you want. Here are ten guidelines:

1.) Know your purpose.
2.) Imitate before you innovate.
3.) Stress communication over artistry.
4.) Headline a benefit.
5.) Break up body copy.
6.) Use readable type.
7.) Use artwork for drama.
8.) Use typestyles as art.
9.) Use color for mood and accent.
10.) Increase client recall with photos.

Graphics embodies your business values and goals.

1.) Know your purpose. Know in advance what you want to say and to whom. Create a visual order which reinforces your central message. For example, a flower shop ad may be pretty and floral. An investment prospectus should have an important look.

2.) Imitate before you innovate. Look at other designs that you find attractive and modify them to your own specific needs. For instance, a coupon should look like a coupon, with a broken line border and cartoon scissors to encourage cutting out. Rules are made to be broken, but have a good reason for breaking them.

3.) Stress communication over artistry. Stress simplicity. Avoid clutter. Organize your text with borders and breaks. Avoid superimposing artwork over text, which is highly distracting to readers. Use graphics to make a point, not to call attention to itself. Ostentatious graphics might elicit, "Look how much they spent!" rather than, "This service must be excellent!"

4.) Headline a benefit. Most people read headlines; far fewer read the body copy. Target your market and name your service in a headline. Put your main sales message or customer benefit in a headline. "Here's How to Cut Health Care Costs..." Avoid ending a headline with a period—it literally means stop. We prefer long dashes, colons, or ellipses.

5.) Break up body copy. Large blocks of text are easier to read if you break them up. Use subheads every few hundred words or less. Lead your reader from theme to theme. Move his eye through the text with symbols, art, and photographs.

6.) *Use readable type.* Make your line lengths less than 55 characters wide. Upper and lower case is easier to read than all capital letters. Upper and lower case letters catch the eye with ascenders and descenders, distinctive bars and curves that push above and below the reading line. In general, the less you write, the larger you can print it. And the larger the type, the more people will read it. Many people cannot read type smaller than 7 point. Newspapers usually are 9 to 12 point. Typewriters use 10 point for elite and 12 point for pica.

7.) *Use artwork for drama.* Art can project and reinforce any marketing theme. Corners and squares look technological. Circles and curves feel biological. Mandalas are hypnotic, transcendent. Use designs that are easy to reproduce in different sizes on letterheads, brochures, and in newspapers. Art that reproduces most easily has strong black and white contrast, bold and clean, much like comic book art or silhouettes. Weak pen lines or light shades don't reproduce well when reduced.

8.) *Use typestyles as art.* There are thousands of typestyles to choose from. The two basic typestyles are serif (with curly hooks at the baseline) and sans-serif (without hooks). Match the type to the job you expect it to accomplish. Serif can be very stylish. Sans-serif feels practical, technological. Serif is more readable for long text; sans-serif is better for brief passages. Big type conveys importance. Tall type, respect. Italics, movement. Bold type, strength. Script (similar to hand-written), the personal touch. Designer typestyles have unique personalities. Your logo type reflects your corporate or professional image.

9.) *Use color for mood and accent.* Use bright, hot colors to draw the eye from a distance. Use cool colors with an established audience. Use a single "spot" color as a visual aid to turn attention to one point. Bright red is the single most attracting color. Most commercial advertising uses basic black and spot red if nothing else—just look at billboards or the brand name products in your kitchen.

10.) *Increase client recall with photos.* Photos lend credibility and create visual impact. Photos increase recall some 26% over artwork alone. People read captions twice as much as body copy. Here's a great place to include a priority message.

Photographs and artwork increase client recall over text alone.

Using Photographs

Photographs add drama, perspective, and visual impact. Use photos in a way that reinforces your words. Create interest, elicit emotion, explain, and accent with photos. Expressions of competence and caring are more convincing when accompanied by photos. Photographs give prospective clients a one-way mirror, the ability to see without being seen. In effect, you offer a no-risk introduction to your service with photographs.

SAMPLE TYPEFACES:

Serif typefaces are best for long passages such as magazine articles and books. The serifs (hooks and curls at each letter's baseline) catch the eye and improve readability. Stylish serif types convey class and culture.

This is a sample of Times Roman 12 point type, a typical serif typeface.

This is a sample of Times Roman Italics.

This is a sample of Times Roman Bold.

This is a sample of Times Roman Bold Italics.

This is a sample of Times Roman Condensed.

This is a sample of Times Roman Expanded.

This is a sample of Times Roman Reversed.

This is a sample of Times Roman Outline & Shadow.

Sans-serif type (no hooks and curls) is very readable for technical pamphlets, class descriptions, and other short passages. Larger, bolder sans-serifs make commanding headlines.

This is a sample of Helvetica 12 point type, a typical sans-serif typeface.

This is a sample of Helvetica Italics.

This is a sample of Helvetica Bold.

This is a sample of Helvetica Bold Italics.

This is a sample of Helvetica Condensed.

This is a sample of Helvetica Expanded.

This is a sample of Helvetica Reversed.

This is a sample of Helvetica Outline & Shadow.

This is a sample of Brush Script 12 point, a type which conveys a very personal feel.

This is a sample of Futura Light 12 point, which has a high-tech look.

This is a sample of Peignot Demi 12 point, a type with an art deco feel.

This is a sample of Palatino 12 point, a serif type similar to Times Roman, but more stylized.

This is a sample of Geneva 12 point, a no-nonsense sans-serif suitable for billing, mailing labels, and business forms.

This is a sample of Utopia 12 point, a strong, clean serif typeface. The body of this book is set in this type.

Each typeface has its own personality. If your text is serif, try using a sans-serif headline for contrast. If your text is sans-serif, try a strong serif or art deco header for variety.

TYPE SIZES AND DISPLAYS:

HELVETICA 4 Point
HELVETICA 5 Point
HELVETICA 6 Point
HELVETICA 7 Point
HELVETICA 8 Point
HELVETICA 9 Point
HELVETICA 10 Point
HELVETICA 11 Point
HELVETICA 12 Point
HELVETICA 13 Point
HELVETICA 14 Point
HELVETICA 15 Point
HELVETICA 16 Point
HELVETICA 20 Point
HELVETICA 24 Point
HELVETICA 30 Point
HELVETICA 36 Point

The larger the type size you use, the more space you need to display it. Note, too, that different typefaces are taller or shorter, wider or narrower, and this affects your copy layout. Whether you justify your lines with even left and right margins, center your copy, or set your type with ragged margins also affects line breaks and spacing requirements. This paragraph has been set two ways: first justified, then ragged left. Ragged type takes up slightly more space. Some designers feel that justified type looks more professional but that ragged is more personal and easier to read. Which do you prefer?

The larger the type size you use, the more space you need to display it. Note, too, that different typefaces are taller or shorter, wider or narrower, and this affects your copy layout. Whether you justify your lines with even left and right margins, center your copy, or set your type with ragged margins also affects line breaks and spacing requirements. This paragraph has been set two ways: first justified, then ragged left. Ragged type takes up slightly more space. Some designers feel that justified type looks more professional but that ragged is more personal and easier to read. Which do you prefer?

Most books and newspapers are set at 9 point to 12 point type. Subheads are usually several points larger than body copy and bolded.

Photos also play to clients' aspirations. Photos dramatize an ideal. So make your photos larger than life. Pose, groom, and dress your subjects a little better, a little prettier, than they appear in daily life.

Here are the main ways to use photographs:

Group
Landscape
Performance
Personal interaction
Portrait
Product
Working environment

Group. Use photographs of a group to show the scope of your enterprise. Staff photos display teamwork and organization. A photo montage of satisfied clients reinforces your track record with visual testimonials.

Landscape photos set off a particular environment. An aerial shot of a wooded campus, a busy cityscape, or a palm studded tropical beach all imply different activities. Use landscape to convey a special mood or to dramatize your location.

Performance photos are useful for dancers, actors, and musicians. Usually these are a skillful blend of portrait and props. Performing artists need portfolios that package them as unique personalities with special talents. There is a "larger than life" quality to performance shots.

Personal interaction can be captured dramatically in a photograph. Show a consultant huddling with a client, a doctor advising a patient, a musician playing for a student, a bodyworker massaging a client's neck. Eye contact between expert and client displays a bond of trust. The client's face can dramatize satisfaction, confidence. The expert's face can show caring, concern. Photographs of clients imply that others endorse your service, a powerful visual testimonial.

Portrait shots personalize any product or service. Prospective clients want to see the faces behind the service. Compose your portrait shots full, three-quarter face, or in profile. Your expression should be natural, a smile of friendship and confidence. Direct lighting minimizes shadows and makes you look open faced and trustworthy. Diffuse lighting smooths away wrinkles. Side lighting creates deep shadows and casts part or all of the face in darkness. This may project an aura of power or a special mood. Back lighting can create halos, almost a "psychic" effect. Portrait shots, for better or worse, sell a service based on personal appearances. Helping professionals want to project caring and concern. Some therapists even lean forward slightly, assuming a "listening" posture. Businesspeople want to project confidence, power, and success in their portrait photos.

Photo captions are read perhaps twice as much as ordinary text. Put important ideas here for impact.

Product shots are the heart of commercial advertising. Advertisers manipulate color, background, and perspective in ways which highlight a product to its best advantage. For instance, a small child eating a hamburger makes the hamburger look proportionately bigger. For your own product shots, include props of known size (a dime, hand, person, etc.) to show scale. Put a product in familiar context and show it in use.

Working environment. Take a "real people" approach and focus on the working environment. Show what you do and how it's done. Emphasize the service rather than the personality. Add specific props for impact—the weaver at his loom, doctor at her desk, lecturer at the podium.

A high quality photograph will add immense value and prestige to any brochure, press kit, or advertisement. Artists and theater people know how effective a good portfolio can be, and the rest of us can learn a lesson here. Don't get cheap where photos are concerned. If you can afford it, hire a professional photographer and pay for a carefully crafted, well lit studio shot. Have prints custom developed in large format.

Use quality photographs in your ads, brochures, flyers, and press kits.

Before you publish a person's photograph, you need to get their permission. (However, if a person is a known public figure, you need no permission, as any paparazzo knows.) Verbal consent usually is sufficient for most artistic or benign editorial uses. However, it is best to obtain written releases when using people's images in brochures, ads, or other commercial contexts. Most camera stores carry standard release forms for sale. Terms of a release may vary. A general release permits you unlimited use of a photograph in any context. Professional models may want to include provisions for additional compensation when photos are used at different times or in different media. If you employ a photographer, ask him to obtain model releases in your behalf.

Ways to Add Color

Learn how to use black, white, and everything in between. The difference between black and white is 100%; there is no stronger contrast. If this seems too harsh, mute the contrast by using grays. The difference between gray and white is 50%. You also can soften contrast by using colors.

There are many different theories of color. Shout at new audiences with loud, primary colors; whisper at established audiences with soft, muted colors. Loud, warm colors make your material visible from a greater distance. Subtle, cool colors convey a sophistication and special mood that may appeal to an established audience. Reds and yellows are warm, eye-catching. Blues and greens are tranquil, pastoral. Beige is classy. Silver and gray are technological, modern. Primary colors are louder; pastels and mixed colors more subtle, sophisticated. Pastels such

SO, YOU WANT TO BE IN PICTURES, BUT YOU HATE TO GET A PHOTO?

Is this you? You need a photograph of yourself to reinforce your professional image, but you've been avoiding it. Try this:

1.) Admit what bothers you. Maybe you think you weigh too much. Maybe you think your nose is too big. Maybe you're uncomfortable with the idea of promoting yourself. Admit what you don't like and tell the photographer. Together you can work around it. A good photographer has many "tricks of the trade."

2.) Highlight your best features. Direct the camera where you want it to go. If you have pretty hands, highlight them. If you have a confident smile, show it. Consider profile shots.

3.) Play down your weaknesses. Use upper body shots if you are "out of shape." Hide wrinkles with soft light. Dress more conservatively if you wish to minimize extremes in height, weight, or some other aspect of physical appearance.

4.) Dilute your presence. If you believe that promotion is narcissistic, direct the action away from yourself. Add one or more people to play the part of your clients. Point toward a blackboard, a book, or some other prop. Focus on the message, not the personality.

Colors can create both physiological and emotional impacts.

as light purple, muted pink, sky blue, and goldenrod are favorite new age colors for magazines and books.

Colors may be seasonal, too. Coordinate with the golds and browns of autumn, the green of spring, the cool blue of summer, and the snow white of winter.

Consider the context in which you use a color. Green can mean ecology and nature, but in business it is also the color of money. Gold is a color with high minded metaphysical significance, but it also means wealth and power in the business community. Raised gold leaf lettering can add a real touch of class to your printed materials.

Wearing grays and blues in business is supposed to convey power and authority. Black is sometimes good, but often overpowering. Beiges and light browns are less threatening, conceivably good for therapists. Red sweaters and dresses always get you noticed. Dark browns are a negative in the "dress for success" literature.

Orange supposedly makes people thirsty. Notice how most fast food places use orange? Bright colors also make people more frenetic. They spend less time in brightly painted rooms. You rarely find a fast food establishment decorated in subtle colors. Muted colors, on the other hand, promote tranquillity. Prison cells painted in pink reduce inmate violence.

There are many ways to add color. The least expensive way is to print on colored paper rather than standard white. Most copy stores keep a variety of standard paper colors which cost you only a small surcharge. The next step up is to use colored ink rather than black. Many printers keep a collection of mixed inks available. Printers usually add an extra charge of $20 or so for washing the press to change colors. After that, you can add a second or third color. On some presses this means that your job will have to pass through the press twice. This can more than double your print costs over basic black and white. Finally, you can print in full color. The full color process requires at least four colors (three primary and black). Initial costs for design, color separations, and press set-up runs several hundred dollars. This makes full color practical only with larger print runs and bigger budgets.

Use grays and colors for mood and to soften contrast.

For brochures and catalogs, here are some low-cost color combinations that almost always reproduce well, even on a mediocre press:

Beige or gray paper, black ink
Beige paper, brown ink
Beige paper, burgundy or purple inks
Light yellow paper, black or red inks
White paper, black and red inks
White paper, black or brown or dark blue inks

For the printed word, avoid using ink colors that may fade, such as light blue or yellow. Also avoid blue ink on blue paper, red ink on red paper, or any other combination that would reduce contrast. Lighter colors may work for screens and background, but they may not be readable in print.

Generally, we recommend printing promotional material in warm colors. It's safer to be loud and be noticed than to be subtle and risk going unnoticed. Once we printed a school catalog in what we thought was a very pleasing shade of green. Student registration dropped 30% that issue. We printed the next catalog in reds and yellows, and student response returned to normal.

Pre-production Analysis

Before you begin production, review your budget and staff resources. Figure what you can do for yourself, in-house with existing resources, and what you'd rather farm out. Are you counting your own time in the equation? If you're designing handmade flyers, your only out of pocket expenses may be printing. On more intricate jobs, labor costs for typesetting, photography, art inserts, paste-up, and distribution enter the equation. If a friend or colleague offers free assistance, ask to see samples of past work before agreeing. Sometimes it's cheaper in the long run to pay a professional. Get cost estimates for everything in advance. You may want to expand or scale down your project based on these factors.

Various design and budget considerations include:

Artwork
Binding and trimming
Ink color
Method of reproduction
Page size and number of pages
Paper stock
Preparing photographs
Print run
Typefaces

Artwork. Hire an artist for sketches if your budget permits. Always ask to see samples of his work so that you can determine if his style matches the effect you want to achieve. You also can purchase artwork "off the shelf" at your local art store. Look at the Dover series of books which contain public domain art available for your use without securing copyright permission. Formatt also has a series of art on acetate sheets which you can cut out and stick on your original paste-up boards. This art is organized by style or subject so that you can purchase just what you need. You can purchase animals, people, lines, borders, classical images, deco designs, and more.

Binding and trimming. Hold together larger documents by folding and stapling. For larger or more sophisticated jobs use glue or special binders. For larger volumes use "perfect binding," or book binding. Explore these options with your printer before you start production. Prices vary with the effect you want to achieve, and this can greatly affect your budget.

Ink color. Full color photographs and art illustrations typically are composed of four distinct screens: black, red, yellow and blue. On the press it takes four plates, one for each color, to reproduce full color. This is why printing in full color can be several times as expensive as one color. If you cannot afford four colors, consider adding a second color to your basic black. A bright second color is almost as eye-catching as full color at a fraction of the cost. Border important paragraphs or highlight titles in your chosen color for dramatic effect.

Full color reproductions are expensive but most eye-catching.

Method of reproduction. There are different printing methods, depending on the number of copies you need. Instant printing on copy machines is cost-effective for up to 100 or so copies. Offset printing, often done the same day or overnight by most commercial copy stores, is efficient for between 100 and 20,000 copies. With offset printing a raised image is made on a plate. This plate is inked and pressed onto sheets which become your copies. If you ask your printer to use plastic or paper plates, it will save you money, especially on print runs under 1,000. Metal plates are more expensive but are higher quality, good for runs up to 50,000 or more. Consider web printing for runs of 5,000 or more. Newspapers are printed on web presses. So are most of their slick commercial inserts. The paper is fed off huge rolls at high speeds, and this can significantly reduce costs for very large runs. Finally, consider silk-screen printing for very accurate reproduction of elaborate artwork. Use silk-screen printing on banners, fabrics, and special surfaces. Since print quality can vary greatly even among similar presses, always see samples of the printer's work before you agree to an order.

Page size and number of pages. Generally, paper is cheapest if you use a standard size: letter (8 1/2" x 11"), legal (8 1/2" x 14"), or tabloid (11" x 17"). With special sizes you may have to purchase larger sheets than you need and then pay extra to trim the excess.

Paper stock. Evaluate paper stock from the standpoint of design and budget. Paper stocks vary with respect to brightness, texture, coating, weight, and fabric content. Cotton improves paper quality with a linen-like texture. Slick or coated stock is better for reproducing fine lined artwork. Newsprint is the least expensive, but tends to be dull and spreads the ink. Paper classifications are not always consistent. A 20 pound rough textured paper may appear thicker than a 50 pound smooth bond. Whiter, brighter paper usually is more expensive than duller paper, except for recycled paper, which often is duller yet more expensive. Quality also varies with each manufacturer. So shop paper—touch and fold it—before you decide.

Shop paper— touch and fold it— before you print.

Preparing photographs. Show prospective photographs to your printer before final layout to make sure that they will reproduce satisfactorily. Notice that printed photographs are composed of patterns of small dots of varying intensity. These are called screens or halftones. Each screen requires a separate camera shot which will cost you $4-$10 additional. Your printer can supply you with a screen of your original photograph, enlarged or reduced to your exact design needs. If you are printing in black and white, try to provide black and white originals, preferably 5" x 7" or 8" x 10" prints. If your original print is color, you may lose some clarity when your printer prepares a black and white screen. Even so, don't convert a color print into a black and white print before ordering your screen. It's too expensive and it doesn't improve your final outcome. Just let your printer make the best screen he can from your color original. If you are reproducing in full color, try to provide original slides, not copies. We prefer Kodachrome for the brightest results.

Print run. Your local copy store probably can print any amount you need from one to 100,000. If your business is new, just print what you expect to use up within a few months or sooner. You probably need no more than a few hundred business cards or stationery envelopes for normal use. If you are mailing or postering, you'll need more. It takes about 100 pieces to generate one paying client. So budget your resources accordingly. If money's tight, trim costs by using cheaper paper, fewer colors, smaller pages, or fewer pages. This way you can still print the number of copies you need.

Typefaces. Select typefaces because they are readable and lend personality to your design. Like people, typefaces can look friendly, imposing, urgent, relaxed, important, happy, fearful—you name it. Computerized laser printing or professional photo-typesetting give you literally thousands of typestyle options. If you need ornamental headlines, there is yet another alternative. Visit your local art store and ask to see their catalog of press-on or rub-on headline lettering.

Allow extra time for production delays and mistakes.

Production Work-flow

Once you've decided on a message, reviewed your budget, selected a graphics medium (flyer, newsletter, brochure, catalog, etc.), and considered design possibilities, production begins in earnest. Organize your production work-flow around these tasks:

1.) Semi-final draft of text
2.) Preliminary sketches of layout
3.) Editing and final draft
4.) Assignment for photos, artwork
5.) Dummy layout
6.) Typesetting
7.) Proofreading
8.) Corrected typeset copy
9.) Final layout
10.) Pre-press, or "blueline" check
11.) Printing date
12.) Distribution date

Set your deadlines for each task before you start. Review each deadline with your support staff; writers, artists, typesetters, and printers, and leave extra time to compensate for delays and mistakes.

Decide in advance whether you are going to contract out for typesetting and mechanical paste-up. Professional typesetting runs $40 per hour and up. Freelance graphic artists typically work for $10-$25 per hour. A two-page newsletter on letterhead stationery might take one hour of typesetting and another hour of paste-up. Every job, of course, is unique. Many printers run full service shops and also will bid on typesetting and paste-up. If you hire a freelance artist for paste-up or design work, make sure that they have production experience. Artists that are not used to working on deadlines tend to run over budget.

If you're a do-it-yourselfer, gather the following essential paste-up supplies for production at your kitchen table. They should run you about $50 and will see you through most small to medium sized projects:

Black border tapes in varying thicknesses
Clear acetate overlay sheets for spot color
Glue stick
Metal ruler
Non-reproducible blue felt-tipped correction pen
Proportion wheel for enlarging or reducing photographs
Public domain clip art books
Scissors
White art tape
Xacto knife with No. 11 blade

Your local art store almost certainly carries these and all sorts of really fun (and expensive!) toys for the professional artist. If you're serious about production work, check out the drafting tables, chairs, light tables, waxers, paper cutters, and....

Unless you definitely want to make paste-up your livelihood or are in serious need of a tax shelter, stick to the short list we've described above. Alternately, you might want to consider computerized, or desktop publishing.

Desktop Publishing

Desktop publishing technology is now very affordable.

Desktop publishing is changing the publishing business. Independent professionals and small businesses now can afford to produce materials in-house rather than contract out to typesetting service bureaus. Computer equipment that in the 1980's cost more than a Rolls Royce is now surpassed by machines that cost less than a Yugo. If you're motivated to learn a couple of software programs, you can typeset and paste up your own flyers, newsletters, and catalogs.

IBM, Apple, and Amiga are top condenders for desktop publishing.

Desktop publishing technology is leapfrogging so rapidly that we hesitate to make specific computer recommendations. Among the major computer companies, IBM and Apple have the widest support, with Amiga an up-and-coming contender. IBM, with over three quarters of the market, is the favorite for accounting and business applications. IBM is less expensive, but it may be too complicated for some casual users. Apple is preferred by many desktop publishers because of its relative ease of use and extensive range of graphics software. Now that Apple and IBM can "network" and the most popular software comes in both versions, the gap between the two has narrowed. If you're already comfortable with using IBM, you'll probably want to stay with it. If you're new to computers, however, take a close look at the Apple Macintosh.

We have to confess that we're Apple addicts. Typing on the Macintosh is almost as easy as using an electric typewriter. Editing is much easier. You can add or delete words or paragraphs without rewriting everything. There are also programs that check grammar and spelling, sort alphabetically, file, and index. We've taught new staffers basic data entry and editing on the Mac in less than an hour. More experienced people help with design and art programs.

We *will* go out on a limb and recommend a specific desktop publishing software program. Aldus PageMaker is a sophisticated design program with an intuitive feel that many artists love to use. PageMaker comes in both IBM and Mac versions. Most people who work in desktop publishing are familiar with PageMaker, even if it is not their program of first preference. Thus, training entry-level job applicants, finding temporary help, or getting technical assistance is easier if you use "Page." If your production needs are specialized, you may prefer other software. There are also less expensive programs if your computing needs are more modest.

Spend some time on a machine to find out if desktop publishing meets your needs. Take a three-hour introductory computer class at a local adult school or recreation center. Find a local copy store or computer center that rents time on their computers. You'll pay around $5 per hour to practice. When ready, you can purchase a basic computer, software, and printer for under $2,000. A better printer with a decent collection of typefaces can cost you at least as much as your computer, but you can wait on this purchase. Many type shops or service bureaus will work from your disks and print your materials for as low $ 0.25 per page.

When you actually decide to purchase a computer, take a knowledgeable computer "hacker" along. Pay for his time if you have to. When the computer salesperson speaks "computerese," have your hacker translate it into English. About one fourth all computers sold, and about half of all software winds up in a closet unused. Even if you think you know what you want, you can be oversold. One of our friends was sold a color monitor when she only needed monochrome for desktop publishing. She spent at least $1,000 more than she had to.

Despite its obvious advantages, desktop publishing is a major business investment, both in terms of dollars and time. Make the investment only if you intend to publish regularly. Your computer probably will cost you more than it saves you in the first year. Desktop publishing can look deceptively easy. More sophisticated art and graphics software programs require extensive training and practice. You'll find basic typing very easy, but trying to produce the flyer you want may turn into a nightmare. Your "executive network" should include that friendly hacker, someone to call when the computer freezes or the printer jams. Once you get the hang of it, watch your productivity soar!

Dealing with Commercial Printers

The three most important rules for choosing a printer are:

1.) Get competitive bids.
2.) Review your order before printing.
3.) Insist that your printer fixes his mistakes.

1.) *Get competitive bids.* Get at least three bids. If the job is large, get the bids in writing. Printers are no more or less honorable than any other profession. It's simply that costs and pricing are not standardized. When we've obtained bids for a particular job, we've found that prices vary as much as 200%.

That's right; some printers charge twice as much as others for the same quality of work. How can that be? Presses are expensive to maintain. When presses are cold, many printers drop their prices. When presses are busy and printers are overworked, prices rise sharply. Just because you're paying more doesn't mean that the job will look better.

Some printers charge twice the price of others for the same job.

If you get a good price once, it doesn't mean that you'll get a good price the next time you use that printer. Some printers "low-ball," or offer a very low bid on your first job, only to raise it appreciably on subsequent work. So, continue to get competitive bids. Ask how long the price is good for. You may even want to line up a backup printer just in case your favorite printer gets too busy (or too expensive).

Compare bids by insisting on a "bottom line" quote. Get an account of everything you're going to pay for, including tax. If applicable, obtain breakdowns for typesetting, screening photographs, enlargements and reductions, color overlays, extra preparation costs. Get samples of paper stock and compare them. If you're printing on two sides, make sure that the paper is opaque and doesn't bleed to the other side. Paper can account for more than half of the costs of printing. So know what you're getting, and accept no substitutes.

Most printers have 30 day billing accounts for regular customers. However, for the best price, offer to pay cash in advance or upon delivery. It's common to receive an extra 2% to 5% discount for cash payments.

2.) *Review your order before printing.* You will pay for any mistakes you make, so check your work carefully. Proofread the phone numbers, dates, names, and addresses one more time. Review your order with the printer regarding paper stock, ink color, press run, folding and binding, and due date. Ask if the photos or overlays are prepared correctly. Get assistance before you go to press. This is more for your protection than the printer's. At least half of all mistakes come from inexperienced customers who don't understand the mechanics of printing.

3.) *Insist that your printer fixes his mistakes.* Printers are human and can make mistakes. If the mistake is serious, such as smudges on station-ery, the printer should reprint your job without charge. If the error is not critical, such as using the wrong shade of blue, negotiate for a reduced price. Insist on your rights, but don't push too far if you want to continue a working relationship with your printer. Our regular copy printer erred on an important job of ours. The type was readable, but a screen was damaged. Most clients wouldn't have noticed, but since our business is media, perfection is critical. The printer apologized and volunteered to reprint the job. However, we couldn't afford the time. Also, we knew that he'd lose money if he had to reprint. So we accepted his alternate offer, a 33% discount off our original price. We saved over $200. The printer still made money. We negotiated a satisfactory (though not perfect) resolu-tion, and our printer still has us for a customer.

Find a good printer and nurture the relationship.

Here's a bonus tip: Count the number of copies you receive. Some printers ask customers to accept a print count of plus or minus 10%. It's the "minus" that bothers us. Would you accept only 900 envelopes if you ordered 1,000? Our mailing house says that one of the biggest delays in labeling comes from short print runs. There's really no excuse for running short by more than 1%, because counting equipment is highly accurate. Quality printers will print a 2% to 5% overrun just for goodwill and to compensate for crumpled or smeared copies. If your count is short, insist on compensation. Demand that the printer either credits your account, discounts your price, or puts your job back on press. If he doesn't make good, find another printer fast.

Once you've found a printer you can work with, nurture the relation-ship. Once a printer knows your tastes, he can give you just the kind of results you want. He can special order a unique ink color or paper, or retouch your photographs to make them look extra good. If you're a regular client, he'll go out of his way to keep you happy!

CHOOSING YOUR LOGO:

A logo is a unique representation of your service using type and/or art. An effective logo has visual impact and tells prospective clients about your service at a glance.

You can spend thousands of dollars on a logo design or you can create your own for next to nothing. Ask your local type shop to run out a batch of a dozen or so sample decorative typefaces from among the thousands available. Experiment with expanding, condensing, and shadowing various typefaces. This might cost you around $50. Find or create a look that matches your business personality:

Smiley Caterers   **Smiley Caterers**

Smiley Caterers   Ｓｍｉｌｅｙ　Ｃａｔｅｒｅｒｓ

Smiley Caterers   SMILEY CATERERS

If your budget warrants, consider hiring a graphics artist who specializes in typefaces to design an original font. This can cost you several hundred dollars.

If you want to add art to match your typeface, there are several ways to go. One inexpensive solution is to go to the library and find old public domain art in books for which the copyright has expired. There's a world of ancient Roman, Greek, and Oriental drawings, 18th Century woodcuts and the like, from which to choose. Another almost free source is the Dover series of clip art, available in book collections at most art supply stores. The images here range from ancient to modern, simple to baroque. Newspapers and magazines typically subscribe to art services which provide them with a wide variety of modern images: business, recreational, regional, seasonal, and famous faces. Subscriptions to these services can be pricey, but if you have a friend in the trade, ask if you can obtain access to theirs. If you use a computer, there's also an abundant supply of computerized commercial art on disks. A collection may run you $25 and up. Last but not least, consider hiring an artist to design your logo.

A good designer can modify an existing piece of art, work from your own preliminary sketches, or generate a truly original design that becomes your own. This can cost you from $250 on up to many thousands of dollars. Don't forget to add your "TM."

Integrated Designs

Featured on the following pages is a package of integrated designs for our hypothetical financial consultant, John Pennysworth. John offers personal financial planning, an investment newsletter, video cassettes, books, and group workshops. He markets his services in a variety of ways, as you can see by the following. And he uses the same logo designs for all of his printed materials:

For posters, standard sizes of paper are 11" x 17" (tabloid), 8 1/2" x 11" (letter), or 8 1/2" x 14" (legal).

For handbills, also consider cutting letter or legal size in half. You stretch your printing budget and create a more compact, personal document.

John Pennysworth's
MONEY & YOU WORKSHOP

With Foremost Financial Expert
John Pennysworth

How You'll Benefit:
1.) Learn where bankers invest....
2.) Discover where the biggest profits are...
3.) Where to obtain unsecured loans at below market interest rates...

Date: Saturday, January 14
Time: 10am to 5 pm
Place: Hyatt Regency
Uppercrust Conference Room
Fees: $249 in advance; $289 at the door.

How to Register: Register by mail, by phone or at the door. Cash, check, and major credit cards accepted. Call 777-555-1234 or write for a detailed brochure: 1442-A Walnut, #51, Berkeley, California 94709

About John Pennysworth:
Entrepreneur—//////// ////// //// //////////// //////////
/////////////// ////////// /////// ///
Investor—//////////// ////////// //////////////// / //////
/////////// ////////// ////// ///
Educator—//////////// ////////////// ////////// ////// ///
/////////////// ////////// ////// ///
Author—//////////// ////////////// ////////////// ////////// ///
///// ////////// /

CALL TODAY FOR A FREE BROCHURE: (777) 555-1234

Here are two different display ads that sell John Pennysworth's services to the public.

The tall ad sells John's expensive workshop and is complete with a detailed registration form. This ad is designed to reach people that already know something about John by reputation or from previous advertising. They are ready to participate.

The smaller ad takes a different approach. This ad, with it's no-risk "free" introduction, is designed to attract new people, to generate hot prospects. Participants at the free event will be invited to sign up for the more expensive workshop, purchase books and tapes, subscribe to John's newsletter, or become his personal client.

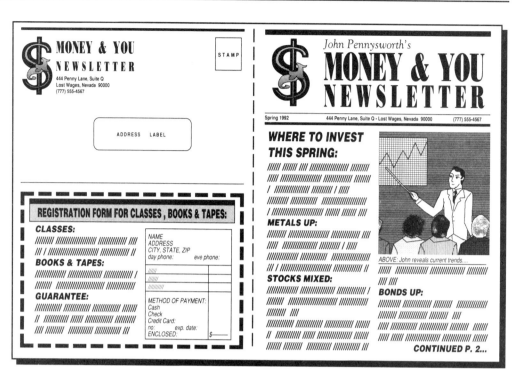

Elements in this newsletter include:

- Masthead
- News
- Photos and captions
- Graph for artistic impact
- Calendar
- Testimonials
- Registration/ order form
- Return address
- Mailing label

The newsletter pictured here is one 11" x 17" sheet folded to create a four page document, each page 8 1/2" x 11". Alternately, you can design a simple one-page newsletter on your letterhead stationery.

Consider the economy of using window envelopes: Type addressee information just once on stationery. Then fold the stationery so address shows through the window on a #9 or #10 window envelope.

Matching stationery and business card.

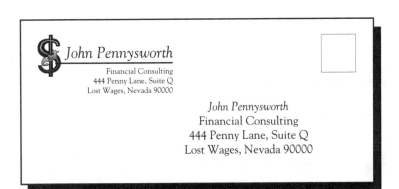

An optional self-addressed postcard or #9 envelope (mailed inside of a standard business size #10 envelope) allows your client to respond quickly and easily.

Pictured below is a six panel brochure designed to fit on standard 8 1/2" x 11" paper. Another option is an eight panel brochure printed on 8 1/2" x 14" legal size sheets of paper. Use the larger size if you need more room to describe your service or to add something extra, perhaps an order form for books or tapes.

Elements in this brochure include:

• Front cover
• Introduction
• Benefits list
• Photos with captions
• Brief biography
• Testimonials
• Registration form
• Address panel
• Call for more information

John Pennysworth's
WORKSHOPS
• When:
• Where:
• Price:

Another benefit of attending, ya, ta da ta, ta ta!

Call today for more information:
(777) 555-4567

REGISTRATION FORM
Name_____
Address_____
City, State, Zip_____
Day phone_____Eve. phone_____
☐ Check here to be on our free mailing list.
☐ Please charge my Visa or MasterCard
Account #_____ Exp. Date_____
Signature_____
Amount _____
Guarantee _____   CHECK ENCLOSED $ [   ]

MONEY & YOU EVENTS

ADDRESS LABEL

John Pennysworth
Financial Consulting
444 Penny Lane, Suite Q
Lost Wages, Nevada 90000

STAMP

MONEY & YOU
CLASSES & CONSULTATION

Consider an alternative four panel format on legal size paper:

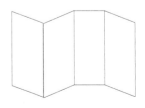

WHY PLANNING IS IMPORTANT...
This introduction targets a specific audience and explains why they need the services of John Pennysworth more than they might think.

Get the hot insider information here in John Pennysworth's "University Without Wall Street" classes. (Highlight an important benefit in a caption. Captions are read twice as much as other body copy.)

HOW JOHN PENNYSWORTH CAN BENEFIT YOU—

• *Financial Independence*
• *Discount Loans*
• *Security*
• *Higher Returns*
• *Insider Information!*

About John Pennysworth...
Here is John's track record, including corporations he's worked with, businesses he's launched, education, special training, and community involvement. This isn't a resume, just a quick, readable summary of achievement.

WHAT JOHN'S CLIENTS SAY—

"I made money on his recommendations."
—*D. Trump*
Real Estate Investor

"His newsletter is great!"
—*M. Griffin*
Entertainer

"My Financial situation has never been better!"
—*L. Helmsley*
Hotel Empress

"With the money he made me, my wardrobe has more than trippled it's size!"
—*Z. Gabor*
Entertainer

John Pennysworth • 444 Penny Lane, Suite Q • Lost Wages, Nevada
(777) 555-4567

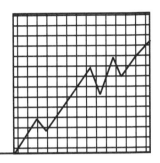

Books
and
Resources

HERE ARE SOME EXCELLENT marketing books and resources with our comments. We believe that this list is extensive and well-rounded. However, by no means is it meant to be complete. The problem is not a lack of resources, but that there are so many. Sorting through what's available and finding the most useful can be a permanent part time job in itself. On some topics there were so many very good books and resources that choosing just one or two became rather arbitrary. If we missed including one that you believe deserves to be on this list, write us. We'll try to include it in a future edition.

1.) Exploring Your Options

Self-Employment or the Career Track?

In Search of Excellence
Thomas J. Peters and Robert H. Waterman, Jr.
New York: Warner Books, Inc., 1982
Here are the success formulas for some of the United States' best run major corporations. And many of the lessons also apply to small business and independent professionals. "Stay close to the customer." "Think independently and competitively." "Share rewards (with your) employees." "Few administrative layers." "Dedication to central values." This book is a valuable overview to business at its best. The emphasis is always on what works. Also see the sequel, *A Passion For Excellence*.

Megatrends
Ten New Directions Transforming Our Lives
John Naisbitt
New York: Warner Books, Inc., 1982
Naisbitt by profession is a consultant to corporations, and that's good for the rest of us. He has a good news way of presenting some powerful ideas. His "megatrends" include decentralization, long term planning, participatory democracy, and networking. Everyone in business is familiar with this best-seller. Also see *Megatrends 2000*, the sequel.

Re-Inventing the Corporation
John Naisbitt and Patricia Aburdene
New York: Warner, 1985
Naisbitt envisions a corporate culture that respects the worker, where "people and profits are inexorably linked." Work should be fun, "a spiritual and mental high." He shows how major companies can adopt many of the qualities of entrepreneurship to stay competitive, keep and reward their employees.

New Ways to Work (NWW)
149 9th Street
San Francisco, CA 94103
(415) 552-1000
NWW, a membership organization, helps provide information on creating permanent, professional part time and job sharing positions. NWW publishes *Work Times,* a quarterly newsletter available to members, helping to find potential job sharers. Visit their resource library and counseling center at the above address, or phone for details.

Are You an Entrepreneur?

Honest Business
Michael Phillips and Salli Rasberry
New York: Random House, 1981
This book offers undisputed practical advice: "Love business." "Go slow." "Focus your Energy." "Pay bills promptly." The authors also recommend several novel approaches: open books to employees and customers; emphasize service over profits; substitute your own labor over high capital investment.

The book fosters caring communities—gentle business for gentle people.

The Growing Seed or Big Splash?

Think and Grow Rich
Napoleon Hill
Meriden, Connecticut: The Ralston Society, 1937
Just for fun, check your library for one of the original "positive thinking" books. Using the examples Carnegie, Henry Ford, and others, Hill describes timeless secrets to success through desire, motivation, organized planning, and persistence. Written during another era when tycoons were heroes, this book reads as new age as any today. "There are no limitations to the mind except those we acknowledge." "Both poverty and riches are the offspring of thought."

Shoestring Start Ups

Entrepreneur Magazine's 184 Businesses Anyone Can Start & Make A Lot of Money
Editors of *Entrepreneur Magazine*
New York: Bantam, 1990
Use this as an excellent source book of business possibilities. The publishers also sell consulting kits to help you start specific businesses.

168 More Businesses Anyone Can Start And Make A Lot of Money
Chase Revel
New York: Bantam Books, 1984
Here's another good reference book on low risk business ventures. Savor the possibilities, but question the author's hard sell, get rich quick bias.

555 Ways to Earn Extra Money
Jay Conrad Levinson
New York: Holt, Rinehart, Winston, 1982
The most complete book of possibilities, but the sections on each business are quite brief. So many businesses, so little space.... Use this book as the ultimate reference.

What Color is Your Package Wrapping?

What Color Is Your Parachute?
A Practical Manual for Job-Hunters & Career-Changers
Richard N. Bolles
Berkeley, CA: Ten Speed Press, 1972
This is the definitive book for corporate job seekers. Get yourself the latest edition. The resource section alone is worth more than the cover price. Practical and readable.

The Three Boxes of Life
Richard N. Bolles
Berkeley, CA: Ten Speed Press, 1978
An introduction to life/work planning, the focus is more inner-directed than Bolles' *Parachute*. The three boxes are education, work, and retirement. The author recommends strategies

for escaping the boxes, integrating learning and leisure, work and fulfillment. A superb book for setting priorities.

Do What You Love, The Money Will Follow
Marsha Sinetar
New York: Dell Publishing, 1987
Not your typical business book, this is a meditation on the spiritual side of work. Discover your right livelihood by following your heart. Your passion for what you love makes hard work seem effortless. Your dedication is a source for excellence.

2.) Marketing: From Concept to Delivery

The McGraw-Hill 36-Hour Marketing Course
Jeffrey L. Seglin
New York: McGraw-Hill, 1990
Here is the best conceptual overview of marketing you can get without going back to school. There's even a final exam at the end. "Take it and get 70 percent or more and McGraw-Hill will send you a handsome Certificate of Achievement!" The book's a dry read, but a handy reference, with solid introductions to research, pricing, distribution, and strategic planning.

Psychological Barriers to Marketing

Growing A Business
Paul Hawken
New York: Simon & Schuster, 1987
You've seen the show; now read the book! The book is even better than the PBS series based on it. Hawken sees business as an arena for personal development, and his insights follow: "Permission of the marketplace is many times more important than capital." "You are the customer, you are the company." "I believe [businesses] are successful *because* they have a broader vision." "If you meet the Buddha on the road, sell him." For Hawken, even Zen makes cents.

Guerilla Marketing Attack
Jay Conrad Levinson
Boston: Houghton Mifflin Company, 1989
Levinson's sequel to *Guerilla Marketing* is practical and down to earth. The author knows what works for small businesses, and he's fun to read.

How to Make Your Advertising Twice As Effective At Half the Cost
Hershell Gordon Lewis
(See Chapter 8.)

Marketing Warfare
Al Ries and Jack Trout
New York: McGraw-Hill, 1986
If marketing is war, these guys are the generals. This book is a fast, fun read. It deserves to become required reading for marketing pros and inquiring minds. But it's not a "how to" book, and the examples aren't always applicable to community based businesses and independent professionals.

Mass Markets Versus Niche Markets

The Marketing Imagination
Theodore Levitt
New York: The Free Press, 1986
In the new edition to this seminal work, the Harvard Business School's marketing guru defends his premise that markets are growing increasingly homogeneous ("The Globalization of Markets"). He explains subtle and hidden values customers put on products and services ("Marketing Intangible Products and Product Intangibles"), shows how to extend product life cycles ("Marketing Myopia"), and more. A classic.

Maximarketing
Stan Rapp and Thomas L. Collins
New York: McGraw-Hill, 1988
This book shows how larger corporations can compete in the declining mass market. Widely hailed as "an essential guide to the new age of enterprise," the irony here is that "maximarketing" is a synonym for the innovative strategic marketing that small time niche marketers have practiced for years. Excellent chapters on database management.

The Next Economy
Paul Hawken
New York: Holt, Rinehart and Winston, 1983
Hawken analyzes the segmentation of mass markets and the decline of the mass economy. He is one of a handful of business writers to incorporate both ecological considerations and ethical values into macro-economics. The book is post-apocalyptic, thoughtful, practical. Specific advice on how the local businessperson can compete successfully against corporate giants. "The next economy will be led by those [whose] lives and work are integrated." A brilliant vision.

Positioning: The Battle for Your Mind
Al Ries and Jack Trout
New York: McGraw-Hill, Inc., 1981
This book is a bona fide classic. In an overcrowded marketplace, not everyone can be number one. Nor should everyone try. Often there is more profit going directly for position number two, or three, or seventy-three. Consider Avis ("We're No. 2") or Seven-Up ("The Uncola.") Find a unique selling position for your service. Make it memorable, or "position" it, in the mind of the prospective buyer. Included: choosing a name, pricing, competition, line-extension. Some, not all, examples can be adapted to local and specialty markets.

Market Entry

"Gateways to Entry"
George S. Yip
Harvard Business Review
September-October 1982
This is an insightful analysis of how market barriers can be exploited to the new entrant's advantage. Also, how the incumbent can protect his market against late entrants. Thoughtful and practical.

3.) Organizing Your Business

Be the Boss:
Start and Run Your Own Service Business
Sandi Wilson
New York: Avon, 1985
Here is a fast-paced, upbeat introduction to small scale free-lancing and service businesses. Solid information on getting started, finding clients, partners, employees, vendors, taxes, and the rest. And some wry asides: "What happens when you lose a steady client…. You didn't want the dumb account anyway. You are drained of all your energy. You are getting a cold…and at your funeral they'll be sorry they took their stupid account sway." Sandi uses humor to combat the scary beginnings.

Running A One-Person Business
Claude Whitmyer,
and Salli Rasberry
Berkeley, CA: Ten Speed Press, 1989
This is probably the most practical, detailed manual you'll find on the day-to-day operations of a micro-business. The authors write from experience. They've visited and consulted with one-person businesses around the world and on every continent. For more information on one-person businesses write the authors in care of The Enterprise Support Center, P.O. Box 77086, San Francisco, CA 94107. ESC also publishes a local newsletter to help the formation of new small businesses.

Nolo Press
950 Parker Street
Berkeley, CA 94710
(510) 549-1976
Nolo Press publishes a comprehensive series of self-help books on small business, incorporations, finance, and law. Contact the publisher for a current catalog. *Nolo News* is a quarterly newspaper which updates development in self-help law. Write for book list and subscription information.

Running Your Business Successfully
A Woman's Guide to Surviving The First Two Years
Peg Moran
New York: Doubleday and Co., 1985
Peg, we know your secret. We read this workbook substituting "he" for "she" and discovered it works equally well both ways. Use this book interactively, filling in answers to a guided series of questions. Themes include: "What Are My Best Profit Centers?" "Are My Advertising and Promotion Producing Results?" "Can I Use Independent Contractors Rather Than Employees?" Also, interviews with successful women in business. A useful planner for any beginner.

Small Time Operator
Bernard Kamoroff, C.P.A.
Laytonville, CA: Bell Springs Publishing, 1977
"How to Start Your Own Small Business, Keep Your books, Pay Your Taxes, & Stay Out of Trouble!" Written in plain English, this is one of the best popular books ever written on bookkeeping, accounting, and small business organization. Kamoroff really knows how to make business accessible to everybody, not just accounting majors. Charts and forms for one year are included. Look for the latest edition.

We Own It
Peter Jan Honigsberg, Bernard Kamoroff and Jim Beatty
Laytonville, CA: Bell Springs Publishing, 1982
"Starting & Managing Coops, Collectives, & Employee Owned Ventures." With forms and friendly text, a readable workbook on forming cooperative ventures. Written by an attorney, an accountant, and a Coop accountant, this book gives solid advice as well as a sense of purpose.

Strategies For Independent Professionals

Empire Building By Writing and Speaking
Gordon Burgett
Communications Unlimited
P.O. Box 1001
Carpinteria, CA 93013
Burgett has built his own small empire in writing, lecturing, and consulting using the methods outlined herein. Write to the publisher for more information and a complete book list.

Private Practice Handbook, Third Edition
Charles H. Browning and Beverly J. Browning
Los Alamitos, CA: Duncliff's International, 1986
This is a very useful volume especially for therapists on how to build their private practices. Specific information on getting referrals from dozens of groups, including free clinics, community mental health organizations, physicians, foster parent programs, other clients, and more. Advice on fee setting, handling no-shows, handling publicity, etc. Filled with real life examples from other therapists.

Start-Up Money

How To Write A Winning Business Plan
Joseph R. Mancuso
New York: Prentice Hall, 1985
Here's how to write a business plan and secure money from lending institutions, venture capitalists, and other funders. Included are three complete original business plans that helped launch *Venture* magazine, Shopsmith, and Storage Technology. This book is very readable considering its institutional and technical focus.

Getting Yours: The Complete Guide to Government Money,
Third Edition
Matthew Lesko
New York: Penguin Books, 1987
Lesko has researched out mainstream as well as some of the most obscure grants you'll never believe. If you're looking for government money for any purpose whatsoever, check out this book.

Start-Up Money
How to Create a Business Plan & Loan Package
to Finance Your Small Business
Mike P. McKeever
Berkeley: Nolo, 1984
How to organize your loan materials and where to present them. Filled with detailed examples and do-it-yourself forms, here is a workbook even a beginner can use.

Your Board of Directors

Robert's Rules of Order Revised
Henry M. Robert
New York: William Morrow and Company, Inc., 1971
People often ask us how board meetings work–at least in theory. Here's how to convene a meeting, introduce a motion, preside over a debate, or draft a set of by-laws. Since 1876, this has been the standard reference text on parliamentary procedure.

Surviving A Recession

How to Prepare for the Coming Depression
A Workbook for Managing Your Money and Your Life
During Economic Hard Times
Mark Friedman
Willow Springs, MO: Nucleus Publications, 1989
Friedman shows how current economic conditions parallel the beginning of the 1929 Great Depression era. More importantly, he provides a very readable, practical guide for getting by during hard times. Friedman advises keeping your assets liquid, living more simply, building community, and learning to laugh! We showed this book to an economics student at the University of California who commented, "Is this a joke? The government won't allow another depression to happen." We believe that the institutional inability to even consider the problem makes a depression more likely! At any rate, the book is useful to anyone experiencing depression, recession, or simply personal hard times.

4.) Your Client Profile

The Baby Boomers

100 Predictions for the Baby Boom:
The Next 50 Years
Cheryl Russell
New York: Plenum Press, 1987
Look no further. This is the ultimate *readable* book of statistics and trends for the baby boom generation. Russell is editor-in-chief of *American Demographics,* a monthly magazine that keeps businesses abreast of consumer trends. Includes predictions about family, children, work, money, business, home, aging, and retirement.

Aging Americans

Successful Marketing to the 50+ Consumer
Jeff Ostroff
New Jersey: Prentiss Hall, 1989
Well organized and thoughtful, Ostroff does more than hand you the facts. He offers concise interpretations and analyses of what it means to grow older and how businesses can market to this audience. The book is literally a course in marketing as applied specifically to the over 50 market. First rate.

Lifestyle Marketing

The Nine American Lifestyles
Arnold Mitchell
New York: Warner Books, Inc., 1984
In the age of market fragmentation, businesses have to know where to target promotional dollars. Personal values affect purchases. "Achievers buy more large and luxury cars; Belongers tend toward 'family-sized' cars; the Societally Conscious purchase more gas-savers; muscle cars are bought by Emulators and Experientials; the Need-Drivens are heavy in the secondhand market." Mitchell is director of Stanford Research Institute's Values and Lifestyles Program, a source of market research for major corporations. A bird's eye view of values that shape the American landscape.

The New Age Publishing and Retail Alliance (NAPRA)
PO Box 9
Eastbound, WA 98245
(206) 376-2702
Marilyn McGuire, Executive Director
This is an alliance of publishers, distributors, retailers, and others involved with New Age materials, books, periodicals, and audio and video cassettes. The NAPRA seeks to serve as a marketing and networking organization that assists in the growth and sales of New Age materials, which focus on topics of human growth and awareness (creates and publishes a New Age best-sellers list, serves as a clearinghouse for New Age information, provides opportunities for members to interact). Publications available to members. Annual conventions and meetings with exhibits.

5.) Researching Your Market

California Small Business Resource Directory
California Department of Commerce
Small Business Development Center
1121 L St., Suite 600
Sacramento, CA 95814
(916) 324-8102
A library reference, a small publication very helpful for those starting out with their own business. Look for similar directories in other states. It is a computer generated directory of small business assistance organizations and it provides direct financial, marketing, management, and employee training assistance to small businesses.

National Directory of State Agencies, 1989
Cambridge Information Group Directories, Inc.
Main Office:
7200 Wisconsin Ave.
Bethesda, MD 20814
(800) 227-3052, in Maryland (301) 961-6750
Lists state agencies by function, for example commerce, consumer affairs, economic affairs, fish and game, food and drugs, real estate, and tourism are some entries. Also lists national associations which represent government officials, has an all state telephone directory for state telephone operators with information and addresses, lists state elected officials and agencies and locator numbers for state agencies and state legislatures. Ask at the reference desk at your local library to see a copy.

Successful Marketing for Small Business
Brian R. Smith
Brattleboro, VT: The Lewis Publishing Company, 1984
Why hire a market research firm? If you are interested in doing the calculations, charts, and pie graphs of market research, there are several useful chapters in this volume. Here are excellent references on business forecasting, data gathering, pricing, and market testing, too. If you passed high school math and still remember how to read a graph, you'll have no trouble with Smith's examples.

Trade and Professional Associations in California
California Institute of Public Affairs
PO Box 10
Claremont, CA 91711.
(714) 624-5212
Published by the California Institute of Public Affairs, this directory lists addresses of all kinds of associations you could contact for further information and possible support. Examples: the American Harp Society, American Institute of Architects, Associated Guitar Composers and Publishers, and Association of Beauty Salon Owners.

U.S. Government Manual published by the Office of the Federal Register, National Archives and Records Administration, has a chapter or sub-heading called "Department of Commerce," which gives further addresses, telephone numbers, and basic information. This book is available for sale by writing to Superintendent of Documents, U.S. Government Printing Office, Washington, DC 20402-9325. and it is also sold at Government Printing Office bookstores located in several major cities. Telephone inquiries should be directed to (202) 783-3238. Other U.S. Department of Commerce publications can be obtained by writing to the Office of Publications at the same address as above.

6.) Your Promotion Campaign

Guerilla Marketing
Secrets For Making Big Profits
From Your Small Business
Jay Conrad Levinson

Boston: Houghton Mifflin Company, 1984
This could be the best book ever written about small scale marketing. Levinson understands entrepreneurs and his approaches are down-to-earth. Extremely useful for storefront businesses, retail trades, and many independent professionals. Details on the Yellow Pages, canvassing, personal letters, radio, television, and other media options. A classic reference that belongs on your bookshelf. Also see the sequels, *Guerilla Marketing Attack* and *Guerilla Marketing Weapons.*

Publicizing and Promoting Programs
Helen Farlow
New York: McGraw-Hill, 1979
Professionals and administrators who market educational and institutional programs will benefit from reading this. Included are checklists, reminders, calendars, marketing glossary, list of newspaper associations, news services, and first-rate academic bibliography. Dry, but information packed. Find it at the library. Plan to take notes.

Profit from Your Money-Making Ideas
Herman R. Holtz
New York: AMACOM, 1980
This solid overview is filled with anecdotes and helpful advice on selecting marketing options. The reference section is a gold mine of free and almost free aids from the federal government and the Small Business Administration. Also listed are catalog houses, mailing list suppliers, newsletters, and business "opportunity" publications.

7.) Personal Marketing

Yearbook of Experts
2233 Wisconsin, N. W.
Washington, D.C., 20007
(202) 333-4904
FAX: (202) 342-5411
The major media frequently refers to this directory as a source of interviews. The publishers will sell you a listing for $225 on up. If you're active as a speaker or author, you'll probably recoup your initial investment and then some. We've heard good secondhand reports about advertising here, but, as with all advertising, there are no guarantees.

Encyclopedia of Associations
Gale Research Company
Book Tower
Detroit, Michigan 48226
(313) 961-2242
A super library reference, this directory lists professional, business and trade associations in the U.S. and Canada. Contact the meeting planners or calendar coordinators to arrange to speak before targeted organizations. Submit articles to organizations which publish newsletters, mags, etc.

Marketing Without Advertising
Michael Phillips
and Salli Rasberry

Berkeley, CA: Nolo Press, 1986
If you offer a specialty service, here are important lessons in niche marketing. Starting with the premise that advertising really doesn't work, the authors detail ways to build word of mouth referrals for your enterprise. Taking care of clients, referrals, networking, and directory listings are among the recommended options. Valuable strategies show how to target prospects who are turned off by traditional advertising approaches.

Public Speaking

Command Productions
Warren Weagant
P.O. Box 2223
San Francisco, CA 94126
(415) 332-3161
Command Productions is an audiotape duplication, packaging, and marketing service with separate production studios in Sausalito, California. Call for details. If you're a good speaker, consider making a professional tape of your best material to use as a teaching aid, calling card, and possibly an extra source of income. One advantage of marketing tapes over books is that you can economically duplicate just one at a time, minimizing your capital investment. By contrast, you generally have to publish a minimum of 1,000 books to arrive at a reasonably low unit price for resale.

Johnson's World-Wide Chamber of Commerce Directory
Johnson Publishers, Inc.
P.O. Box 455
Eighth Street and Van Buren
Loveland, Colorado 80537
(303) 667-0652
Available at your public library or direct from the publisher, this is a directory of chambers of commerce worldwide. You or your publicist may want to schedule speaking engagements as part of a publicity or book tour.

National Speakers' Association
5201 North 7th Street
Phoenix, Arizona 85014
(602) 265-1001
This is a national association of speakers and trainers, with local branches in major cities. Their meetings provide useful contacts and professional training aimed at institutional markets. For meeting planners, their membership directory is an excellent source of speakers, too.

Public Speaking for Private People
Art Linkletter
Indianapolis, New York: Bobbs-Merrill, 1980
The avuncular television personality is also a surprisingly gifted writer. This book reads like the spoken word, full of human interest and warmth. Especially good advice for the inexperienced or occasional speaker: The Non Joke Teller's Guide To Telling Jokes; Making Friends With Your Audience. We confess we took to Linkletter's folksy inspiration.

Speakers and Lecturers: How to Find Them
Gale Research Company
Book Tower
Detroit, MI 48226
A two volume "directory of booking agents, lecture bureaus, companies, professional and trade associations, universities, and other groups which organize and schedule engagements for lecturers and public speakers on all subjects." Volume 1 has the names of the companies and Volume 2 has speaker biographies. Speaker and lecturer bureaus are arranged alphabetically and include bureau name, address, telephone number, as well as details of the general program, topics, and terms and arrangements for lectures. Bureaus listed range from the Institute of Certified Financial Planners to the Talent Enterprise, which presents lectures on ESP.

Speaking for Money
Gordon Burgett and Mike Frank
Communication Unlimited
P.O. Box 1001
Carpinteria, CA 93013
Here's an extremely practical guide to earning money as a public speaker. Includes a short list of speakers bureaus who hire non-celebrities. Write for a complete book list on related topics: how to sell your writing, self-publishing, consulting, etc.

The Eloquent Executive
William Parkhurst
New York: Times Books, 1988
If you're a quick study, you'll love this fast read on public speaking. Written like a business brief, this book covers everything once over lightly, with lists and "Instant Reviews."

The Public Speaker's Treasure Chest, Fourth Edition
Herbert V. Prochnow and Herbert V. Prochnow, Jr.
New York: Harper & Row, 1986
This book is a combination "how to" and a handy reference for "humorous stories," "amusing definitions," "interesting lives," "selected quotations," "biblical quotations," and more. Consider getting this one for your bookshelf if you speak in public regularly.

Toastmasters International
PO Box 10400
2200 N. Grand Ave.
Santa Ana, CA 92711
(714) 542-6793
Terrence J. McCann, Executive Director
Founded in 1924 for men and women who wish to improve their communication and leadership skills. Toastmasters meetings are a way to meet people who enjoy public speaking. From shy novices to experienced professionals—everybody is encouraged to participate and hone their skills. Supportive, inexpensive, fun. For a contact in your city consult your phone book or contact Toastmasters.

Sideline Teaching

Learning Resources Network (LERN)
1550 Hayes Drive
Manhattan, KS, 66502
(913) 539-5376
LERN is a national membership organization which publishes several newsletters and sells books by mail on all aspects of organizing and marketing non-credit programs. LERN also offers consulting to organizations and sponsors seminars and conferences for school administrators and education marketers. LERN member organizations include university extension schools, parks and recreation centers, independent open universities, and art centers.

Meeting Planners International (MPI)
3719 Roosevelt Boulevard
Middletown, Ohio 45042
ATTN: Manager of Education
(513) 424-6827
Their Directory of Supplier Members and Planner Members includes people who plan meetings and supply services for meetings. Also inquire about their annual resource guide to books and articles on this subject. Conferences throughout the country. Their materials are vital for school and program administrators to stay competitive. Call or write for a complete list of books and publications on teaching, administration, and sideline consulting.

The Teaching Marketplace
Make Money With Freelance Teaching, Corporate
Consulting, And On the Lecture Circuit
Bart Brodsky and Janet Geis
Berkeley, CA: Community Resource Institute Press, 1991
Everything you need to attract students, organize and sell classes to schools and corporations and, if you choose, to freelance on your own. For independent professionals who want to reinforce their expert image by teaching, school administrators who want to improve the bottom line, performing and fine artists who want extra income, and businesspeople who want classes to attract new clients or customers. Order from your favorite bookstore or direct: (510) 526-7190.

Corporate Consulting

Advice, A High Profit Business
Herman Holtz
New Jersey: Prentice-Hall, 1986
Practical guidelines on the how-to's of consulting, public speaking, seminars, newsletters, books, and specialty publishing. Lots of details and information you can use.

American Society of Training and Development (ASTD)
600 Maryland Avenue, S.W.
Washington, D.C. 20024
(202) 484-2390

This society provides information on seminar planning and implementation. Especially recommended for individuals targeting corporate and institutional clients. Local branches in major cities conduct regular meetings. Contact their office for details.

The Consultant's Handbook
Stephan Schiffman
Boston, MA: Bob Adams, Inc., 1988
Excellent marketing advice for how to build a consulting practice using telemarketing, client presentations, and solicitation letters. The strategies are practical. The book is an easy read, too.

The Contract and Fee-Setting Guide
for Consultants and Professionals
Howard L. Shenson
New York: John Wiley & Sons, 1990
This has the most detailed, specific information on proposal writing and contracts that you'll find anywhere. Includes sample proposals which literally set you up in business.

Writing Articles

Getting Published
A Guide For Businesspeople And Other Professionals
Gary S. Belkin
New York: John Wiley & Sons, Inc., 1984
This book's an excellent guide to getting published. It includes a 34 page appendix with prime leads for query letters.

How To Sell More than 75% Of Your Freelance Writing
Gordon Burgett
Prima Publishing & Communications
P.O. Box 1260 B1
Rocklin, CA 95677
(916) 624-5718
Burgett helps you to focus on low risk strategies and make them work. He's very practical and readable. If you're aiming to write non-fiction articles, this book delivers on its promise. If you can't find this one at your bookstore or library, contact the publisher directly. Ask for a complete book list.

Simpson's Contemporary Quotations
The Most Notable Quotes Since 1950
James B. Simpson
Boston: Houghton Mifflin, 1988
Better than *Bartlett's Quotations* if you're going to give a speech, here are quotes from current names in news, literature, sports, and entertainment.

14,000 Quips and Quotes for Writers and Speakers
E. C. McKenzie
New York: Greenwich House, 1980
Lots of usable material to spice up your speeches and presentations.

Writing Books

Authors' Publishing Services
Publishers Distribution Service
121 East Front Street
Traverse City, MI 49684
(616) 929-0733 or (616) 929-3808
Small press publishers and independent authors, ask about *The Professional Book Production Kit,* a comprehensive marketing system for independent publishers. Includes names, address labels, and phone numbers of book distributors, reviewers, major media, catalog buyers, bookstore buyers, and much more. If you're serious about marketing, this kit is well worth the price: $125.

Self-Publishing to Tightly-Targeted Markets
Gordon Burgett
Communication Unlimited, 1989
P.O. Box 6405,
Santa Maria, CA 93456
Burgett's one of our favorite writers of "how-to" books relating to publishing and speaking. He's always well organized and very practical. This book in particular offers detailed, low risk strategies for targeting specialty readerships. Follow Burgett's formula and you'll greatly improve your chances of making money with self-publishing.

The Complete Guide to Self-Publishing
Tom & Marilyn Ross
Cincinnati, Ohio: Writer's Digest Books, 1985
There are lots of fine books on self-publishing. We like this one in particular because of the Rosses' generous, detailed advice on marketing and promotion. Includes how to get reviewed, testing and tracking ads, publicity tours, distribution outlets, contracts, and more. Nobody seriously considering self-publishing should be without this book as a desk reference.

The Insider's Guide to Book Editors and Publishers, 1990-1991
Jeff Herman
Rocklin, CA: Prima Publishing and Communication, 1990
The first third of this book shows you how to make introductions and write query letters. Two thirds of the book contains the names, phone numbers, and addresses of publishers and key acquisitions editors. What a time saver!

The Marin Small Publishers Association
P.O. Box 1346
Ross, CA 94957
(415) 454-1771
Network with other self-publishers through the MSPA. Founded in 1979, MSPA may be the most comprehensive source of self-publishing information in the United States. MSPA publishes a newsletter, sells books on writing, production, and marketing, and conducts seminars in the San Francisco Bay Area. These people are really supportive! The annual conference is worth a trip to the West Coast from almost anywhere.

The Self-Publishing Manual
Dan Poynter
Parachuting Publications, 1980
Post Office Box 4232
Santa Barbara, CA 93103
Learn from one of the most successful self-publishers. Poynter is great on specifics. For example, he includes photographs demonstrating how to organize your book by spreading stacks of material over your living room floor. This is one of the first and best books available on the topic. Poynter is also available for private consulting.

Whitehall Company
1200 South Willis Avenue
Wheeling, ILL 60090
(708) 541-9290
Whitehall specializes in printing books in runs as small as 1000. A family run business, they are good people to work with, economical and, more importantly, very reliable. No haggling on prices: They'll send you a rate sheet with size, quantity, and color options.

Writer's Market
Where & How To Sell What You Write
Glenda Tennant Neff, Editor
Cincinnati, Ohio: Writer's Digest Books, 1990
This book is a tremendous library resource that any serious writer should purchase for his own. Includes over 4,000 places to sell your articles, books, fillers, greeting cards, novels, plays, scripts, and short stories. And there are a series of succinct, well-written articles all about the business of writing and how to break in.

8.) Direct Marketing

"Selling Lite"

Non-Manipulative Selling
Tony Alessandra, Phil Wexler, & Rick Barrera
New York: Prentiss Hall, 1987
Forget every cliche you know about selling. The authors assume you're a real human being, not a sales machine. They even advise not to push too hard, to avoid feeling guilty. These are practical and professional strategies to influence people to buy, rather than to "sell" them. This book gives you a better way to do your job.

Telemarketing Tips

You Can Sell Anything By Telephone
Gary S. Goodman
New Jersey: Prentice-Hall, 1984
Here are solid, classic telemarketing strategies. "We're all telephone salespeople." Goodman's right, of course. More to the point, he makes us feel good about using the telephone to accomplish our professional goals. "Real professionals like themselves, and it shows." He tells how to warm up prospects, "Send them a telephone smile." He makes appeals to quality,

"Sell yourself by being 'sold' yourself." He recommends specific opening and closing techniques for just about any occasion, "There is an answer to every objection." This fellow actually sold wine by describing it over the phone!

Newsletters

Editing Your Newsletter
A Guide to Writing, Design and Production
Mark Beach
Portland, Oregon: Coast to Coast Books, 1982
The author makes it easy for anybody to publish a newsletter. The minimum requirements are access to a typewriter and a copy machine. Build in the components of news, gossip, and advertising. This book is especially strong on design elements, with plenty of samples, logos, photos, and graphics. Did you know, for instance, that people spend 41% of their time looking at the upper left quarter of a newsletter page, but only 14% of their time on the lower right? Plan your page accordingly.

Direct Mail

Direct Marketing Success
What Works and Why
Freeman F. Gosden, Jr.
New York: John Wiley & Sons, 1985
Gosden explores the range of direct marketing strategies, including direct mail, telemarketing, catalogs, and interactive television. He makes important distinctions between newspaper advertising and direct mail flyers (they're more personal, often lengthier). He explains test marketing, coding, order forms, costs, and schedules. Recommended for anybody spending $1000 or more annually on mailings.

Mail Order Moonlighting
Cecil C. Hoge, Sr.
Berkeley, CA: Ten Speed Press, 1976
"The first thing to remember is that there are no simplistic solutions.... contrary to the get-rich-quick ads." Amen. The author's advice is to go slow, to develop a feel for what works by testing and evaluating. He shows what items have been big sellers and how to anticipate new hits. He recommends testing with split-runs (half of a test circulation gets ad A, half gets ad B; the best pulling ad goes into mass circulation). Also: barter options, cost analysis, building your business, and more. This book will not intimidate the novice, yet includes some sophisticated approaches for advanced marketing.

More Than You Ever Wanted To Know About Mail Order Advertising
Herschell Gordon Lewis
Englewood Cliffs, N.J.: Prentice-Hall, 1983
If you're serious about learning mail order techniques, take a look here. This book is jam packed with more suggestions than you'll be able to try in several years of mail order marketing.

9.) Publicity in the Mass Media

How to Get Free Press
Toni Delacorte, Judy Kimsey, and Susan Halas
New York: Avon Books, 1984
Here is a practical guide for individuals and groups to approach the mass media. Includes distinctions between managing editors, city editors, assignment editors, reporters and researchers, and how to approach them. Detailed descriptions of press kits, sample news releases, publicity stunts, planning calendars. Also, "How to Raise Hell for A Cause...PR for Environmental and Consumer Groups and the Arts." Creative and resourceful.

How to Get on Radio Talk Shows
All Across America Without Leaving Your Home or Office
Joe and Judy Sabah
POB 24147
Denver, CO 80224
(303) 722-7200
The Sabahs offer a book, a cassette tape by the same name, and a sets of 500+ mailing labels of radio talk shows. They price their information high, but it's still a lot cheaper than hiring a secretary to collate and type this data yourself. Book includes details on obtaining an 800# service, getting VISA and MasterCard merchant capability, and developing a press kit that works. Especially recommended if you're a self-published author who is selling and fulfilling your own book orders. Write or call for details.

How to Publicize Your Way to Success
Bonnie Weiss
San Francisco: Catalyst Publications, 1985
A publicist and local radio show host, Weiss has neatly distilled what you need to know about developing a publicity campaign in just 79 pages. Expert advice on how to create a polished, professional media image. Excellent references to national publicity resources: TV and radio, newspapers, writers, columnists, wire services, etc. Free San Francisco Bay Area media lists are included. Send $14.95 to Catalyst Publications, POB 4384, San Francisco, CA 94101.

Getting Publicity
Martin Bradley Winston
New York: John Wiley & Sons, Inc., 1982
"Who? What? Where? When? Why? How?" These are the questions to answer when selling your story to the media. The author shows you how to produce clean, journalistic prose. Then he covers the rest: editorial contact, meeting the press, headlines, photographs, printing, and tracking release placements. Applicable for small budgets or big. Solid, proven strategies from a nationally recognized professional publicist.

Ayers Directory of Publications
Ayer Press
One Bala Avenue
Bala Cynwyd, Pennsylvania 19004
(215) 627-1303

This directory lists U.S. and Canadian newspapers and magazines, their personnel, and basic audience demographics.

Broadcast Yearbook
1735 De Salle St. N.W.
Washington, DC 30036
(202) 638-1022
This directory lists television and radio stations in the U.S., Canada, and Latin America.

News Bureaus
Richard Weiner, Inc.
888 Seventh Avenue
New York, NY 10019
(212) 582-7373
This is a directory of newspaper and magazine wire services and news bureaus.

U.S. Publicity Directory
John Wiley & Sons
605 Third Avenue
New York, NY 10058
(212) 850-6000
This directory lists all U.S. newspapers, television, and radio stations, magazines, business and financial publications, and their personnel.

10.) Advertising That Pays

Advertising Age
740 Rush Street
Chicago, Illinois, 60611
This magazine is a must read for those who work in advertising. It's a combination of *Business Week* and *Wall Street Journal.* Check your local newsstand.

Advertising—How to Write the Kind That Works
Revised Edition
David L. Malickson and John W. Nason
New York, Charles Schribner's Sons, 1982
Malickson is a college professor of advertising; Nason is a director of marketing. The book is a fortuitous blend of theory and practice, an excellent introduction to print and broadcast advertising.

How to Advertise
Kenneth Roman and Jane Maas
New York: St. Martin's Press, 1976
Here's a tidy little volume, still current, that presents the ABC's of advertising. It's especially useful if you're about to hire an ad agency or work with the broadcast media.

How to Make Your Advertising Twice As Effective
At Half the Cost
Hershell Gordon Lewis
Chicago, Ill: Bonus Books, 1990
"The title sounds like hype," was our first reaction. But Lewis knows how to deliver on his promise. There's lots of cost-cutting, practical advice here. Avoid common mistakes that could cost you hundreds of times the price of the book.

Ogilvy On Advertising
David Ogilvy
New York: Crown Publishers, Inc., 1983
Ogilvy, the urbane ad man, creates million dollar campaigns, but basic lessons of style, composition, and copy writing are quite adaptable to modest budgets. The book is lavish with full page reproductions, many in color, of sophisticated magazine and TV ads. Ogilvy recalls numerous successes, admits to a few glorious failures. Though not a conceptual book, it's good storytelling and you'll learn by example.

Romancing The Brand
David N. Martin
New York: Amacom, 1989
"Besides Ogilvy, is there any other outstanding book about corporate advertising by an ad agency executive?" Yes, and this is it. Martin is more conceptual than Ogilvy, more organized and better referenced. The prose is crisp and the examples are warm and real. Why do we think "Scotch" when we think tape? How do you use drama in an ad? How do you spend more to make more?

The Complete Guide to Advertising
Torin Douglas
New Jersey: Chartwell Books, 1984
Here is a comprehensive introduction to corporate advertising written by a respected journalist and commentator. Included: why ads work; how to choose an agency; how to write ads; selecting the best media; commissioning photographers; typefaces; budgets. Chockful of color and black and white ads, illustrations, and a complete glossary of advertising terms, this book makes a superb home reference. Especially good for marketing professionals or prospective agency clients.

Understanding Media:
The Extensions of Man
Marshall McLuhan
New York: Signet Books, 1964
McLuhan's classic helped to revolutionize the way we understand media and its impact on culture. Brilliant, heady, and entertaining, this book chronicles our transition from the Gutenberg age to the electronic age. "The medium is the message." Or is it "massage"?

Why People Distrust Advertising

Doublespeak
William Lutz
New York: Harper & Row, 1989
Lutz is a combination of George Orwell and Ralph Nader, alerting us to the myriad of linguistic corruptions perpetrated by business and government. Welcome to the world of distortion and misdirection. The chapters on advertising and labeling are most relevant to marketing.

Media Sexploitation
Wilson Bryan Key
New York: Signet, 1977
Beyond *Subliminal Seduction,* Key uncovers more hidden messages in television and print advertising. Airbrushed penises and vaginas, dirty word graffiti, pedophilia, and worse are revealed. Includes 49 eye-popping photographs. After this book, you won't even be able to read *Lady's Home Journal* in innocence.

Subliminal Seduction
Wilson Bryan Key
New York: Signet, 1974
"The mind is quicker than the eye," according to Marshall McLuhan in his introduction. Do greedy advertisers insert secret sexual arousals to spur wasteful consumption? Author Key uncovers subliminal appeals in words and pictures. Ravings of an overactive imagination? Perhaps. But McLuhan adds perspective: "It is fascinating how long this world–starving and impoverished as it is–will tolerate the incredible self-indulgence which has come to be known as the American way of life."

The Hidden Persuaders
Vance Packard
New York: Pocket Books, Inc. 1957
This was the first popular book to expose the psychology of advertising. Why do men think of a mistress when they see a convertible? Why are women in supermarkets attracted to red? Why does children's cereal crackle? There's a revelation on every page.

11.) Writing to Persuade

A Manual of Style
Chicago: University of Chicago Press
Every working author, advertiser, and editor should have at least one standard reference guide close at hand. This one is very complete and includes manuscript preparation, style, grammar, design, and typography. The rules vary among reference guides. This one's a favorite, and it's our bible. Get yourself the latest edition.

Confessions of an Advertising Man
David Ogilvy
New York: Antheneum, 1963
More than an autobiography, the chapter "How to Write Potent Copy" is worth the price alone. Some sample advice: "Always include the brand name in your headline." "Avoid superlatives, generalizations, and platitudes. Be specific and factual." "You should always include testimonials in your copy." "Another profitable gambit is to give the reader helpful advice or service." Ogilvy's instincts made his ad agency one of the largest.

How to Make Your Advertising Make Money
John Caples
New York: Prentice-Hall, 1983
The premise of this book goes to the heart of our philosophy of persuasive writing. From the introduction: "If an ad gets poor results, it is dropped. If an ad gets good results, it is run again and again. Every decision regarding advertising is based on facts. No decisions based merely on opinions are tolerated." This book is chockful of successful ads, sales letters, lists of words, phrases, headlines, and sentences that have worked for the author, an ad agency executive.

How to Write, Speak and Think More Effectively
Rudolf Flesch
New York: Signet, 1946
Another library classic. Don't let the publication date deter you. Flesch's two page inset, "The 25 rules of effective writing," is one of our all-time favorite teaching aids. Samples: "Write about people, things, and facts. Write as you talk. Put yourself in the reader's place. Go from the familiar to the new. Use verbs rather than nouns." If you want to improve your writing, check it out.

12.) Graphics With Impact

Desktop Publishing By Design
Ronnie Shushan and Don Wright
Redmond, WA: Microsoft Press, 1989
This book, beautifully designed itself, shows the potential for desktop publishing as applied to journals, magazines, flyers, posters, catalogs, brochures, and newsletters. Cutting edge technology applied to classic design and typography concepts. Examples on almost every page.

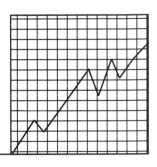

Index

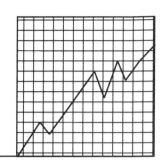

About The Authors

Iₙ 1974 Bᴀʀᴛ Bʀᴏᴅsᴋʏ, a University of California Berkeley political science graduate, founded Open (Education) Exchange with the approval of his Board of Directors and a pledge of $100.

Bart took $1.50 and ran a classified advertisement for "teachers wanted" in a local newspaper. Another $3.00 went for 500 posters which Bart stapled to telephone poles near the Berkeley campus. About 150 people responded to the call. Each was told that there was to be a new "open university" starting in the San Francisco Bay Area. Anyone could teach any topic of their choosing. There would be no grades, no credits, and teacher salaries and administration would be funded entirely from student tuitions. Bart asked each prospective teacher to put up $10 to $15 risk money for every class they listed. Open Exchange would register students and split the fees at the conclusion of class. The first catalog cost less than $550 for typesetting and printing and raised over $750. Open Exchange was "in the black" with the very first issue. After they saw the catalog, the Board delivered their check for $100.

Teachers were paid from the very first issue, but all staff labor, including Bart's, was unpaid for about the first year. Janet Geis volunteered to help with production of the second catalog and soon became indispensable. With her background in journalism and corporate training, Janet helped make the organization grow. By 1979 Open Exchange was grossing almost a half million dollars annually. In the same year Open Exchange registered over 17,000 students in about 1,500 non-credit "mini-classes."

In 1980 *Open Exchange* was expanded from a catalog of classes to a directory of professionals. Doctors, lawyers, teachers, artists, businesspeople, therapists, individuals and organizations, were invited to advertise and promote their services. This new format gave Janet and Bart more time to pursue varied interests, including writing and consulting. In 1984 Janet and Bart were walking down a street near the Berkeley campus when they came upon a telephone pole crowded with posters. Brittle and yellowed, but quite intact, was one of Bart's original posters with the headline, "Teachers Wanted!" Bart remarked that he had placed it low on the pole so that it wouldn't get covered up so quickly. Even though the phone number had changed, they left the ten year old poster on the pole.

In Fall 1991 *Open Exchange* celebrated its seventeenth anniversary. With almost 1/3 million Bay Area readers, each edition contains about 1,000 listings for classes, business and therapy referrals. Janet and Bart have worked with over 5,000 teachers, businesspeople, artists, and therapists. They have consulted with school administrators at major universities. Their specialty is in evolving low-risk business strategies which help people find or create the work they love.

Janet and Bart are available for lectures and public speaking. Contact them in care of the publisher, Community Resource Institute Press.

Reader: Review This Book!

Here's your chance to talk back to the authors. Do you have a story you'd like to share? Please forward your comments, bouquets, and brickbats to Community Resource Institute Press, 1442-A Walnut Street, #51, Berkeley, California 94709. Phone (510) 525-9663. We'll incorporate your suggestions or anecdotes into future editions.

Rate this book's content—(CIRCLE ONE: Excellent; Good; Fair; Poor)

Rate this book's writing style—(CIRCLE ONE: Excellent; Good; Fair; Poor)

Will it be useful to you?—(CIRCLE ONE: Excellent; Good; Fair; Poor)

What was your favorite part?

What would you change or delete?

Do you have a story or anecdote to share?
(Attach a sheet with additional comments.)

Please photocopy and remit—

FINDING YOUR NICHE...
ORDER FORM

Support your local bookstore! Ask them to order Finding Your Niche. *Or order direct:*

Please send me _____ copies @ $15.95: $_____
Postage and handling–add $2 per order
(Save money by ordering several copies):   _____2.00
CA residents–add applicable sales tax or $1.32/book :   _____
CHECK OR MONEY ORDER ENCLOSED: $_____
Order with credit card by mail or phone (510) 525-9663:
VISA, Master, or AMEX#_____   Expires_____

Name_____
Mailing Address_____
City_____ State_____ Zip_____ Phone_____

Mail to: COMMUNITY RESOURCE INSTITUTE PRESS
1442-A Walnut, #51 • Berkeley, California 94709 • (510) 525-9663

NOTES:

NOTES:

NOTES: